THE POLITICS
OF FOREIGN AID

THE POLITICS
OF FOREIGN AID

AMERICAN EXPERIENCE IN SOUTHEAST ASIA

By JOHN D. MONTGOMERY

Published for the
COUNCIL ON FOREIGN RELATIONS
by
FREDERICK A. PRAEGER, *Publisher*
New York · London

FREDERICK A. PRAEGER, PUBLISHER
64 UNIVERSITY PLACE, NEW YORK 3, N.Y.
49 GREAT ORMOND STREET, LONDON, W.C. 1, ENGLAND

First published in the United States of America in 1962 by
Frederick A. Praeger, Inc., Publisher
64 University Place, New York 3, N.Y.

Second printing, 1963

Manufactured in the United States of America

Gift. Peter M. Swartz

PUBLICATIONS OF THE
COUNCIL ON FOREIGN RELATIONS

To the emeriti of
"a fellowship in learning"

ACKNOWLEDGMENTS

This study is a distant cousin to my earlier examination of American efforts to install democracy in Germany and Japan in the period of military government and economic rehabilitation following the Second World War.* During the course of that work I began to speculate about the comparable and only vaguely expressed political purposes of our use of foreign aid throughout the non-Communist world, and about the operations intended to achieve them. When in 1957 I received an invitation to spend two years in research and teaching in Viet-Nam, I decided to take the opportunity to explore these questions further. The research that followed led me into a full-scale study of the politics of giving and receiving aid; it also convinced me that the whole subject was far more complex than either practitioners or students of our foreign aid programs had yet realized. The result is not a brief for any theory of foreign aid, but rather an attempt to apply reasoned analysis to the subject, particularly in the light of actual operations in the field.

For the original impetus of this study I am therefore indebted to the Operations Research Office of Johns Hopkins University and a John Simon Guggenheim Foundation fellowship; for the opportunity to begin a close examination of American aid operations, to Michigan State University's Viet-Nam project; and for the means of completing it in book form, to the Council on Foreign Relations.

* John D. Montgomery, *Forced To Be Free: The Artificial Revolution in Germany and Japan* (Chicago: University of Chicago Press, 1957). This in turn was based on studies of the purge and denazification I prepared for the Operations Research Office of Johns Hopkins University.

During my period of investigations in the field American Ambassadors Elbridge Durbrow (Viet-Nam), U. Alexis Johnson (Thailand), Everett Francis Drumright (Republic of China, Taiwan), and Walter P. McConaughy (Burma) lent me their personal support and assistance. In Viet-Nam the successive chiefs of the United States Operations Mission, Leland Barrows and Arthur Z. Gardiner, fully cooperated with my project, not only by generously granting me long and searching interviews, but also by introducing the project to their own staff members and to the mission chiefs in Laos, Cambodia, Taiwan, Thailand, and Burma, to whom I am also grateful. During the next eighteen months I conducted some three hundred interviews with administrators and experts engaged in all forms of technical and economic assistance. To each of the technicians who submitted to the interviews, prepared materials for me, and thereafter checked my statements, I am deeply grateful. Commissioner Clifford H. Willson of the Joint Commission on Rural Reconstruction, Taiwan, assisted me by correspondence after I had left the island, where the JCRR had been so helpful. C. Hart Schaaf, Executive Agent of the Committee for Coordination of Investigation of the Lower Mekong Basin, was a most perceptive guide to United Nations and other regional activities in the Far East. At a late stage, officials of the Agency for International Development in Washington were most helpful in correcting and bringing up to date a number of the statistics in this book.

Among my colleagues in Viet-Nam Professor Howard Hoyt of Michigan State University offered some penetrating and informed suggestions on the sections devoted to problems of internal security; and Professors Milton Taylor and Robert G. Scigliano and Associate Dean Ralph Smuckler of that institution and Professor W. Y. Elliott of Harvard University wrote helpful comments on portions of the manuscript. I am grateful to J. Price Gittinger, the imaginative and efficient agricultural economist who not only stimulated my interest in the land reform programs in Viet-Nam and Taiwan, but also suggested, wisely, that the Council on Foreign Relations would be the ideal sponsor for this project. Many officials of the governments of Viet-Nam, Thailand, Taiwan, and Burma were helpful to me, but because of the nature of their positions I think most of them would prefer to remain anonymous.

My indebtedness to the Council on Foreign Relations is greatest of all. George S. Franklin, Jr., Executive Director, introduced my project to the American ambassadors in all the countries I visited. John C. Campbell kept a kindly eye on my peregrinations before I arrived in New York, and he and Anthony Pearce edited the drafts and final copy of this book. Philip E. Mosely and William Diebold, Jr., helpfully reviewed parts of the manuscript. The Council staff shortened my labors in several important phases of the study. I wish to express special thanks to William Henderson, Richard P. Stebbins, Donald Wasson, Vivian Weaver, Lorna Brennan, Sandra Collison, and Toni-Susanne White; and to Helena Stalson, who gathered most of the source material used in Appendixes I and II. I am also grateful to my colleagues at the Council serving as research fellows during my stay there, Russell H. Fifield and Henry G. Aubrey, who were backboards for some of my ideas and fruitful sources of information.

In a series of stimulating meetings, members of a Council Study Group discussed my working papers, which constituted an early draft of this book. They did not stint themselves in criticizing and enlarging upon it and in supplying me with valuable material, ideas, and introductions; several wrote long comments that were especially helpful. I therefore wish to express my thanks to all members of the group, consisting of Leland Barrows, Jonathan Bingham, Lincoln Brownell, Joseph Buttinger, Emile Despres, Michael T. Deutch, Karl W. Deutsch, Russell H. Dorr, Milton J. Esman, John S. Everton, John Exter, Wesley R. Fishel, Huntington Gilchrist, James P. Grant, Samuel P. Hayes, Jr., Albert O. Hirschman, George F. James, Col. Amos A. Jordan, Edmund H. Kellogg, Daly C. Lavergne, Isador Lubin, August Maffry, Stacy May, John H. Ohly, Karl Pelzer, Frank D. Rosebery, Frank Schiff, Joseph Slater, Ralph Smuckler, Jr., Edwin F. Stanton, Frank N. Trager, David B. Truman, James Warren, Warren Wiggins, Charles Wolf, Jr., and Kenneth T. Young, Jr. Ian Michael Wright served as rapporteur for the meetings.

Professor Carter Goodrich of Columbia University was an ideal chairman. He presided at each of the seven meetings with a genial humor that matched his firm but intelligent and creative leadership of the discussions.

Professor William O. Brown and my other colleagues at the

African Studies Program at Boston University were most sympathetic with certain of my shortcomings as director of the Center for Development Research and Training because of my preoccupation with Southeast Asia and with the completion of this book. My wife, who suffered and enjoyed with me the Vietnamese, New York, and Boston phases of this study, has made continuing sacrifices in its interest.

I do not intend by this series of acknowledgments to share the responsibility for the judgments and recommendations contained in these pages, but only to express my gratitude to those who contributed to my present understanding and knowledge of foreign aid.

J. D. M.

June 1962

CONTENTS

THE POLITICS
OF FOREIGN AID

INTRODUCTION

Foreign aid is a political force abroad and a political issue at home, irrespective of its successes and failures. Its purposes and its achievements, its origins and its operations, its giving and its receiving, all involve conflicts of ideology and power. This has been true whether the receiving countries were mature societies or the newly emerging and underdeveloped nations we shall be considering in this book. In aiding Europe and Japan, America was helping to rehabilitate established industrial states possessing still active traditions of parliamentary democracy. There common political purposes, together with a basic economic similarity, provided the foundation for a genuine partnership that may not be possible between the United States and the underdeveloped countries.

Specialized studies that have already enriched our understanding of the economics of growth in underdeveloped countries, of the implications of social change, and of the art of rendering technical assistance have tended to isolate their subject matter from the politics of foreign aid. Anyone who has participated in foreign aid operations or read newspaper accounts of the annual presentation of mutual security programs to Congress knows that these studies of economics and of techniques often represent an abstraction. A study concentrating on the politics of foreign aid may produce an abstraction as well, rather than a totality; but an understanding of foreign aid operations as a whole cannot be reached without it. This book represents a preliminary effort to identify and to interpret those neglected political dimensions.

A study of the politics of American aid ought to consider at least three separate aspects of the whole: the relationship between domestic pressures and the foreign policies involved; attitudes and

3

responses in the receiving countries; and the international implications of foreign aid. None of these can be treated exhaustively, even in a study that focuses on a single geographic region. Accordingly, this book will alternate between general considerations and specific cases and examples treated at some length. Such a combined approach, while not without its dangers, has real advantages over either a general and largely theoretical discussion of issues or a detailed history or finely drawn descriptive analysis of the microscopic incidents of foreign aid. It permits the policy issues to emerge and clothes them in the vitality of immediate experience.

International politics lie at the heart of foreign aid and, indeed, are the very reason for its existence. On the American side, whether the primary motivation is to hold the line against further Communist expansion or to establish mutually beneficial relations with the receiving states, aid programs are the instruments of a general political strategy, although it may not always be clearly defined or consistently pursued. From the standpoint of the receiving countries as well, whether the main concern is with security, economic growth, or prestige, the programs are intended to serve the national interests in a world full of danger. Where the two sets of purposes coincide, presumably, is in the common interest of both sides in preserving and strengthening the independence of the receiving countries against external attack or subversion. This is the political background, sometimes seen differently from the two sides, against which the total aid levels, the nature of the projects to be undertaken, and the allocation of resources within a receiving country are decided.

International politics on the local or regional scale also play their part. In general the shifting balance of international power among states in a given region, as they jealously eye the sums of American money available, can be very persuasive as to the need for avoiding favoritism and thus tends to increase aid levels throughout the region. Prudence dictated a matching of aid to neutralist India with increases to allied Pakistan; the distribution of surplus grain as aid to India induced a Thai foreign minister to offer his resignation because of the anticipated loss to Thailand's rice exports; the pressures of regionalism have encouraged countries to accept projects in which their own technicians and economists had little interest. And within individual countries the political stresses of the cold war have directly influenced the shaping of aid programs regardless of economic factors, as when projects have been discontinued because of Communist propaganda against them or when refugees from communism have forced the adoption of new programs.

Politics in a narrow sense, the primarily domestic factors in the granting and in the receiving state, determine the climate in which foreign aid programs take shape and in which they are put into practice. No analysis of what foreign aid can do and how it works can properly ignore these two sets of pressures.

Evidences of domestic American politics in foreign aid are not difficult to find. The mutual security legislation itself betrays its influences. American shipping interests, small businessmen, farmers, and marine insurance companies are protected by the law. Foreign aid legislation has also paid homage to the sentiments of those opposing the seating of Communist China in the United Nations, those favoring the political federation of Europe or a joint organization of Asian states, and those who hope that the competitive free enterprise system will be used overseas to achieve the economic development for which U.S. aid is proffered. If a congressional act could bring the privileges of self-determination to the Communist satellites, foreign aid would already have toppled the Soviet empire. The divided party support for foreign aid, the congressmen's occasional use of public hearings to exploit popular suspicions, and efforts by private groups to influence the administration of mutual security funds provide further evidence that foreign aid is not, and cannot be, left exclusively in the hands of the experts in economic and technical assistance.

Foreign aid may become a center of political controversy in the host country as well. It is usually administered on behalf of the donor country by men and women who are cultural strangers, and received by a government that wavers between intellectual gratitude and emotional resentment. Its uses are subject to pork-barrel treatment not unlike those attending substantial public works programs in the United States but without the sobering reflection in the host country that constituents' money is involved. The motives behind it may be closely scrutinized by governments to whom East and West are geographical reference points rather than political opposites. It is circumscribed by administrative requirements alien to the traditions of the host government; it is often tied to unsought advice, and it is subject to retrospective attack by American journalists and congressmen exercising what seems like extraterritorial authority. It may even be the occasion for American efforts to introduce democratic ideas and procedures within a well-established autocracy.

For the successes of foreign aid, both governments assume responsibility; for its failures, neither. And not all the changes it introduces are equally desired by the two. It is not surprising that an Indonesian cabinet was forced to resign because it had accepted U.S. aid, or that General Marshall, recalling the failure of U.S. aid to "save" China, ruefully admitted: "I have tried every important individual in that Government and they greeted me in the most sympathetic fashion and did nothing."[1]

America has given foreign aid to many underdeveloped countries, but our experiences in these countries are not equal in importance and interest. Since a primary objective of foreign aid has been to check Communist expansion, we have perhaps most to lose and most to learn from foreign aid given in the face of the enemy in the areas under the heaviest pressure. Among the most critical American experiments in foreign aid, certainly, are those taking place in Southeast Asia in lands lying on or near the perimeter of an aggressive, truculent power in control of mainland China, where Laos already bears witness to an experiment which did not succeed. This study, in consequence, concentrates upon four countries in that area which are most immediately threatened: Viet-Nam, Thailand, Burma, and Taiwan. All four know that they live under that threat, and their policies both internal and external offer a variety of responses to it.

Viet-Nam and Taiwan, having emerged as functioning states out of a military struggle against communism, have been firmly committed to continue the struggle against it. Thailand, the home of the Southeast Asia Treaty Organization, has been allied to the Western powers, the Philippines, and Pakistan in a defensive stance. In spite of some misgivings about Western policies in the cold war, Thailand sent troops to serve with the United Nations in Korea, and its active role in SEATO reflects a general desire for regional solidarity and collective security against Communist ag-

[1] *United States Foreign Policy for a Post-War Recovery Program,* Hearings before the House Foreign Affairs Committee, 80th Cong., 2d sess., February 20, 1948 (Washington: GPO, 1948), p. 1570.

gression. Burma, morally sympathetic to the West, has been politically neutral and open to aid from both East and West.

The success or failure of our aid programs in Southeast Asia is thus a major, urgent issue. Of almost equal importance is the relevance for other operations, as far away as Africa or Latin America, of our complex and varied experience in this area; for in many ways the four countries studied have provided a laboratory of foreign aid. While each new situation will be dominated by unique and unpredictable circumstances, we can learn much from our present efforts to strengthen the free nations of Southeast Asia against the Communist tide.

American aid in these four settings represents in its purposes a variety of goals and in practice a cross section of loans, grants, project and nonproject assistance, technical advice, military aid, defense support, special assistance, and most of the other devices available under the mutual security legislation. Collectively, they demonstrate most aspects of the politics of foreign aid.

Not every type of aid operation, regrettably, can be fully examined in a book of this scope. In particular, the "purely military" aid programs, the political and economic significance of which may often outweigh that of financial and technical assistance, have remained shrouded in security restrictions: governmental bodies, even military agencies themselves, have refrained from making or permitting a detailed study of their full implications, with the exception of the pioneering Draper Report.[2] The general size of the programs is publicly known, as is their purpose of strengthening the receiving countries against aggression and subversion, but many aspects of the policies and the "politics" on both sides necessarily remain obscure. Roughly half of the American effort in Viet-Nam and Taiwan is therefore not subject to the same kind of analysis that can be applied to the economic and technical side, and virtually the entire U.S. aid program in Laos has been so wrapped up in military considerations that a reasoned analysis of it can hardly be made at this time. The present study, therefore, while always mindful of the existence of the military programs and their relationship to the nonmilitary, confines itself to the latter aspects of U.S. foreign aid in Viet-Nam, Taiwan, Thailand, and Burma.

[2] The President's Committee to Study the United States Military Assistance Program, *Composite Report* (Washington: GPO, 1959).

Foreign aid policy in practice, like most diplomacy, consists not of a body of doctrine but rather of many specific decisions which shape, as much as they are shaped by, a number of general and ill-defined principles. To approach the subject mainly from the experience of operations in the field may be hazardous to abstract preconceptions, but it should contribute to a better understanding of the situations that produce policies. Some simple facts about the people who administer the programs abroad and the conditions under which they do so, for example, may be more illuminating than a discussion on the relative merits of project and nonproject aid. The capital cities of Southeast Asia provide an unfamiliar and exotic setting for the work of American technicians and administrators. All are officially designated "hardship posts," for reasons which remain a mystery to transient visitors who see only the graceful, tree-lined boulevards and luxury-priced shops of Saigon, the magnificent temples of Bangkok and Rangoon, and the bustling activity of Taipei. Tourists and visiting officials, living for a few days in the air-conditioned hotels or enjoying whatever luxuries the hospitality of the American community can afford, are more conscious of the summer sports than of the enervation that results from constant exposure to the tropical climate. The limitations of the local scene, the barriers of customs and culture, the lack of sanitation and low standards of public health—all contribute to fraying the nerves and depressing the morale of the Americans resident there, despite the best of will and the firm intention on their part to adapt to the environment and to understand and help the local population.

The U.S. Operations Mission in Saigon in 1958 had some 180 American employees. Whether the number was too large is a question. Whether the level of competence was above or below average is another. Whatever the best judgment on those points may be, it is a fact that in any given month roughly 40 per cent of American official personnel visit the dispensary for medical reasons other than immunizations, and that illness reduces the productivity of the aid mission in Viet-Nam by 20 per cent. The dispensary itself, staffed—or rather understaffed—with military personnel untrained in tropical medicine, is unable to cope with the incidence of disease. During a four-month period the 1,500 Americans provided the dispensary with 42 cases of amoebic dysentery, 180 of bacillic dysentery, 9 cases of hepatitis, 2 of malaria,

4 of dengue fever, 28 of ascariosis, 4 of giardiasis, 3 of pneumonitis, 5 of tapeworm, 16 of pinworms, and 1 of liver fluke. These figures do not include many cases treated privately, for some Americans preferred the overworked missionary doctors of the Seventh Day Adventist hospital. Other hazards to health were more alarming: sporadic dissident raids and terrorist outrages outside of Saigon, and on dramatic occasions in the city itself, have restricted the activities of American advisers and have even taken the lives of a few. Failure to recognize facts of this kind will jeopardize an understanding of one very important factor in foreign aid: the personal factor.[3]

The case studies given at length in this book are selected and presented to illuminate the processes by which policy questions are identified and resolved and to measure the political impact of various forms of aid. But since neither the policy-making process nor the general effects of foreign aid will be exhaustively treated here, perhaps it will be wise to state at the outset the main propositions of this book: that foreign aid as a political instrument of U.S. policy is here to stay because of its usefulness and flexibility; that its permanence must be more solidly based on increased understanding and support in America, and its usefulness assured by greater flexibility in the field; and that the country approach—the location of responsibility for planning, coordination, and operational decisions in the field, where American representatives are in direct contact with the governments and peoples being assisted—offers the most promising means of attaining common objectives and of meeting the complex political requirements for success.

This book is not, then, a history of American aid programs in Southeast Asia. It makes no attempt to describe the events of the last few years in Laos and Viet-Nam, where increased Communist pressure has brought new conditions of crisis and threatened the very existence of independent governments. There is certainly a story to be told about the place of American aid programs in

[3] The writer has prepared in collaboration with Vietnamese colleagues a series of studies of administrative operations that will help illuminate the context in which foreign aid is offered. See John D. Montgomery and the NIA Case Development Seminar, *Cases In Vietnamese Administration* (Saigon: National Institute of Administration, 1959). See also John D. Montgomery, "Crossing the Culture Bars," *World Politics*, July 1961, pp. 544–560.

American foreign policy with respect to both of those countries. It is on military and economic assistance that the United States is relying for the critical margin of victory over the Communist effort to win control of Viet-Nam. But the story told in these pages is a different one. It concerns the process by which economic aid is provided to underdeveloped nations by the United States: how it bears on relationships between governments; how it affects, and is affected by, political attitudes and social institutions; how it advances or thwarts the political purposes of both parties. The case studies, mostly taken from the period of the late 1950s, are pointed toward the "why" and the "how" of foreign aid. Thus, although they do not describe the fast-changing current situation, they illustrate the basic issues which lie behind it.

There are four major parts to this study of the politics of foreign aid. First, it examines the complex and at times contradictory objectives of our foreign aid programs. Then it turns to the practical problems of mutual aid between sovereign nations, using case studies to illuminate both the political friction which arises between the granting and the receiving country in spite of a clear and explicit common interest, and problems which flow from the intrusion of special national interests. The third part is an analysis of the complicated administration of American foreign aid, including recommendations designed to increase the flexibility and the impact of our programs. Finally, an attempt is made to clarify the profound issues of political principle which arise in American aid to underdeveloped countries, perhaps the most extraordinary partnership between nations ever recorded.

The political theory of foreign aid has lagged behind its practice: in part, because we have not fully grasped the fundamental changes which have altered the very nature of traditional international relations; in part, because we have been more concerned with clear results than with clear language. While the elaboration of theory may not be in itself of great significance, we cannot let our programs be determined merely by the nature and dimensions of each emergency as it arises. If the need for America to support free nations against invasion and subversion and chaos is no longer an emergency but a permanent and central fact of our place in the world, it is surely worth while to explore the political factors on which sound policy depends.

I INTERNATIONAL PURPOSES AND
ACHIEVEMENTS OF FOREIGN AID

AMERICAN AID to underdeveloped countries has been variously interpreted as a self-serving device dictated by national interest and as an unprecedented act of altruism. The use of a single program for diverse military, political, economic, and humanitarian purposes has at once confused the American image and obscured our main objectives. Seemingly contradictory operations are involved when the United States supplies a country with weapons and military advice, encourages economic development and social improvement with loans, grants, and technical assistance, and seeks to relieve human distress by gifts of food and medical supplies. Because it has been easy to justify each of these operations in its own terms, we have tended to postpone the intellectual and moral task of establishing a system of priorities among the orders for guns, plows, schools, and alms. In contrast to the apparent disorder of American purposes, Soviet foreign aid appears simplicity itself, serving immediate political objectives in the hope of achieving eventual domination. American society, on the other hand, responding to complex internal pressures that are ignored or absent in the U.S.S.R., produces paradoxes in its foreign relations that are difficult to explain and rationalize even among ourselves.

Since the Second World War, power and conscience have been at the two poles of American foreign policy. The nation that spent $4 billion developing the atomic bomb two decades ago has since spent that much per year as the originator and sustainer of foreign aid. American aid has sprung simultaneously out of a concern for world security and a hope for decency and justice; to describe it as simply a manifestation of our national conscience could be as misleading as to recognize only its implications for national security. Neither *Realpolitik* nor humanitarianism has alone dominated the diplomacy of American foreign aid. In varying degree both have been present.

Apart from the danger of oversimplifying our manifold objectives in each of the underdeveloped countries to which aid is offered, it must also be recognized that the practical results of aid are often unrelated to our intentions. Some countries, possessing relatively developed economies and extensive administrative resources, have been able to absorb vast amounts of American aid with corresponding benefit, while far smaller amounts of aid can disrupt the economies and corrupt the bureaucracies of others. Even military aid intended to strengthen the prospects for political stability against external forces can disturb the domestic balance and regional position of a group of aid recipients. When dealing with peoples still on the edge of the modern world, we must acknowledge the great distance in power and wealth and habit of mind between America and the nations struggling with the problems of independence. Foreign aid seems to possess inherent contradictions: it cannot "induce growth," "encourage democracy," or even "strengthen military posture," without influencing in other ways both the donor and the recipient of aid funds, and even, to some extent, other countries not directly concerned. We cannot always tell, in short, what we are "buying" with foreign aid. But if simple arithmetic, or indeed the most sophisticated mathematical calculation, provides no direct answer to that question, there is still room for analysis and political judgment, and it is in terms of the purposes and achievements of aid that its potentials must be first assessed.

1. The International Potentials of Foreign Aid

In its various forms, U.S. aid has worked toward a foreign policy goal that may be called a *stable* and *decent* world order. The complementary and sometimes contradictory elements in this ultimate objective appear in many statements of basic American policy. In 1948 President Truman urged "the development of a world order in which each nation feels secure under law," and requested assistance to "free nations in creating economic conditions under which free institutions can survive and flourish. . . ."[1] The Mutual Security Acts make provision for two kinds of aid related to "stability": "measures in the common defense," to be accomplished through military aid and supporting programs, and economic aid, "designed to promote economic development, and to assist in maintaining economic and political stability." A third form of aid, clearly related to achieving "decency" as well, is technical assistance to help "the peoples of economically underdeveloped areas to develop their resources and improve their working and living conditions. . . ." Stated in this form the two purposes are complementary; nevertheless, the United States has sometimes favored stability by supporting a regime that offered little decency to its citizens, while our efforts to encourage greater decency or justice have sometimes threatened a stable but authoritarian order.

"Stable" in the context of foreign aid objectives does not mean "static," although American policy has sometimes confused the two. Stability cannot be achieved in either internal or international affairs by the mere avoidance of change. An irresistible dynamism pervades twentieth-century politics: of the nearly one hundred national constitutions now in existence only nine are as many as fifty years old. American policy has generally been to favor institutional changes abroad that will support political and economic demands for improvement without degenerating into civil disorder. "Stability" in the underdeveloped world suggests the consolidation and defense of national independence and the building of institutions that will prevent disorder and permit steady progress.

The second component in this formulation of American policy, promoting a "decent" world order, is a complex and ill-defined objective which, nevertheless, has at times decisively influenced American action. Decency is not just a standard of international relations; it has to do with how people live. A response to requests for aid that will improve living standards may also require the United States to exhibit concern for the political and social conditions of life in other countries. At the same time, our commitment to safeguard the independence of nations calls for self-

[1] Address at Berkeley, California, June 12, 1948, *Documents on American Foreign Relations*, v. 10, ed. by Raymond Dennett and Robert K. Turner (Princeton University Press, for the World Peace Foundation, 1950), p. 17.

restraint from meddlesome intervention. While this problem cannot be resolved by invoking universal principles, the general American practice has been to exercise influence by means of example and informal suggestions, except where a nation's stability appears to be gravely threatened by internal authoritarian practices. In the spring of 1960, a few months before Syngman Rhee was overthrown in Korea, the United States officially warned him that popular resentment against his denial of political rights was reaching a critical level, and the favorable American attitude toward reform was a factor in the success of Rhee's political opponents. Yet in the same year, demands by opposition groups for similar American intervention in Taiwan and Turkey were ignored, partly, no doubt, because political tensions in these countries were deemed not yet to have reached the danger level. The same consideration appears to have operated in Viet-Nam, where American advice on civil rights was given gently (if at all) in spite of serious popular dissatisfaction with the policies of President Ngo Dinh Diem. But after a second coup in Korea and a change of administration in Washington Vice President Johnson was to issue similar advice to Diem less than a year later. Not long afterwards, however, guerrilla activities forced the United States into an anticlimactic withdrawal from its insistence on reform, a decision based ultimately on military rather than political considerations.

The concept of "decency" has thus involved at first considerations that are primarily economic, such as the standard of living, the production and distribution of consumer goods, and various institutional encouragements to growth. In the fulfillment of these economic requirements foreign aid has a direct contribution to make, taking different forms in various semi-industrialized or predominantly agrarian societies. But the exercise of American influence has been strongly conditioned by the receptiveness of the host government and the attitudes of the existing economic leadership. In the social order as well, American policy may be to favor "decency" in community relationships or in the treatment of ethnic and religious minorities, but its influence has been exerted with great deference to local conditions and the often contrary indigenous forces at work. The deliberate role the United States may play in the politics of other countries, for however noble a cause, is severely limited; indeed, what it involuntarily accomplishes may be more important than what it can achieve directly toward the stated purposes of its foreign policy. Foreign aid has a vast potential, both positive and negative, and its consequences are not always fully predictable, much less controllable.

The use of foreign aid on behalf of creating a stable world order has been generally (and perhaps too narrowly) conceived along military lines, largely because of the urgency of this aspect of the Communist challenge. In practice, however, action aimed at economic, political, and social results has also played a vital part in the efforts to promote stability. The American diplomatic response to the cold war began with a series of defensive moves throughout the non-Communist world, where alliances were formed, allies were provided with arms and economic support, and neutrals were strengthened so that they could better defend their independence. Beyond this, foreign aid has also contributed to international stability by encouraging regional organization and progress in various parts of the world. In Asia, these efforts have transcended such military arrangements as the Southeast Asia Treaty Organization (SEATO); they include economic and cultural programs, both within and outside formal military alliances. The rationale for substantial American support to regional organizations assumes that cooperative participation on the part of the newly independent countries contributes to their national sense of dignity and self-respect and thus creates a stronger community interest in the prospects of self-fulfillment outside of Communist direction.

The negative potentials of military aid are also impressive. A successful approach toward the somewhat evasive goal of military security for a particular nation may threaten the larger aspects of regional stability. Better military resources available to the existing regimes may contribute to regional instability by encouraging intraregional rivalry and heightening the seriousness of the apparently inevitable border incidents. (The Vietnamese incursions across the Cambodian border in recent years, for example, present a picture of attacks, defensive moves, and counterattacks on the part of two nations that are under the protection of SEATO, both employing American arms.) Military aid also tends to improve the political position and capacity of a national army to the point where it may become an independent source of political strength. It may then either seize power or exercise a preponderant influence over the civil aspects of government. In a country riven by civil strife, military aid may serve only to arm contending factions and to make their struggle more violent and more destructive to national unity and stability.

Another untoward effect of programs centered on military aid is the likelihood that waste and corruption may arise from the large sums involved in extending military supplies and in supporting a civilian economy so that it can afford a military effort beyond its means. If waste is viewed as the unintended enrichment of one sector of the society, its unsettling consequences in a country undergoing political and economic development may threaten the "stability" and "decency" for the sake of which the aid was offered—a melancholy condition already apparent in Laos and Cambodia.

Finally, there is the danger that the deterrents afforded by U.S. aid will fail, and that the equipment and wealth supplied through American funds will be captured and used by Communist guerrillas or invaders. As the veterans in Chiang Kai-shek's armies can testify, this is more than a theoretical possibility. Military assistance as a means to political stability is, in short, an important foreign aid potential, but not all possible consequences of military aid are favorable to American objectives.

Military assistance and its corollaries obviously do not exhaust the approaches taken through foreign aid toward the kind of world order favored by American policy. Although military aid is primarily concerned with stability, it may also introduce a sense of national purpose, habits of discipline, and progress in education and health that will in turn improve the decency of living conditions. Similarly, economic aid may help to stabilize society as well as give promise of higher living standards. Technical assistance may strengthen the administration of government as well as raise economic productivity. Aid dollars can import commodities which appease consumer demands and check the disturbing effects of inflation. Construction projects of all kinds—schools, roads, dams, and hospitals—can help meet rising expectations, encourage further capital development programs, and also bring prestige to a regime. Thus economic aid contributes in various ways to stability: a well-administered government and a steady economy can minimize popular discontent, and a government's demonstrated concern with the economic future of an ambitious society can enlist public confidence. These forms of aid are primarily contributions to the "decent" order favored by American opinion and policy: better health, better education, better public service, and better living standards as ends in themselves, self-justifying alike to enthusiastic technicians and to skeptical congressmen. Nations in which all citizens increasingly have a stake in society are nations which can better preserve their independence and will themselves have a stake in a peaceful world order.

On the other hand, the negative potentials of economic aid are almost as appalling as those of military assistance. The consequences of economic aid are also much more difficult to predict, since they are caught up in obscure processes of economic and social change. When an industrialized nation attempts to inject resources or techniques or practical energy into the lives of underprivileged and sometimes apathetic people, an act of faith is involved. In order to reduce a one-crop country's dependence on a precarious international commodity market, an aid program may attempt to diversify agriculture, only to see its efforts run dry in the sands of custom. On the industrial side, the establishment of any modern factory may impose unbearable burdens of a practical order on the limited skills and the ingrained habits of workers, on irregular power supplies, or on inadequate distribution services. Even the success of such foreign aid projects may cause severe economic inequities and social friction.

Instead of regarding such economic growing pains as part of the costs of progress, the peoples of underdeveloped countries are likely to consider them as a hidden penalty attached to a supposed gift. Since America is the source of most foreign aid, the United States suffers proportionately in public esteem. Uneven growth benefiting certain segments of the economy more than others leaves dissatisfaction, and "misdirected" aid (and most aid may seem misguided to those who themselves do not benefit from it) sometimes arouses more resentment than no aid at all. Economic development tends to create new economic or bureaucratic elites who may exploit foreign aid to weaken traditional forms of leadership; other dynamic new classes that arise as a result of greater educational and economic opportunity naturally reach out for political power. These new forces are well able to bring chaos in the course of their struggle to replace existing regimes.

Faced with the facts of inevitable political turmoil as well as social problems that may not be solved for generations, the well-meaning American may risk frustration merely through the normal quota of errors in judgment. Perhaps our principal error lies in committing ourselves to a work where success requires nothing less than the attributes of divinity—infinite compassion, infinite wisdom, and infinite power. The symbol of our predicament is a great modern hospital, staffed and equipped to the highest standards, which today cures a score of babies of severe dysentery and tomorrow will send them back into the swamps where they may die at leisure. The achievements of foreign aid may create new desires faster than the possibilities of meeting them, thus making the inevitable disappointments appear all the greater and more unjust. Worst of all, the gap between the rich and the poor nations is increasing; productivity and income continue to rise faster in the United States and Western Europe than in the underdeveloped countries of Asia, Africa, or Latin America.[2] Foreign aid in itself can never close that gap. The rising expectations of the world's poor are insatiable, because the rapid spread of education and the gradual improvement of technology induce needs faster than backward economies, even with the best of development plans, can supply them. Those who presume to offer aid must therefore bear the burden of their inability to satisfy the very expectations they encourage. The purposes of foreign aid represent a horizon which, as one approaches it, moves further away.

This formidable list of positive and negative potentials surely poses the question of the "net value" of foreign aid: why have it at all? The main answer lies in the positive achievements of our aid programs, which in practice have far outweighed any negative effects. Moreover, any decision to avoid the risks of aid by stopping it would leave a still more hazardous alternative: a withdrawal from the underdeveloped world which could abandon the possibly decisive third of humanity to communism. Renewed colonialism is impossible for the West; complete reliance on private initiative

[2] Between 1950 and 1960 the average annual per capita income in one hundred underdeveloped countries and territories increased by about $10, a rate of increase of about one per cent per year. Among the industrialized nations as a whole the rate in the same period was about 2.5 per cent and the absolute gain in the decade was over $200. Paul G. Hoffman, *One Hundred Countries, One and One-Quarter Billion People* (Washington: Albert D. and Mary Lasker Foundation, 1960), pp. 21–22.

and investment, on the other hand, would probably lead to neglect of public development essential to economic and political progress. Finally, exclusive reliance on the United Nations or other multilateral means would involve intolerable risks that the programs would be totally inadequate or unsuited to our foreign policy objectives. Since American foreign aid appears to be necessary and inevitable, the real issue is how to improve our operations.

The only reasonable prospect for effective American policy toward the underdeveloped countries lies in the direction of more purposeful foreign aid programs, which must be closely integrated with other forms of our economic and political diplomacy. In many cases American purposes appear clear enough to begin with, but in the process of their implementation the original clarity of our concern with stability and decency becomes obscured. Some loss of clarity is inevitable, due to the combination of obstructive friction and deadening routine that goes with a great administrative machine; but some indeterminate part of the uncertainties in our practice must be traced to confusion in principle. While the total purpose of foreign aid, no more than the totality of values in our civilization, cannot be resolved for all time into one neat formula, it is equally clear that foreign aid requirements will increasingly force the United States to discover a means of balancing our many concerns, both in the formulation of policy and in its application to the special circumstances of each underdeveloped country. As will be shown in the following studies of our aid programs in four countries of Southeast Asia, the main challenge of foreign aid is the task of building the elements of a decent and stable world order by means that are basically political—that is, by practice of the art of the possible within the context of ordered purposes.

2. Objectives and Programs in Four Southeast Asian Countries

U.S. aid to Taiwan, Viet-Nam, Thailand, and Burma has been dominated by the military menace and subversive activities of Communist China. This central fact is acknowledged in the American efforts to reinforce political, military, and economic structures in this threatened region. In the "front-line" countries of Taiwan and Viet-Nam military aid and "defense support" economic programs have been offered in amounts and designs related more to military than to economic needs. In Thailand, where a pro-Western alignment and strong national support of SEATO have served as the rationale for aid, a lower degree of Communist pressure has permitted the development of a much more modest and less crisis-ridden program. A third type of aid has been the token economic programs (incidentally involving some very large tokens of American concern) recently provided to neutralist Burma. These contrasting situations will serve to illustrate the range of foreign policy problems affecting the American aid program in Southeast Asia.

It would not be too fanciful, perhaps, to describe the political moods of these four countries as the four seasons to which American aid had to adapt itself in the late 1950s, before occasional subversion had developed into a major Communist guerrilla war: Viet-Nam, the springtime, ready to bloom when current storms passed, warmed with the pride of nationalism, boisterous, but suffering occasional chilly winds reminiscent of past troubles; Thailand, the mid-summer, languid, torpid, agreeable, flourishing but unhurried; Taiwan, the fall of the year, economically busy and aggressive but somewhat restive over future U.S. policy, and fearful of losing its claim to the mainland and perhaps its own international status; and Burma, once gripped by the icy winter of neutralism, where hostility to U.S. aid was gradually thawing before the friendly winds from the West.

Viet-Nam

The American aid program in Viet-Nam was offered and accepted in the wake of revolution, civil war, threatened invasion, and Communist infiltration. Everything that foreign aid could offer was needed in Viet-Nam: military arms and advice, generous grants and loans, technical assistance, foreign exchange for commercial imports, and even political support. The primary objective was survival; and, in the early years of the country's independence, the prospects of achieving even this were far from good.

From its earliest days South Viet-Nam seemed destined to precarious membership in the family of nations. Created by the Geneva truce of 1954 which divided the nation at the 17th parallel, the young country could not sign the documents which gave it existence but barred it from joining SEATO (although the terms of the Southeast Asia Treaty did provide protection to its frontiers). At once an offspring and a victim of cold war politics, South Viet-Nam could not become a member of the United Nations where a Soviet veto was certain. It could feel no security even in its own neighborhood, for relations with its neighbors were marked by a series of border incidents involving Cambodia and Laos as well as Communist-ruled North Viet-Nam.

As part of a former French colony, many of Viet-Nam's political institutions and traditions were derived from France, but the fierce Asian nationalism that rejected colonial status surged on until it had also banished many of the cultural benefits of Western rule. The nation's intellectual leaders, the finest products of French education in Viet-Nam, continued to respect their teachers while preferring that they remain in France; but their attitude toward America was ambivalent. Unable to deny their country's dependence on American aid and advice, they had been taught to regard American culture as mechanical and inferior. The presence of American technicians and teachers, clearly necessary to the economic and intellectual development of the nation, was paradoxically regarded as something approaching a debasement of the Sino-Vietnamese and the French cultural traditions.

The Communists used every available resource, first to discredit, then to undermine and destroy Vietnamese President Ngo Dinh Diem, a resolute Catholic who had opposed communism throughout his career. But he won out over formidable domestic rivals and over the Communist challenge as well. Even after Viet-Minh forces were officially withdrawn from South Viet-Nam on May 18, 1955, Communist violence and sabotage continued year after year. After a few years this menace was temporarily abated, but by mid-1959 fifteen to twenty assassinations of government officials were being reported every month,[3] and this terrible toll was soon to be multiplied many times. In 1960 and 1961, after major Communist advances in neighboring Laos had opened new routes of invasion and supply from the north, Communist Viet-Cong forces reintroduced a major guerrilla war resembling that of the early 1950s. To violence in arms was added assault by words. Radio broadcasts from North Viet-Nam, China, and other Communist

[3] *Current Situation in the Far East*, Hearings before a subcommittee of the House Committee on Foreign Affairs, 86th Cong., 1st sess., August 14, 1959 (Washington: GPO, 1959), p. 323.

countries harassed the Diem regime with a steady stream of charges, including fantastic accusations which were, nevertheless, often deemed worthy of an official denial.

In spite of this relentless siege, Viet-Nam served, together with South Korea and Taiwan, to check the Communist advance in Asia; and it is not surprising that these three countries have consistently received some of the largest allocations in the U.S. mutual security budget. Apart from large military grants, the programs of American economic aid have also been impressive.

America spent an estimated $3.5 billion on Indo-China during the war years 1950–54; of this amount $2.6 million was administered by the French for the agreed purposes of prosecuting the war and restoring a condition of security. Most of these funds represented purely military aid: for the three fiscal years 1950–52, assistance to the French Union forces for Indo-China amounted to some $800 million, and for 1953 and 1954 almost $1.8 billion.[4] Thereafter, from 1955 through mid-1960, the United States extended military aid grants of about $500 million directly to Viet-Nam, within the limits laid down by the Geneva agreements.[5]

In the period before the armistice of 1954, U.S. economic and technical assistance to Viet-Nam, both north and south, was probably about $70 million (less than 3 per cent of military aid), some three-fifths of which consisted of commercial imports. At first this aid was administered with the rather uncomfortable support of the French embassy, but when Ngo Dinh Diem became prime minister, it began to go directly to the Vietnamese government. Thereafter, almost all of it took the form of grants from the Foreign Operations Administration and its successor, the International Cooperation Administration (ICA). Those grants came to

---

[4] *Report on Indochina*, by Senator Mike Mansfield for the Senate Committee on Foreign Relations, 83d Cong., 2d sess. (Washington: GPO, 1954), p. 1. See also Appendix I-A.

[5] Chapter III, Article 17, of the Agreements of the Geneva Conference on Indo-China on the Cessation of Hostilities in Viet-Nam, prohibited "the introduction into Viet-Nam of any reinforcements in the form of all types of arms, munitions and other war material, such as combat aircraft, naval craft, pieces of ordnance, jet engines, and jet weapons and armoured vehicles" except on a replacement "basis of piece-for-piece of the same type and with similar characteristics." Even these were to be introduced only through stated ports of entry, and after notification to the joint commission and the international commission, which retained inspection privileges.

$322 million in fiscal year 1955 and then tapered off somewhat, though the figure never fell below $170 million until 1961. The total by mid-1960 was $1,311 million in grants, in addition to $82.4 million in loans.[6]

By virtue of its size, the American aid program played a very important role in the national finances of Viet-Nam. Local currency accumulated in American accounts by the commercial import program was used to pay the salaries of the 150,000 members of the armed forces. The International Monetary Fund estimated that U.S. aid, exclusive of the substantial indirect benefits gained by taxing American imports, directly supported 40 per cent of all budgetary expenditures in Viet-Nam; in addition, the United States financed over 80 per cent of Vietnamese imports in fiscal 1958, in spite of the reduction in aid level that year.[7] The level of aid was unchanged in fiscal 1959; but because of an increase in the Vietnamese budget, the American contribution declined to about 34 per cent. In recent years, taxes on American-financed imports supplied about one-third of the budget, leaving another third to be raised from Vietnamese sources.

The total specifically designated "project" aid provided by U.S. "defense support" and technical assistance grants to Viet-Nam from 1955 to 1960 amounted to $175 million. Nearly half of these funds were earmarked for transportation, with lesser sums for agriculture, industry, mining, public health, education, and public administration. Nonproject aid came to $1.1 billion in the period 1955 through 1960. An additional $70 million was provided from sales and grants of surplus agricultural products under Public Law 480 and nearly $30 million was approved for loans by the Development Loan Fund (DLF).

Among other sources of aid, the French government continued to offer cultural services to the universities and lycées and extended a $14 million treasury loan and $22 million in export credits in March 1960. German and French industrial groups also performed

[6] Agency for International Development, *U.S. Foreign Assistance and Assistance from International Organizations,* July 1, 1945 through June 30, 1961 (Washington: GPO, 1962), p. 40. For an analysis of American aid in Viet-Nam, Taiwan, Thailand, and Burma, see Appendix I.

[7] In 1958 U.S. authorizations were decreased by 30 per cent from the previous year's total; but because of aid funds still in the pipeline, the actual amount of aid decreased by only 15 per cent.

technical services for newly developing Vietnamese industries; the Colombo Plan nations supplied teachers and professors; UN technicians appeared for short-term assignments at the request of the Vietnamese government; agricultural and other technicians were sent by Nationalist China; and the Japanese government, in fulfillment of a reparations agreement, was preparing to construct a power dam at Da Nhim—a project which had been previously denied American aid on the ground that it was uneconomic.[8]

The great bulk of foreign aid to Viet-Nam, therefore, was in grants from the U.S. government. That the country was living so largely on American subsidies was a fact bound to have political consequences that neither nation could ignore. Inevitably the experience in Viet-Nam provided a great quantity and variety of useful evidence on how such aid may serve the needs of the receiving country and the foreign policy objectives of the United States.

Taiwan

American economic aid to Nationalist China began in October 1947, in the midst of civil war, as a direct relief operation. By the China Aid Act of 1948 the program was enlarged to include economic assistance, which was to be coordinated through an all-Chinese Council for U.S. Aid (CUSA, established on May 13, 1948) and the Joint Commission on Rural Reconstruction (JCRR, established August 4, 1948). After the loss of the Chinese mainland, the American aid programs were designed to reinforce the economic and military strength of Taiwan as rapidly as possible, and, at the same time, to contribute to the island's long-range economic development. A total of nearly $1 billion in mutual security aid was spent on the island between 1951 and 1960, not including the $1.7 billion provided in strictly military assistance.

While in the past few years increasing emphasis has been placed

[8] The report by Maurice R. Scharff, George Schobinger, Franklin J. Leerburger, and Day and Zimmermann, Inc., revised June 1, 1957, recommended against completing the whole Da Nhim project because of its cost ($40–55 million) and the fact that by 1975 it would produce more than double the anticipated power needs of Saigon. However, the American engineers favored the first two stages of the Japanese project (scheduled for completion in 1972) and recommended for U.S. financing a smaller hydroelectric project at Tri An Falls, increased thermal installations, and a distribution system for Saigon. The final request for a $12.7 million American loan (later reduced to $10.7 million) was approved by DLF in November 1960.

on DLF loans and grants intended to accelerate domestic investment, American economic aid to Taiwan (which averaged $102
million a year between 1951 and 1958) has been mostly classified
as "defense support," of which more than half was granted in the
form of agricultural and other commodities. Substantial sums have
also continued to be allocated to technical assistance in agriculture, health, education, industry, labor, housing, engineering, and
public administration. In 1959 the amount provided for all types
of American aid was $340 million, consisting of $100 million
for defense support, technical assistance, development loans,
and the agricultural commodities (PL 480) program, and $240
million in military aid. The American staff in that same year
comprised 75 ICA employees working for the mutual security
mission, 13 more employed by the JCRR, and about 100 on
private contracts. The relatively small size of this staff, especially in agricultural projects, could be explained by the number
and quality of Chinese technicians available and the high degree
of cooperation between the two governments.

American aid to Taiwan has been complicated by the political
necessities and ambitions of the Nationalist government, especially
its unwavering determination to regain the mainland; for while
American aid was designed to defend the islands, the government
of Chiang Kai-shek chose to nourish itself on the myth of "the
return." As a result of American pressures, the Nationalists reluctantly renounced in 1954 the unilateral use of force (although they
continued to prepare for reconquest). The prolonged stay on
Taiwan was officially considered a temporary expedient, permitting a regrouping of forces in anticipation of the collapse of the
Communist pretenders.[9] Whatever private reservations there may
have been about Chiang's prospects for reuniting China, the
Nationalist civil servants were officially in the position of awaiting
the restoration of their effective authority over the entire mainland.

[9] President Eisenhower's statement at a news conference on October 22,
1959, that "42 or more nations . . . recognized the independence of Formosa"
elicited the response from President Chiang Kai-shek that "Taiwan and the
China mainland are an inseparable entity that will some day be reunited by
the Nationalists." (*The New York Times*, October 26, 1959.) A year later he
predicted that this would come to pass in three to five years (same, October
10, 1960). When the *Free China* fortnightly was expelled from the Taiwan
Magazine Association, the charge was that it was "preaching the hopelessness
of attempting to regain the Chinese mainland" (same, September 24, 1960).

The implications of this commitment were immediate and practical. In the view of the Nationalist government, it was necessary to maintain a high level of military preparation against three eventualities: rendering aid to mainland counterrevolutionaries, supplanting the Communist army after the restoration, and protecting Taiwan against Communist assault. The United States, without committing itself to the first two objectives, agreed to support the defense of Taiwan with nearly $2 billion in military aid between May 1951 and October 1960. It also contributed the protection of the Seventh Fleet, which blocked any Communist invasion through its control of the Formosa Strait.

The government in Taipei has been determined to keep its "representative" character for all of China's provinces, among which Taiwan was only one, and that of minor rank. Extensive efforts to develop the island's economic independence were therefore considered unimportant except as evidence of the continued dynamic of Nationalist China. The will to return also excused the "mainlanders" from trying to absorb large numbers of Taiwanese in a government intended to rule the whole of China. Among the 31,320 civil servants of the central government in 1959, only some 5 per cent were Taiwanese.[10] On the other hand, about 65 per cent of the 145,874 provincial and local civil servants were native to the island. About 30 per cent of the enlisted men in the army were Taiwanese, but nearly all of the roughly 100,000 officers were refugees from the mainland.

American aid has been used to pay some 75 per cent of the costs of the 635,000-man Nationalist army. Occasionally an effort was made to shift this military priority in favor of the economic growth of Taiwan, but seldom with success. When the bombardment of Quemoy and Matsu was renewed in the fall of 1958, for example, ICA officials on Taiwan offered to arrange for emergency funds on the condition that the Nationalist government would institute austerity and tax measures designed to improve its economic position. Before accepting this proviso, the Chinese government requested the emergency aid directly and unconditionally

[10] This term refers here to residents of Taiwan before 1948. All Taiwanese, including newcomers from the mainland, are technically Chinese, but some families have lived on the island for three to four centuries. The official language of the government of the Republic of China (Mandarin) differs from the dialects spoken by most Taiwanese (Amoy and Hakka).

from Washington. In spite of the fact that the United States was already providing added resources to the military build-up at that time, Washington promised the additional aid as requested. Because military urgency had obscured and even overwhelmed other considerations, the Chinese could safely ignore most of the economic recommendations made by the U.S. aid mission.

In its basically military orientation, the American aid program in Taiwan resembled that of Viet-Nam. But because of the favorable U.S. relations with all levels of the host government, the presence of thousands of highly trained Chinese technicians and professional men, a strong industrial base bequeathed by two generations of Japanese occupation, and a pragmatic attitude toward industrialization and private enterprise, the economic progress on the island was impressive indeed. Socially, too, the condition of the peasant farmers had been significantly improved. In spite of Chiang's personal military government, the Nationalists' truculent foreign policy, and a waning international prestige, Taiwan offered proof that American military-based aid could contribute to important social and economic objectives as well.

Thailand

The Communist threat to Thailand has been relatively remote, and internal politics there have been orderly, if not actually somnolent. American aid to the country, freed from crises, could be less urgent and less directed to military purposes than the programs in Taiwan or Viet-Nam. Until the Communists made their spectacular advances in Laos in 1960 and 1961, that country served as a protective buffer, shielding Thailand from strong and direct Communist pressure.

Thailand had been receptive to Western influences for well over a century. As the only people in Southeast Asia who had never been subordinated to European rule, the Thais are singularly free of the anti-Western, nationalistic sensitivities which prevail in the region. Foreign technicians have long been advising the government and engaging in various forms of commerce, and by 1959 over two thousand young Thai were studying at public expense in forty-two different countries, approximately half of them in the United States. Modern principles and practices had been absorbed into the native tempo of change, and students returning from abroad offered no threat to established society, generally occupying humble positions until they had reintegrated themselves in the conservative culture.

In the past decade, Thailand's foreign policy has placed the country squarely in the Western camp, with few signs of wavering.[11] The country gave strong support to the United States' position in the United Nations and elsewhere, being the first UN member to send troops to support the "police action" in Korea. It also outlawed its Communist party for domestic as well as diplomatic reasons. Occasionally, however, Thai officials wondered if overt pro-Westernism was the wisest course. In spite of their avowed neutralism, Cambodia and India received so much American aid that certain officials of the Thai foreign office would sometimes make ironic offers to "flirt with communism" or "mismanage the currency," thus rendering their country more in need of aid. More serious, after the Communist gains in Laos, was the obvious concern over the will and ability of the United States to defend Thailand's independence and the questioning of the value of SEATO.

American aid to Thailand carried military overtones, as elsewhere along the perimeter of the Communist world, but it was less conditioned by immediate prospects of invasion than the programs in Viet-Nam or Taiwan. Considered as a prospect for American aid, Thailand was a long-independent nation which offered to its Asiatic neighbors an example of relatively stable self-government and a relaxed *laissez-faire* political economy. Taken together with its unimpeachable diplomatic orientation and interest in improving relations with Southeast Asian neighbors, these political considerations added up to justification for an American aid program designed to strengthen its regional position, stimulate economic and technological development, and encourage a continued alignment with the West.

If military aid to Thailand was relatively crisis-free, American economic aid was similarly unspectacular. It was not a response

[11] Some wavering was evident when popular criticisms forced a premier to deny that the United States was "controlling" his government. Even newspapers under the patronage or control of leading members of the government joined in denunciation of "official pro-Westernism." (*The New York Times*, August 18, 1954, January 14, 1956, June 10, 1957; *The Christian Science Monitor*, September 13, 1957.) Such criticisms were stilled, however, when Sarit Thanarat seized power in October 1958.

to pressing need; indeed, Thai living standards were already higher than in most of Southeast Asia. The land was far from crowded, some jungles having been hardly explored; and although agricultural production depended upon a single rice crop each year (about half the land's potential), hunger was rare. The agricultural economy supported 85 per cent of Thailand's 25 million people and provided over three-fourths of her foreign exchange earnings. For that reason, fear of future American rice dumping or market restrictions was of greater concern to the Thai government than our entire aid program. But Thailand was able to find markets for her rice, the currency was sound, and there was no important flight of capital. The tax burden was relatively light: assessments were modest and only 40 per cent of the taxes were collected.

Being relatively free of the periodic crises that dominated American aid in Viet-Nam and Taiwan, Thailand offered the occasion for some deliberate experimentation in the development and administration of technical and economic aid. The easy relations between American and Thai technicians and the absence of suspicion made possible searching inquiries into both the means and the prospects for introducing administrative reform and social improvements. Thailand was not afflicted with the cultural inferiority complex and nascent nationalism that had hampered free exchanges in Viet-Nam, and the role played by public criticism was not as serious an obstacle as it proved to be in Burma. On the other hand, although American-sponsored projects were designed as close parallels to government activities so that successful American innovations could be officially accepted and absorbed, neither the tradition nor the mechanics existed for planning and executing quick, dramatic changes. Ten years were still required to close out the nation's books and prepare its annual financial reports, and statistics—where available—were prepared informally or based on arbitrary assumptions.[12] Decisions were often difficult to obtain. In the absence of strong government leadership the aid mission

12 According to an authenticated account, a few years ago the government of Thailand prepared a statement of its annual rice consumption by estimating the population and multiplying that number by 143 (the average annual consumption of rice in kilograms in a neighboring country). When the resulting figure was questioned, the Ministry of Health supplied a new factor, 135, as the "minimum caloric requirement," and thus a new "corrected" figure was obtained.

itself, in effect, often determined development priorities whenever it engaged in a review of its own program, and gave advice accordingly. At first, in response to the many technical needs of the country, American aid represented a proliferation of activities, but continuing reviews gradually reduced these to a relatively small, uncontroversial core in each field of operations.

In the ten years following signature of the first agreement on September 19, 1950, the United States earmarked $265 million to Thailand in economic and technical aid, including regional projects. U.S. aid provided over $55 million for transportation, nearly $15 million for health and sanitation, and substantial funds for programs in agriculture, welfare, education, and other public services. In addition to these direct grants, the ICA mission assisted in developing a number of large projects financed by loans from other U.S. agencies. All of these American projects were designed to introduce gradual and steady improvement in the national income.

From 1950 to the fall of Dien Bien Phu, U.S. aid was largely devoted to technical assistance and relatively small projects, ranging in total cost from $6.5 to $9 million per year. But when it was feared that the Viet-Minh victory in Indo-China presaged a general Communist advance, the program was expanded to include more important projects, principally public works and capital improvements of strategic value. These long-range projects were financed largely by "defense support" funds. Economic grants authorized for 1955 amounted to $46.5 million, five times the sum available in 1954. Grants for military construction, electric power, highways, communications, and malaria eradication continued thereafter at a high level, and additional loans were expected to provide power, water supply, and other self-liquidating public utility projects. The gradual reduction in the annual level of American grants between 1955 and 1960 was made in the expectation that technical and economic asisstance would be increasingly financed by loans and other means. As a matter of fact, loans in 1958–60 by the Export-Import Bank and the Development Loan Fund amounted to $14 million and $22.5 million, respectively, and regional projects from 1956–59 assigned $12.8 million to Thailand.

Military considerations continued to grow in importance, however, until by 1959 a fourth of Thailand's national budget was devoted to defense and some ninety thousand men were in uniform; but even these developments did not produce economic crisis. U.S. military assistance, while not comparable with the programs in Viet-Nam or Taiwan, contributed $285 million from 1951 to mid-1960, a total higher than the nonmilitary effort. Nevertheless, while strong political and military purposes underlay American aid, it proved generally possible in Thailand to develop programs in accordance with technical and long-range economic considerations.

Burma

The circumstances under which U.S. aid was offered to Burma provide a sharp contrast to the three programs just described. There the American effort was only a small part of a full spectrum of foreign aid extending from West to East: a large Ford Foundation program specializing in agricultural and technical education; Colombo Plan aid consisting of visiting professors and scholarships from Australia, Canada, New Zealand, and Great Britain; Japanese reparations to the amount of $200 million together with a $50 million economic cooperation agreement; extensive technical assistance from Israel; sterling credits offered by India against future rice deliveries; Yugoslav technical and military advice; and aid from Communist China and the Soviet Union.

Taken together these varied foreign contributions became increasingly important to the Burmese economy. In the fiscal year 1957–58 the Burmese government relied upon foreign grants and loans for 46 per cent of its capital expenditures, and this dependence rapidly increased, to 74 per cent in 1958–59 and then to an estimated 82 per cent in 1959–60. Much of the government's own contribution to public investment was based on deficit financing of one kind or another; indeed, it appears that in 1959 only 70 per cent of the national budget could have been financed from public revenue, including both taxes and the profits from government enterprises.

The American program in Burma was not occasioned or dominated by military considerations as in Viet-Nam and Taiwan, nor was it sustained by the political accord which underlay American operations in Thailand. Indeed, since we were not permitted to bring any political purposes into Burma, our work there might be thought to constitute an important example of attempted cooperation strictly for economic development. Yet even this presumably neutral purpose raised political issues. Suspicions of the West led Burma into vacillations that hampered long-term planning, while the many sources and kinds of aid posed special problems of coordination and integration. In the fiercely neutralist context of Burma, it was of the utmost importance that the United States commit itself to a few clear and acceptable objectives. But our purposes were diffuse, our operations uncertain.

It was not entirely unpredictable that American aid in Burma would immediately come under attack, for the psychology of Burmese neutralism includes an extraordinary sensitivity to possible conditions attached to foreign grants or loans. On August 17, 1951, the *Nation* (a generally pro-Western English-language daily) complained: "It is true that the [American] aids have no strings attached to them [to] which we so strongly objected, but we [must not] overlook the fact that the aids themselves are strings." An explanation of this statement may be found in a Member of Parliament's suggestion, made on the following day, that the American aid agreement should be abrogated because it gave the United States "a foothold in Burma in its capitalistic expansion." A few months later the *New Times of Burma* stated that Asian countries receiving U.S. aid "should be grateful to Mao Tse-tung," because it was "only when China [had] completely turned Communist" that the program in Asia was deemed a useful part of American foreign policy. When the Economic Cooperation Administration was redesignated the Mutual Security Agency, this change of name was made a major issue by the Burmese press. Finally, the U.S. government, in the words of a local headline, "Bow[ed] to Burmese Opinion" by deciding to allow the Burmese program to be known simply as technical and economic aid.[13]

The final crisis was occasioned by the presence of Kuomintang troops who, after the Nationalist collapse in China, had crossed the northern frontiers of Burma and settled in sparsely populated areas. Reports that U.S. supplies were reaching these Kuomintang troops via Thailand led to stinging rebukes and a public warning:

[13] *New Times of Burma*, August 21, September 13, 1951, January 17, 20, 22, and April 13, 1952; *Union Gazette*, September 13, 1951, January 14, 23, and 25, 1952; *Nation*, January 22, 23, 25, and 29, and February 14, April 13, and June 12, 1952; *The Burman*, January 22 and 25, April 13, 1952. For a fuller discussion of the Burmese press, see Chapter III.

"Burma must be careful of American duplicity under which she gives aid under M.S.A. while she does nothing to curb the Kuomintang for undermining Burma's political and territorial integrity."[14] The Burmese government eventually asked the American aid mission to withdraw, alleging that the United States was "aiding and abetting Chinese Nationalist troops . . . who . . . have been conducting aggressive action against the Burmese Army, since last December." After a similar complaint was made before the United Nations in April 1953, the United States was requested to bring its entire aid program in Burma to an end. Burmese government officials stated that it would be immoral to accept U.S. aid while Burma was complaining about its treatment by the United States before the United Nations.[15]

The United States began to dismantle its aid program on June 30, 1953, and our staff of 130 was soon reduced to half in preparation for a complete withdrawal. A "rump" mission had to remain, however, to administer some projects already under way, since Burma had actually received only $13 million in U.S. aid out of the $28 million that had been committed. Technical assistance contracts with private American firms, part of the aid program, were taken over by Burma.

There is some evidence that once the sense of obligation to the United States had been removed by this drastic action, the government of Burma "recognized more frankly the value of U.S. help and friendship."[16] So long as a sense of obligation remained, however, the Burmese were not able to free themselves of fear that their neutrality was somehow being weakened by the mere acceptance of U.S. aid. These problems were still to dominate American aid to Burma when a new program was undertaken, by invitation, three years later.

[14] *New Times of Burma*, April 22, 1952. The issue of American aid to the Kuomintang forces in Burma, directly or through the Nationalist government on Taiwan, troubled Burmese-American relations for a decade. The purpose, the extent, and even the existence of such aid have never been officially acknowledged.

[15] Charles Wolf notes that the level of American aid to Burma was already sharply declining, suggesting that the gesture was not as costly as it appeared. *Foreign Aid: Theory and Practice in Southern Asia* (Princeton: Princeton University Press, 1960), p. 151.

[16] Tillman Durdin, in *The New York Times*, June 11, 1953.

In February 1957 the Burmese government requested a resumption of American assistance. At first, the Burmese wanted loans, and these were promptly offered in the form of two agricultural surplus agreements. It was agreed that $32 million in local currency proceeds of the sale of imported American cotton and other surplus commodities would be authorized for economic development loans. In the same year the United States contracted to purchase Burmese rice for distribution in Pakistan; Burma was to be paid $1.1 million in American currency, to be used to educate Burmese scholars in the United States and to pay the salaries of short-term U.S. technicians. In March 1957 the Export-Import Bank negotiated a loan of $25 million for development assistance from mutual security dollar funds, and in May 1958 a $10 million loan was signed for police equipment, primarily for transportation and communications. The grand total of $67 million[17] was to be used to support many varied projects, including land restoration, forestry and timber extraction equipment, reconstruction of the Kabo diversion dam, the Union of Burma Applied Research Institute, telecommunications, spare parts for a rice mill financed in part by the former American aid program, rice handling and processing equipment, various craft for inland waterways and fleet improvement, airport development, Rangoon water supply and sewerage, village and town water supply, the Rangoon General Hospital, and the police equipment program.

The United States resumed its offers of grant aid as well, largely as a friendly response to Burmese requests for demonstrations of "good faith." Early in 1959, when Ne Win reversed Burma's loan policy and asked for large grants, in addition to the loans, the American ambassador promptly sought $37 million for the Mandalay-Rangoon highway and for university buildings. No funds had been budgeted for those purposes, Congress and the administration both having expressed a preference for handling capital requests on a loan basis; nevertheless, it was argued that, for political reasons, a grant, especially if it was offered promptly, would help overcome neutralist fears of onerous conditions and simultaneously demonstrate the extent and seriousness of U.S. interest in Burma. At the end of June 1961, the Agency for International Development (successor to ICA) reported that construction of the

---

[17] Later reduced to obligations totaling $60 million.

university buildings had begun and that a survey of the highway
project had been completed.

American aid to Burma in its second phase thus represented a
scattered but useful series of projects requested by the Burmese
government, which administered them directly or through contractors working under its supervision. As of September 1959, only
a skeleton ICA staff (consisting of eight officials and four clerks)
remained in Rangoon. This twelve-man crew, not organized as a
separate mission, was attached directly to the U.S. embassy; at
the same time, it was carried on Washington payrolls rather than
being paid out of embassy funds in order to avoid conveying the
impression that it was a permanent addition to the regular diplomatic staff. Other American technicians were brought in for short
periods to evaluate proposed projects, help prepare documentation
for Washington, or supply technical information; experts from the
Army Corps of Engineers supplied technical advice on the highway and university construction projects, and technicians from ICA
missions in neighboring countries were called in as consultants.
Such a small staff, almost unique in U.S. foreign aid operations,
was a recognition of the Burmese desire for "action, not advice."

In a gesture of national self-assurance, early in 1959, the Ne
Win government terminated major foreign contracts for engineering and economic planning, although the firms involved had been
in the country for nearly a decade. This was only partly an economy measure: the new government acted out of the conviction
that it "had enough reports" and that now it was time to use
foreign technicians, if at all, to build, supervise, and perform.
The functions of planning would be carried out by the Burmese
government.

Burma's neutralist position made it possible to accept aid from
many sources, but it reduced the aid projects themselves to a
series of unrelated gifts. The desire for "action, not advice" resulted in competitive offers of impact projects conveying images
of prestige and power. The effort to avoid any appearance of neo-
colonialism led to a rejection of fundamental, "social overhead"
projects that would influence the direction and tempo of future
change. Neither the West nor the East could function at maximum effectiveness when both were compelled to operate at such
remote distances from those engaged in national development
planning.

Summary of Objectives

The range and complexity of objectives served by American foreign aid are suggested by the variety of programs in these four Asian countries. If the threat of Communist violence had caused the original entrance of foreign aid into the region in the interests of promoting stability, it did not entirely obscure our later efforts to serve the goals of decency where conditions permitted it. Crisis forced the United States to act, but it did not always determine the character of the actions that resulted. If military considerations were indirectly responsible for American contributions to public health, expanded conceptions of education, and civic action programs of community development, perhaps the practice of international politics was simply illustrating a rather cynical theory suggested by a New England preacher of colonial times in explaining capitalism: "God will have us live by helping one another, and since Love will not do it, Covetousness shall."

The basic objective of U.S. aid to the threatened countries of Southeast Asia was to increase their capacity for independence and their political stability, thus enabling them to resist Communist invasion or subversion. In the following chapter it will be shown that direct attempts to increase political stability (for example, American plans for reforming the internal security arrangements of Viet-Nam) are among the most difficult tasks of foreign aid, coming very close to the vital center of national sovereignty on which new nations are so touchy. It follows that most of our efforts to increase strength and stability have been more indirect. In general the objective of encouraging political stability in Southeast Asia involved various forms of aid touching upon the host government's relations to the people, whether by improving the government technical services and public administration in Taiwan, Viet-Nam, and Thailand, for example, or by encouraging land reform programs in Taiwan and Viet-Nam. Support to non-Communist governments in the divided countries of China and Viet-Nam helped them demonstrate a viable alternative to their rival Communist regimes, and also offered time for developing efficient and representative government on a broadened basis of popular support. In Thailand the evidences of American aid were used as a symbol of the benefits of a pro-Western alignment that might otherwise have been politically unpopular. In Viet-Nam, Thailand, and Burma aid was intended also to strengthen the government's ability to deal with subversion.

Because Communist China has repeatedly declared its determination to overrun Taiwan and to assist the "unification" of Viet-Nam under Communist auspices, it was urgent for the United States to provide direct military support. Large amounts of weapons were provided to the two countries most actively threatened; Thailand also received military supplies, and even Burma accepted small shipments of arms for its police forces. The United States maintained military advisory groups in Taiwan, Viet-Nam, and Thailand and also provided defense support aid to enable these countries to support larger armies.

A third approach was to provide financial and other assistance to promote economic stability. The United States has pursued this goal in Taiwan, Viet-Nam, and Thailand, largely by efforts to compensate for the inflationary effects of military aid and to balance capital growth with generous supplies of agricultural surplus goods and other consumer items. Such goods were intended to achieve both economic and political ends: they were expected to stabilize prices, reduce inflationary pressures, and support popular living standards. Furthering general economic stability was considered a desirable end in itself, and also, coupled with economic growth, a method of minimizing the appeal of Marxist experimentation. It was, of course, too broad an aim for the smaller aid program in Burma, but even there the hope was that some contribution toward it might be made.

Even in the shadow of the bamboo curtain it was possible to use aid funds to finance and stimulate economic growth. In all four countries grants or loans were made for capital development; in Taiwan, Viet-Nam, and Thailand a special effort was made to employ new and existing capital equipment efficiently by developing managerial and technical skills, and in the same countries the United States used its influence to encourage the adoption of governmental policies designed to stimulate growth. Growth, it was thought, would serve the needs of the people, strengthen their will to independence, discount the Communist example of forced industrialization, and bring about a closer integration among the economies of the rich and poor nations.

These objectives and approaches were realized in an uneven and, at times, unexpected fashion; and in some cases they were not achieved at all. But in view of the difficulty of the undertakings, the United States has not been unsuccessful.

3. The Cold War Background

In most American aid projects in Southeast Asia, no matter how insignificant in scope or how apparently nonpolitical in character, the cold war has lurked somewhere in the background. If foreign aid began in this region as an instrument of the American policy of containment, the response of the Communist states included attempts at political sabotage as well as direct competition through the introduction of aid programs of their own. In both offensives, Communist success was certainly no greater than that of the United States. In Viet-Nam, ultimately, the Communists had to resort to direct military methods in order to undermine the impact of steady progress achieved with American help. That change in tactics, which became apparent in 1960, magnified the scope of the problem, but it was a sign of the aid program's success, not of its failure.

Communist activity added an important dimension to U.S. foreign aid administration. It is unwise to undertake any project without calculating its chances of success from the standpoint of technology and economics, and its diplomatic prospects in terms of the bilateral relationship between giver and receiver; but in the context of the cold war it proved necessary to consider as well its implications as seen from Peking and Moscow and its effect on the Communist powers' relations with the receiving government. Whether introducing a palatable and economical source of nutrition in Viet-Nam or offering technical assistance to national planning in Burma, the United States has found itself confronting formidable competition.

The Tilapia Fish Story

The Tilapia fish project was one of several early American efforts to help the Indochinese peasants. Because of the benefits the program was expected to bring, it was hailed in advance as a symbol of benevolence and a triumph of technology, although the entire program cost less than $20,000. The tilapia, a hardy and easily bred native of African lakes which had been successfully transplanted to a number of Asian countries, was advertised as a miracle fish because it had great nutritional value and could multiply and grow rapidly almost anywhere. Thanks to a widespread and successful publicity campaign, popular demand soon exhausted the stocks that had been shipped in by air in 1952. The program was at first successful; indeed, so successful that the Communist radio in the north and the Communist cadres in the south embarked upon an all-out campaign to discredit it. The most imaginative attack on the tilapia fish also proved to be the most effective: lepers were induced to eat it, then to display themselves in village after village, where Communist agents interviewed them to "demonstrate" that eating the exotic American fish induced leprosy. The Communists (probably with the help of fishermen and fishmongers fearing the competition) systematically defamed the tilapia throughout Viet-Nam, with the result that the fish became almost unsalable even in relatively sophisticated Saigon.

The American aid mission responded by quietly withdrawing from the tilapia program, except in highlands areas where the Communist propaganda was less effective and where the fish was best suited to the environment. It was concluded that the American information services could find better employment than defending the tilapia. Other fish, in some cases of a better quality, were introduced in the areas previously served by the tilapia breeding stations. But some Vietnamese officials, who had cosponsored the tilapia and felt personally committed to its fate, bestirred themselves to retaliate against the Communist propaganda. A province chief produced an old farmer who, despairing of his chance of surviving a serious case of tuberculosis, had stopped working (and rested); had lost his home (and lived outdoors); and for the sake of economy had eaten plentifully of the unwanted fish (and improved his meager diet). After some months his evident recovery was attributed to the powers of the ubiquitous tilapia. Finally, in October 1958, the U.S. mission published a report from Vinh-Binh province stating that the farmers "now fully realize that they were fooled by Communist propaganda," and quoting one farmer as saying that "the Communists, instead of hurting the American aid program, harmed our livelihood. In spite of my grey hair, I did not realize that their sayings were groundless. Nevertheless, these lies have opened up our eyes to many things; the reopening of our fish ponds is a warning to these

liars."[18] Apart from such occasional reactions, however, the tilapia
remained in disrepute; for years few Vietnamese were willing to
eat it.

Not all Communist attacks on American aid programs in Viet-
Nam were equally successful. An effort to discourage the use of
American fertilizer by poisoning dogs with it and pointing to the
danger of indirectly introducing it into human food had little
effect. At the same time, the U.S. aid mission developed more
effective methods of counterattacking Communist propaganda.
When inspired rumors about the malaria eradication program
suggested that after homes were sprayed with DDT an American
agent would come to collect for the service, the Americans answered by publishing articles and showing newsreels describing the
work of the malaria eradication teams, some of which had photo-
genically journeyed by elephant in the course of spraying the
million houses on their schedule. Each release included a statement that this was a free service offered by the Vietnamese government with American aid. The Communists responded to this more
effective approach by substituting intimidation for propaganda
and by the more drastic means of kidnapping or assassinating team
members.

Competitive Giving in Burma

Although the Burmese government had terminated the American aid program in 1953, partly to minimize cold war maneuvering
and dangers to its neutrality, it soon turned to the Communist
countries for aid because of a ruinous decline of the world prices
of rice. Barter agreements were offered by the Soviet Union, China,
and several East European countries, providing for an exchange of
Burma's surplus rice largely for costly capital goods. According
to the 1956 agreement with the U.S.S.R., annual shipments of
400,000 tons of rice were to be exchanged between 1956 and 1960
for machinery, plant equipment, cement, newsprint, chemicals,
and medicine; lesser commitments for rice deliveries were also
made to China, Czechoslovakia, East Germany, Rumania, Poland,
and Bulgaria, in exchange for capital goods and some consumer
items. In 1957, when world rice prices rose again, these exchanges

[18] *USOM News Release*, 142/58, October 7, 1958. *Le Song* reported on
July 8, 1959, that 52,900 tilapia fish were bred during the previous year in
Thanh Giao, Le Phong, and Duc Khanh.

were no longer profitable for Burma, and a second look at the prices, quality, and suitability of the Communist equipment suggested a reversal of the Burmese course.[19] Annual shipments to the U.S.S.R. were cut from 400,000 to 100,000 metric tons, and those to China from 150,000 to 50,000, while those to Poland were cancelled. These unfortunate experiences were somewhat offset by other aid from the Communist bloc, and some experts warned that Burma might again be tempted to enter into negotiations with the East if competition from surplus U.S. rice entering the Asian market should become more acute.

In the meantime, direct aid from the Communist bloc had already been introduced. The Bulganin-Khrushchev visit in 1955 culminated in the offer of a technological institute. In March 1956, Mikoyan visited the country and offered a 200-bed hospital at Taungyi, a theater seating 1,800, a sports and cultural center with a 50,000-seat stadium, buildings for agricultural and industrial exhibitions, a conference hall to accommodate 100,000, a 206-room hotel, and a swimming pool. After a visit by U Nu to Moscow, a thirty-man Soviet economic mission came to advise on cultural and industrial development and to supervise construction of the proposed projects. Although these projects may have been offered in good faith, U Nu's cabinet was nevertheless unwilling to accept "gifts" from any great power on the ground that it might undermine Burma's neutral position. The final agreements, therefore, provided for "gifts" of Burmese rice of "equal" value to "the people of the Soviet Union" over an estimated twenty-year period.

Burma's devotion to principle had its economic drawbacks. Because the projects had been born out of Communist whims and Burmese impulses rather than from a reasoned priority of economic

[19] According to some sources, the price paid for Burmese rice shipments to the U.S.S.R. in 1957 was 20 per cent below the price Japan was paying for the same amount and similar grades of rice. It was also charged that Communist goods were overpriced in comparison with free-world sources by as much as 10 to 20 per cent. According to an official Burmese analysis, a value of 102 million kyats was received for 208,000 tons of rice shipped to "barter countries" in 1954–55, as compared with 743 million kyats for 1,422,000 tons shipped elsewhere. *Economic Survey of Burma*, 1956 (Rangoon: Director of Information, 1956). The average figures would be 6 per cent less from Communist sources than from the Western world. John Seabury Thomson asserts that "Burma estimates her loss between 10 and 30 per cent on all barter agreements to date." "Burmese Neutralism," *Political Science Quarterly*, June 1957, p. 278.

needs, the decision to pay for Soviet aid resulted in uneconomic planning and bad timing. Upon second thought it became necessary to seek ways of diverting the gifts to other uses. The technological institute, patterned after the famous Moscow model, was later tentatively rescheduled to become part of the engineering school of the University of Rangoon; the "gift" hotel had proved unreasonably costly and was scarcely a sound project. Eventually Burma suspended the construction of the sports complex completely and delayed building the industrial and agricultural exhibition halls on the unexceptionable grounds that it would first be desirable to develop industries that could turn out the exhibits.

The principal Chinese projects in 1957–59, on the other hand, proved to be reasonably practical: a new 40,000-spindle textile mill and additional facilities for an existing mill produced results superior to those obtained by an older mill designed privately by an American firm, because the latter had been equipped to use long-stable cotton and yielded an appalling waste of materials when supplied with Burmese short-staple cotton. In spite of the errors in judgment obligingly made by the Soviet Union, American technology was by no means certain of success in competition with the Communist bloc.

The desire to find an independent basis for national security, coupled with a growing sense of self-confidence, further fostered neutralism until it became almost a religion in postwar Burma. The government obviously was more comfortable with aid from nations outside the major blocs, if it could get it. Moreover, neither Soviet nor American technicians could be obtained as cheaply as those from other sources. American technicians cost the Burmese government in 1959 some $1,000 per month, more than twice as much as technicians from Israel ($400) or Yugoslavia ($350–$400); while comparable Soviet technicians cost $768 plus an additional $420 for a Russian interpreter (usually Russian-English) who was required for each technician under the agreement. Housing, transportation, and other perquisites were about the same for all technicians. The Americans were willing to supply technicians without charge, but this was no advantage because of Burmese attitudes toward foreign "charity."

When American aid returned to Burma after the Burmese had learned by experience some of the difficulties of dealing with Communist countries, relations were still anything but easy. Specific

American responses to requests often seemed to the Burmese uncomfortably like those of the Sino-Soviet bloc. By force of circumstance the program was somewhat haphazard, piecemeal, and not closely coordinated on either the Burmese or the American side. The American projects were designed to rival the propaganda effect of the Russian "gifts," except that they were, hopefully, to be economically useful as well as politically impressive. Like the Soviet projects, U.S. grants were offered free of restrictions and with the hope that, if they proved successful, the Burmese government might be disposed to further and more beneficial relations with the donor.

In spite of all these gestures, suspicion of American motives remained. An "exposé" in the American Scripps-Howard press alleging waste in the Viet-Nam program and the criticisms implied in *The Ugly American* were subjects of special comment among Burmese officials. As a member of the national planning staff pointed out to the author, the Burmese government wanted to approve every proposed American technician in advance in order to get "decent chaps" instead of "the other kind." The general preference for using American companies that had no experience in the Far East was based on the desire to avoid those who had "learned how to bribe government officials."

Cooperation proved more difficult in neutralist Burma than in allied countries which were our partners in the cold war, and the presence of multiple and competing forms of aid rendered each project less effective there than it would have been as part of an integrated program. But whatever the degree of alignment with the United States, even purely technical and apparently insignificant aid projects in Burma and other parts of Southeast Asia showed the marks of world politics. In few cases could the economic and technical standards developed in the United States be applied to projects undertaken in the shadow of the cold war.

4. Some Achievements of Foreign Aid

Any estimate of the extent to which American aid in Southeast Asia accomplished the international objectives set for it must be speculative. The objectives were not only imprecise in themselves but they were subject to modification with the changing times; and there were neither causal chains attached to the political developments of the past decade nor the means for observing what would have happened if American aid had not intervened at all. Accountants' reports can give a detailed list of where American dollars went, but they cannot state what they achieved.

This study is more concerned with problems and failures than with achievements. But a reasonable perspective on both the realities and potentialities of foreign aid requires a recital of accomplishments, based not on an accountant's or warehouseman's reckoning, but on a general assessment of the political consequences of American operations in the four countries under consideration. The estimates that follow are not intended to anticipate the conclusions of the study; they are rather the accomplishments of foreign aid as seen by its practitioners and closest observers, a part of the broad background of purpose and achievement against which the problems and the failures may be judged.

The Achievements in Viet-Nam

In spite of numerous criticisms, the Viet-Nam program has been cited both by official and by unofficial sources as a model of what American aid can achieve.[20] In 1954 the politics of Viet-Nam were commonly described in the Western press, not without some justification, as "anarchy," Ngo Dinh Diem as "inept," and his government as ready "to fall of its own corrupt weight."[21] Senator Mansfield considered the outlook "grim and discouraging"; he was even recommending that in "the event that the Diem government falls . . . the United States should consider an immediate sus-

[20] Even Albert Colegrove's denunciation, the most celebrated "scandal" report of the Viet-Nam program (see below, Chapter V), conceded at once: "True enough, we have accomplished our main mission. We have kept Viet-Nam from Communist conquest and from economic collapse." Scripps-Howard newspapers, July 20, 1959. See also *Current Situation in the Far East*, House Hearings, 1959, cited, p. 23 and elsewhere; American Friends of Vietnam, *Aid to Vietnam—An American Success Story* (New York: Author, 1959); *Criticisms of the Foreign Aid Program and Comments Supplied by the Department of State, the International Cooperation Administration, and the Department of Defense*, for the House Foreign Affairs Committee, 86th Cong. (Washington: GPO, 1959), pp. 102–112; David Hotham, "U.S. Aid to Viet Nam—A Balance Sheet," *The Reporter*, September 16, 1957, p. 30; "The Tough Miracle Man of Viet Nam," *Life*, May 13, 1957, pp. 156–176.

[21] C. L. Sulzberger, *The New York Times*, December 8, 1954; "Mr. Diem Loses Favour," *The Economist*, October 8, 1955, pp. 129–130.

pension of all aid to Vietnam and the French Union forces there. . . ."[22] Even a year later, the Senator observed: "Apart from the support of the United States, [Diem] enjoyed little international confidence," adding that even in his own country the Vietnamese President's authority was effective only in the large cities.[23]

In many ways Viet-Nam was not yet a nation. While communism had imposed its brutal but effective order in the northern provinces, the truncated southern half seemed to lack the authority and sense of unity needed to hold its warring factions together. The Geneva truce of 1954 had resulted in a temporary partition, pending the anticipated reunification of the country in 1956 by means of free elections, and, before the new government in Saigon could even establish itself, its overthrow was threatened by Communist guerrillas from the north and three dissident factions in the south. The French had no confidence in Diem, and among the Americans in Saigon there was much debate over the advisability of committing the United States to his uncertain cause. When the decision was taken, late in 1955, U.S. aid began as a "crash" program that had to neglect economic development and other long-range considerations.

Only a few months later Senator Green described the setting: "Rarely if ever in history has a state come into being amid such inauspicious circumstances: arbitrarily split in two at the end of a bitter 8-year war; suddenly given independence after a period of colonialism during which the colonial power made no effort at all to train civil servants or to prepare the people for self-government in other ways; faced with an influx of 800,000 refugees from the north; confronted with open rebellion on the part of pirates and bandits masquerading as religious sects; threatened by Communist infiltration and subversion; and . . . with virtually no economic resources." Indeed, he concluded, the "most impressive thing about Vietnam is that it exists," an outcome in which "United States military and economic assistance and United States

[22] *Report on Indochina,* for the Senate Committee on Foreign Relations, 1954, cited, pp. 2, 14.

[23] *Viet Nam, Cambodia, and Laos,* Report by Senator Mike Mansfield for the Senate Committee on Foreign Relations, 84th Cong., 1st sess. (Washington: GPO, 1955), p. 1.

political support have played a vital part."[24] Within two years of the establishment of Diem's government U.S. aid was able to develop from an urgent concern with security to a broader program which included assistance for economic recovery and development.[25] American aid had not accomplished the building of a nation unaided, but few—least of all President Diem himself— would argue that Viet-Nam could have survived without it.

The achievement in Viet-Nam meant more than survival alone, however, even though the attainment of certain other objectives was to remain in doubt. The machinery of government was made more efficient and, for a time, more responsive to popular demands; gradually Diem's regime built up a degree of political consensus, as well as a strong national army. The inflationary effects of a major defense effort were curbed, and economic productivity was increased. Finally, a slow improvement in civil liberties took place in both urban and rural areas, although progress in this field did not completely fulfill American hopes. In each case the means employed by the government itself were nourished by American funds or were adopted in response to American suggestions. The political failures of Ngo Dinh Diem[26] were chargeable to American hesitance as well as to Vietnamese indifference. But in spite of the tremendous proportion of the national budget supported with aid dollars, the ultimate decisions at all levels were made by Vietnamese, sometimes, as will be demonstrated later, over American protest; and the responsibility for the achievements of the Republic of Viet-Nam remained Vietnamese. It would be absurd to suggest that Diem was anti-Communist because of American aid or that the durability of his regime was bought with U.S. dollars. But without this support it is difficult to conceive of

[24] *Technical Assistance in the Far East, South Asia, and Middle East,* Report by Senator Theodore F. Green for the Senate Committee on Foreign Relations, 84th Cong., 2d sess. (Washington: GPO, 1956), p. 14.

[25] Cf. "The Role of Foreign Aid in the Economic Recovery of Vietnam," in *Aid to Vietnam—An American Success Story,* cited, pp. 75–84. Three phases of recovery are listed in this paper: restoration of internal order, 1955–56; preparation for development, 1957–58; and beginning of development, from 1959 on. Cf. also Leland Barrows, "United States-Vietnamese Cooperation: The ICA Program Since 1955," same, p. 33.

[26] These are detailed in Adrian Jaffe and Milton C. Taylor, "A Crumbling Bastion: Flattery and Lies Won't Save Vietnam," *The New Republic,* June 19, 1961, pp. 17–20.

any means whereby the regime could have developed resources leading to those results.

One of the most dramatic achievements of aid in cooperation with local efforts was "Operation Exodus," an emergency program involving the transportation, settling, and resettling of hundreds of thousands of refugees from Communist North Viet-Nam. During the ten months following the 1954 partition more than 786,000 refugees were evacuated, largely by French planes and ships. Assistance for moving and settling the refugees came from many diverse sources: the governments of Great Britain, Australia, West Germany, New Zealand, and the Netherlands; the UN Children's Fund; and a number of private American agencies, including the National Catholic Welfare Conference, the Junior Chamber of Commerce, and CARE. But the overwhelming contribution came from the U.S. government, which undertook 97 per cent of the costs, supplied technicians and advisers, and gave vast stores of supplies and capital equipment. The American contribution was $55 million in 1955 alone, including $44 million for immediate relief and resettlement and $11 million for transportation provided by the U.S. navy. In 1956 another $37 million was contributed for the permanent resettlement of over 300,000 northerners.

American, French, and Vietnamese technicians and administrators had to deal with two thousand to eight thousand refugees a day arriving in Saigon to "squat" on the boulevards, along the docks, and in the old Opera House. In a matter of months the refugees were resettled, at least temporarily, while surveys and plans were under way for the creation of over three hundred resettlement villages. In one giant reclamation project at Cai San, 47,000 northerners were grub-staked until they could support themselves. This program, the consequence of an international agreement, represented an opportunity to demonstrate to the world a popular rejection of communism in a region where Marxism had a strong intellectual appeal. But it was also unmistakably more than a propaganda gesture, and if humane considerations were not actually used to justify the program to the U.S. Congress, their presence was evident enough from the magnitude and manner of the American participation in a remarkably successful refugee project. Faults in administration and planning and problems of internal coordination, some of which had tragic results, were not hard to find. But they were insignificant beside the achievements.[27]

The Achievements in Taiwan

In American policy Taiwan represented far more than a military bastion that had to be firmly held. It was a symbol of free China. Thus Taiwan's position as custodian of the traditional values of Chinese civilization offered extraordinary prospects for positive American aid operations that could enhance it. Throughout Southeast Asia, Nationalist China was generally considered a government in exile vainly awaiting the reversal of a judgment of history. But American advisers believed that, regardless of the chances of such a rebirth, an aggressive assertion of economic drive and educational leadership from Taiwan could have an impact on the attitudes of the Overseas Chinese throughout the region and could give the island a more substantial and permanent role in the politics of the Far East. In both of these respects American aid was to have an important part. Large amounts of military aid had not enabled the Nationalists to maintain control of the mainland, but successful evacuation and gradual rehabilitation of morale enabled Chiang's government on Taiwan to offer a limited but positive challenge to Communist China's aspirations.

As in Viet-Nam the fundamental fact that Taiwan remained free of Communist control was the main achievement of American policy, and specifically of American aid. From the demoralized remnants of the Nationalist forces a powerful army was created on Taiwan. On the economic side, U.S. aid enabled Chinese entrepreneurship to arrive by 1960 at a stage where the island was said to expect self-sustaining development within five years.

The economy of Taiwan could easily support its population (9.5 million, including two million refugees from the mainland), if not the military effort it was compelled to sustain. The island's rice yield was among the highest in the world, averaging for its

[27] See "Administrative Planning for the Cai San Resettlement Project," "The Cai San Tractor Loans," "Boundary and Land Questions at Tan Mai Village," and "The Commissar and the Law," in John D. Montgomery and the NIA Case Development Seminar, *Cases in Vietnamese Administration* (Saigon: National Institute of Administration, 1959). Some critiques of the refugee program appear in Richard W. Lindholm, ed., *Viet-Nam, the First Five Years* (East Lansing: Michigan State University Press, 1959), pp. 45–103.

two yearly crops 4.8 metric tons per hectare; of its annual production of 1.8 million metric tons, 10 per cent was exported. This
technical triumph in agriculture was strengthened by one of the
most successful land reforms in history, which led to an increase
in over-all production and greater shares for the individual farmer
and his family. The Joint Commission for Rural Reconstruction
is the author of these remarkable achievements. Its operations
are entirely financed by the United States, partly with direct dollar
aid but mainly with local currency from the "counterpart funds,"
although over half of the cost of the projects supported by the
JCRR is borne by local sponsoring agencies.

Industrial development on Taiwan started from a base well
established during half a century of Japanese rule. The Japanese
industries were taken over by the Nationalists after World War II,
and most of them remained under government ownership and
control. But private Chinese enterprise, stimulated by new opportunities and reinforced by a variety of aid programs, developed
rapidly; by 1960 there were an estimated 20,000 industrial enterprises each employing twenty to forty workers.[28] The government
further proposed to sell to private owners those public enterprises
which were not directly related to national defense and were not
major public utilities, thus raising funds to be plowed back into
economic development. Chiang's government also rescinded its
policy of buying shares in nominally private enterprises, announc-
ing that it would no longer invest "in those enterprises which
private owners can operate except in public utilities and in those
enterprises that are pilot plants or in the nature of demonstrations."[29]

In the seven-year period 1952-58 agricultural production increased by 41.6 per cent, and industrial production by 85.6 per
cent. Real national income rose by 50 per cent and the real income
of every person on Taiwan by 24.4 per cent (taking into account

[28] The estimate is derived from ICA sources and from figures supplied by
the Nationalist government. See *The Department of State Bulletin*, April 11,
1960, p. 573. Cf. Department of State, *The Republic of China*, Publication
6844 (Washington: GPO, 1959), where the figure is given as 14,000 (p. 34).
This relates to "separate manufacturing and processing enterprises."

[29] C. T. Yang, "Direction of Economic Development," *Free China Review*,
November 1959, p. 16; Premier Chen Cheng, "Economic Outlook of Free
China," oral report to the first meeting of the 25th session of the Legislative
Yuan, February 16, quoted in *Free China Review*, March 1960, p. 49.

the large annual population growth which averaged over 3.3 per cent).[30] The American-sponsored Small Industry Loan program had already lent $11 million, and both the China Development Corporation (founded in 1959) and the China Productivity Center (dating from 1955) offered managerial and technical services.

The most serious economic problem of the island was a continuous inflation, a regressive form of taxation which permitted the government to pay off its debts in cheap money. Between 1949 and 1958 the value of the currency had dropped to less than a third of its former value in relation to the American dollar. The government did not, however, manipulate its exchange rate to absorb these losses, which was taken as evidence of its good faith in using American aid dollars for the purposes intended rather than syphoning part of them into the general treasury for its own use. Chinese officials often cited this fact in comparing favorably the forthrightness of their government's dealings with the United States with those of Viet-Nam and other countries receiving large amounts of aid.

The record of economic, military, and political achievements on Taiwan was marred by continuing tension between the native Taiwanese and the refugee mainlanders. Differences in custom and language between the newcomers and their Taiwanese cousins were not eased by efforts to teach Mandarin in the schools (which, incidentally, paralleled a decision made by the Red Chinese for the mainland). This language program tended to alienate parents even though it facilitated communication with officials from Taipei: some villagers noted that visiting dignitaries tended to address their questions to children because of the higher probability of being understood when they spoke Mandarin. Because so many of the nearly two million Nationalists who had withdrawn from China in 1949 were educated and respected members of the old elite, they far overshadowed in sheer numbers the professionally and technically skilled classes native to Taiwan. When the Nationalist government was transferred to Taiwan, the same group of officials performed essentially the same functions as they had in China. It was obvious, entirely apart from their military strength, that these mainland groups would dominate the islanders, who had been previously curbed by nearly two generations of

[30] C. T. Yang, "Direction of Economic Development," cited, p. 14.

Japanese domination; but the Taiwanese, understandably, were dissatisfied with their subordinate role.

The mainland monopoly of important administrative, judicial, and military posts was rationalized by the Nationalist government's claim that it represented all of China, rather than the single province of Taiwan. The Taiwanese, for their part, were aware that their payment of taxes supplied most of the government's internal revenue and that their drafted soldiers provided nearly half of the lower ranks of the army. In spite of some improvements in economic and political opportunities, the native islanders wanted greater representation in the government, and their leaders even hoped that the United States would intercede "to insure the placing of Taiwanese parties on the ballot in future elections."[31] Careful of its relations with the Chiang government, the United States declined to intervene in Taiwan's politics, despite the so-called "Herter Doctrine" that had made its appearance in Korea in 1960. Further improvements in the political lot of the Taiwanese people would improve the stability of the island, but attempts by the United States to use its aid as a political lever—even assuming they would be effective—could easily impugn the independence of the Nationalist government and affect other American objectives. The unresolved problem testified to some of the limitations of foreign aid as an instrument of diplomacy.

Results in Thailand and Burma

In Thailand, in the absence of crisis diplomacy, the United States offered a much smaller program and scored few dramatic achievements. In spite of a lack of public enthusiasm for the American military aid program and an evident concern lest the association affect its ability to maintain an independent foreign policy, Thailand's alignment with the West was unequivocal. Yet without the benefits of American aid, the costs of her participation in the Korean War, her restrictions on trade with China, and her solid support of the Southeast Asia Treaty arrangement could have endangered her domestic and international position. As it was, the government maintained its pro-Western alignment with no sacrifice of public support or evidence of economic hardship.

Achievements of the aid program in Thailand may more justly

[31] Jacques Nevard, in *The New York Times*, June 1, 1960.

be measured by financial and technical standards than in Viet-Nam, where local projects had to be activated quickly in order to counter the inflationary effects of large expenditures on military aid. The relative lack of urgency permitted more fruitful experimentation in the administration of projects as well as greater Thai understanding and acceptance of U.S. technical and procedural requirements. The projects supported by U.S. aid were mainly in the fields of fiscal administration, community planning in education and health, and agricultural extension services. At the same time a large number of university and other private groups—twenty-two in mid-1959—worked on introducing gradual institutional changes that could take place without disturbing the calm flow of events characteristic of Thailand. Presumably the political, social, and even economic achievements of American aid under such favorable conditions will in the long run offer a more favorable return than the crisis programs characteristic of Viet-Nam or Taiwan.

Achievements in Burma were necessarily modest. The programs were small, and the experience of having them cut off by the Burmese made the United States especially prudent. When invited to return in 1957, the United States accepted Burma's neutrality on her own terms, offered no suggestion of alignment with SEATO or other pro-Western associations, and restrained even the impulse to render advice on the fundamental requirements for national development. The new program, basically a symbolic gesture of friendship, still served to balance Soviet economic efforts in Burma and permitted a real, though almost imperceptible, movement to the West. The U.S. project grants, together with a small program supplying military equipment to the police, provided tangible and acceptable support for Burma's efforts to maintain political and economic independence. When the U Nu government returned to power in 1960, it did not choose to reverse the favorable attitude of the Ne Win caretaker regime, and further U.S. support was forthcoming when the new government requested it.

The token program in Burma did not yield optimum technical results from either the American or the Burmese viewpoint. American technicians, who were absent or, at best, remote from operating responsibilities, were skeptical of the effectiveness of official Burmese planning and supervision. Burma itself was to find that coordinating assorted aid from numerous public and private sources strained its understaffed planning and operating agencies. The difficulties were illustrated—and in this one case successfully resolved—in the land restoration project under the Agricultural and Rural Development Corporation. This effort was designed both to resettle surplus urban population on abandoned lands and to diversify agricultural production with a view to restoring foreign exchange earnings. Since the war millions of acres of rice land had gone out of cultivation; at the same time, while rural production declined, the national population increased from 16 million to 20 million, indicating a constant movement toward the cities. The four-year resettlement project included restoring water control dikes and channels and plowing the land, as well as relocating the surplus urban population. The UN Food and Agriculture Organization and the Colombo Plan nations contributed experts to train farm machinery operators and mechanics; Russian technicians worked on the introduction of long-staple cotton, soil surveys, and the survey and design of two dams; Israeli experts advised on pump irrigation, and the U.S. Development Loan Fund helped to finance the project. The planning and integration of these international aid activities into a coherent program remained, of course, a responsibility of the Burmese.

Neutral Burma attracted aid from many sources and, while each offer was relatively small, each was also free of political or economic conditions. The considerable burdens of establishing planning and operating priorities, inviting donor participation, and supervising project performance fell on the Burmese government alone. While that task might have been accomplished much more efficiently by a single external agency working with the government, Burma was not prepared to try the experiment. Foreign aid to underdeveloped countries must often sacrifice administrative efficiency to national self-determination and self-reliance.

Regionalism

In addition to these achievements in the individual countries of Southeast Asia, American aid programs contributed also to a slowly developing regionalism. Under U.S. sponsorship several countries in the area undertook cooperative planning and joint operations designed to serve both mutual security interests and the needs of economic and cultural development. The implications of sustained U.S. military and economic support tended to encourage a climate of stability and to identify foreign aid as more than a series of responses to immediate threats. It is indicative of the American desire to avoid the appearance of a purely military defensive diplomacy that the United States began using its foreign aid programs to give SEATO broader purposes than those of mutual defense. SEATO, designed to afford a response to military challenges, was beginning to offer means for encouraging regional cooperation for cultural and economic purposes as well: scholarships, professorships, exchanges, economic surveys, and special training programs. The vast Mekong River development project, extensive programs of international communications and transportation, and increasingly important cultural exchanges were all supported partly or entirely with American funds. The capitals of Southeast Asia were still more closely linked to London or to Paris than to each other,[32] but there was evidence that increasing exchanges within the region might alter this relationship. Where in 1952, for example, fifty Southeast Asians were studying in other countries in their region, the number had increased to 1,500 in 1959.

For reasons already suggested, a great variety of regional programs was sponsored by the U.S. aid mission in Thailand. The American effort to encourage regionalism took place on a project-by-project basis, however, rather than as a coordinated program to establish or support Thai leadership. The malaria control program in Thailand, for example, provided the first evidence that complete eradication of the disease was technically feasible. Under the guidance and financing of the U.S. mission in cooperation with the Thai Ministry of Health and the World Health Organization, the project provided a coordinating center for the activities of similar units in Burma, Cambodia, Laos, Malaya, and Viet-Nam. A communications program represented the largest of the U.S. regional programs, involving a projected network for Thailand, Laos, and Viet-Nam (Cambodia declining to participate), for military, naval, police, civil aviation, and commercial uses. A regional program in English instruction was set up by ICA in 1958, with headquarters in Bangkok and linguistic study teams from the University of Michigan in Viet-Nam and Laos. ICA

[32] See William Henderson, "The Development of Regionalism in Southeast Asia," *International Organization*, November 1955, pp. 463–476.

helped to establish a program in marine research in Viet-Nam and Thailand, with the expectation that Cambodia might later join, and also proposed a regional study of insects and pests, intended to include Burma, Cambodia, Laos, the Philippines, Thailand, and Viet-Nam, in the hope of creating conditions leading to efficient control and quarantine of pests common to the entire region.

In the Mekong River development project, under the sponsorship of the United Nations' Economic Commission for Asia and the Far East, surveys were jointly arranged by Thailand, Viet-Nam, Laos, and Cambodia for the development of navigation, irrigation and power dams, and mineral resources along Southeast Asia's great waterway. The United States had invested $2.5 million on one such survey by 1959, and much more extensive outlays were anticipated. Important contributions from several other countries had been received even before the United States had subscribed its aid. France offered $500,000 in equipment; Canada, aerial mapping assistance; Iran, petroleum products; New Zealand, four jet-propelled boats; Britain, a scientific vessel; Japan, a $500,000 tributary study; and India, a supply of rain gauges.

SEATO headquarters in Bangkok, although principally occupied with military matters, were also becoming an important center of economic planning for Southeast Asia. Under SEATO sponsorship the United States financed a contract with the University of Hawaii to institute a program for training skilled workers throughout the region, and another with Colorado State University for advice in establishing a graduate school of engineering to be open to students throughout Southeast Asia. American support also went to international cooperative programs in technical assistance sponsored by the Colombo Plan, the International Labor Office, and the United Nations. Regional aid programs are always difficult to establish and complex to administer, but at least half a dozen were operating successfully by 1959, and other possible fields of activity were under consideration with strong support from the Thai government.

The recent cooperative enterprises should not obscure the fact that Thai relations in the region had not been always uniformly friendly. Relations between Thailand and Burma, of nearly equal size and population, both deeply Buddhist, and each dependent upon the export of rice and timber, had never been close. Burmese attacks on Thai villages accused of arming Nationalist Chinese troops in Burma reflected a background of centuries of intermittent distrust. Exchanges of state visits in 1955, however, including expiatory gifts from Burma, provided a basis for negotiating projects of interest to both countries. Thailand's similar difficulties with Cambodia, however, arising out of border questions, have resulted in threatened closures and the temporary severance of diplomatic relations. The Thai concern with possible Communist infiltration applied to Laos as well as Cambodia. In 1955 Thailand proposed that the SEATO Council in Bangkok consider the question of the Communist threat in Laos, inspired and supported from North Viet-Nam, a proposition which Laos resented as an interference in a domestic question. Even in 1960, Thai interest in rumored pro-Communist activities of the Laotian government provoked sharp criticism from that country. Viet-Minh activity among refugees living in Thailand was also a serious matter between the governments of South Viet-Nam and Thailand, especially after the latter agreed in August 1959 to permit the Communist government of North Viet-Nam to supervise the evacuation of 50,000 Vietnamese refugees from the Indo-China wars.

Regional projects were also supported by American aid missions in the Philippines, Viet-Nam, and Taiwan. An important project for providing higher education to Overseas Chinese in Southeast Asia was instituted not only to project the image of Taiwan as the protector of Chinese culture, but also to weaken the drawing power of Peking among Chinese emigrants throughout the region. In some respects it was inconsistent for the United States to encourage Chinese students living abroad to complete their education in Taiwan, and at the same time to urge Overseas Chinese communities to find means of integrating themselves with their adopted countries. But the more pressing political realities in the struggle for Chinese support were to overrule the policy favoring integration.

The total population of the Chinese communities in Southeast Asia was estimated at more than twelve million. Of these, nearly three million lived in Thailand, where 60 per cent were described by the government as sympathetic to communism.[33] Their in-

[33] Dennis Warner, "Peking and the Overseas Chinese," *The New Republic*, January 12, 1959, p. 14.

fluence in Thailand, as elsewhere, was out of proportion to their numbers, their social prestige, or their actual political power, for nearly all of the private businesses in Thailand not owned by Westerners were in the hands of Chinese entrepreneurs. Almost one million Chinese emigrants lived in Viet-Nam, where native-born Chinese were "granted" Vietnamese citizenship in August 1956, with the alternative of being barred from their traditional trades. In the Philippines, about 200,000 of the total population of 21 million were Chinese. All were barred from trade. In Singapore, 80 per cent of the population of 1.7 million were Chinese. In Malaya the 2.35 million Chinese constituted well over a third of the total population. Another 2.5 to 3 million Chinese lived in Indonesia, where the government first discriminated against the small but growing minority favorable to Nationalist China, and then by enforcing restrictive measures against the entire Chinese community provoked a bitter dispute with Communist China. All in all, because of the wealth and the human potential of the Overseas Chinese throughout the region, and because of their symbolic "uncommitted" position, they were important both to Taiwan and to Communist China.[34]

When Vice President Nixon visited Southeast Asia in 1953 he expressed concern over the fact that ten thousand Chinese nationals living in that region were leaving their adopted countries each year to complete their education,[35] many in Communist universities. He recommended that an effort be made to counter this trend by developing educational facilities on Taiwan capable of challenging the Red Chinese intellectual leadership. Taiwan already enjoyed the most elaborate program of mass primary edu-

---

[34] On December 8, 1958, the *New York Herald Tribune* quoted a report by the Overseas Affairs Department of the government of the Republic of China stating that $35 million of capital investment had come to Taiwan from Overseas Chinese, largely during the previous two years. Reports in 1959 and 1960 reflected disappointment in the actual Overseas Chinese investments in Taiwan, however.

[35] This figure includes those coming to the West. On July 7, 1953, *The Times* (London) estimated that seven thousand Chinese in Southeast Asia would go to mainland China for an education in that year, which was perhaps the peak of the Red Chinese efforts to attract their overseas countrymen. Only two thousand had gone in 1952 and three thousand in 1951. Robert S. Elegant, *The Dragon's Seed: Peking and the Overseas Chinese* (New York: St. Martin's Press, 1959), underestimates the extent and success of the Nationalists' Overseas Chinese education program.

cation of any province in China, thanks to two generations of Japanese rule; but the facilities for secondary and higher education were far from adequate to meet the postwar demands on Taiwan. U.S. aid accordingly financed the construction of almost all the new educational facilities for the Overseas Chinese. The U.S. mission spent 172.7 million New Taiwan dollars between 1954 and 1960 for the construction of special educational facilities.

The number of students coming to Taiwan as a result of this program increased from 60 in 1951 to 885 in 1954 (the first year of operations), finally rising to 7,017 to 1959 (2,564 from Hong Kong; 1,231 from Viet-Nam; 894 from Indonesia; 775 from Singapore and Malaya; 454 from Korea; 406 from Thailand; 170 from the Philippines; and the rest from other countries of Southeast Asia). Because of the superiority of the Taiwan educational facilities over those available to Overseas Chinese in their various adopted homelands, and because the selection was not academically discriminating at first, the quality of the students did not compare favorably with that of the native Taiwanese.

The reaction of the other countries to the education of a somewhat unpopular Chinese minority was not reassuring. In Viet-Nam and Indonesia, in spite of the almost desperate need for professional and technical men, the governments refused to re-admit these students upon completion of their studies, although they had been willing enough earlier to permit their departure for Taiwan. In other countries, where such restrictions were not adopted, alumni from Taiwan still encountered great difficulty in establishing themselves appropriately in their adopted homelands. Only in Hong Kong and Macao were they welcomed. In view of the fact that non-Chinese students returning from Western countries to their homes were given preference, one may conclude that the resentments against the Overseas Chinese alumni were a result of prejudice against Chinese rather than foreign education as such. The Chinese communities abroad were probably all the more isolated from their neighbors as a result of this program. Experience was beginning to suggest that the more educated and ambitious members of the Chinese communities were the very ones whom the nationalistic societies of Southeast Asia were most reluctant to absorb.

The program also aroused mild criticism from the Taiwanese, who sometimes resented the fact that the construction of new facilities for their less qualified cousins from overseas was given preference over the development of educational facilities for themselves, an argument which ignored the fact that the buildings and equipment were to remain in Taiwan for use after the program was completed. On the whole the Nationalist government showed less enthusiasm for the program than its potential would have suggested, except as a building operation. Indeed, seldom has a program designed to provide education where its need and political advantages were so obvious met with such indifference. To students given an opportunity to complete their education in the context of their own finest cultural heritage, the benefits of the program were self-evident. But its political success was inextricably linked to the future prospects of Taiwan.

Regional programs, however useful in themselves, were by no means automatically acceptable to all Southeast Asian nations. Programs supported by U.S. foreign aid were for the most part technical and politically harmless, and indeed were often chosen for that reason; but politics were never very far in the background. The very fact of foreign support usually made it certain that political questions could not be avoided. Some real progress was made, but no giant strides could be taken toward a regional economy until the governments were ready for it.

Conclusion

This brief tally of the achievements of foreign aid is revealing in part for what is left unsaid. It is not, of course, an evaluation, but it does suggest some of the basic potentials and limitations of U.S. foreign aid. It cannot be argued, for example, that American aid has converted enemies into neutrals or neutrals into allies; indeed, American aid probably has not changed any foreign or domestic policies in Southeast Asia that affect vital national interests of those nations. Moreover, when governments have failed to respond to their own pressing domestic or international needs, American assistance has never been able to compensate for deficiencies in national authority. Finally, the exponents of aid have not claimed for military and economic assistance the power to guarantee the survival of a nation hemmed in with vastly superior military forces or infested with guerrillas.

Within these limits, much has been accomplished: decisive support has been given to governments seeking to maintain their independence; trends of international and domestic policy that will contribute toward stability and decency have been sustained; and, at times, the United States has even been able to encourage internal forces that promise greater respect for human rights and more responsible and more representative government. Foreign aid has shown a usefulness and versatility that have earned it a distinctive and permanent place in the arsenal of peace. The practical difficulties and far-reaching consequences of this vital part of our foreign policy require an intensive, continual, and critical scrutiny, carefully tempered with a sympathetic understanding of the limited possibilities of American action in each political situation.

II PROBLEMS OF MUTUALITY IN
FOREIGN AID

Oₙₑ ᴏꜰ the most confusing aspects of foreign aid is the deceptive quality of the mutuality that is supposed to exist between the governments extending and receiving aid. Diplomatic enthusiasm tends to exaggerate the common purposes between cooperating countries, even to the point of overlooking genuine differences of interest and policy. Recognition of the strong political, military, and economic forces that have led countries to ally or to associate themselves with the United States should not be permitted to obscure the divisive factors. Countries participate in American aid programs for many different reasons, and mutually supported programs are carried out in different ways and with unequal degrees of enthusiasm. Even in projects developed out of undoubted common interest, matters of technique have sometimes led to vigorous controversy. To will the end is not always to will the means.

The areas of greatest mutuality in foreign aid, presumably, are those affecting the ends of "security" and "economic development." For underdeveloped countries, each of these elements represents an unimpeachable objective of sovereignty and even a prerequisite of national survival; yet for the United States, neither objective has a simple or a constant value for purposes of planning and carrying out an aid program. If "security" is taken to mean adequate military protection against a Communist invasion, it can easily be interpreted in the receiving country as a cold war issue involving only the United States and the Communist bloc; if the term is restricted to the establishment of domestic law and order, the United States risks interfering with a sensitive matter of national sovereignty no matter what it proposes. Even "economic development" is subject to varying interpretations. Is the purpose of development to be defined as economic autarchy, higher agricultural production, rapid industrialization, improving immediate living standards, a favorable balance of trade, or some combination of these and other aims? Curiously enough, disputes over aid which is intended to serve an avowed common purpose may, on occasion, rival the vehemence and ill will generated by "strings" obviously designed to serve strictly unilateral ends. Problems of mutuality, illustrated by cases described in this chapter, have sometimes proved more thorny than those resulting from certain unilateral and even conflicting policies discussed in Chapter III.

1. Internal Security Problems: Three Cases from Viet-Nam

American military and "defense support" aid is designed principally to maintain the political integrity and economic stability of nations threatened by Communist violence. The possibility of direct invasion by Communist China or her Viet-Minh satellite has strongly influenced the character of the program in Viet-Nam and Taiwan; but a still more urgent threat in Southeast Asia is armed Communist subversion, which Burma, Laos, Viet-Nam, and Malaya have already experienced. Throughout the area the prospect of indirect armed aggression has markedly increased since this pattern was used so clearly and so successfully in Laos.

The problem of internal security in South Viet-Nam, recently accentuated by the increased tempo of assassination, sabotage, large-scale guerrilla warfare, and even regular military operations, has existed since the establishment of the state in 1954. The Communists' decision to concentrate on paramilitary warfare has served them well; for it promises military gains without the likelihood of an encounter with the full force of American military power. American troops are not the answer to subversion and should not be deployed in strength in the absence of a full-scale Communist invasion. At the same time, the necessary forceful action by the Vietnamese government against Communist operations often requires drastic and unpopular repressive measures, thereby encouraging disaffection within the ranks of its own people. Direct or indirect American aid against subversion, however tempered with respect for the principle of national self-determination, may take on for many Vietnamese the appearance it is given by Communist propaganda, that of a cynical disguise for an imperialistic desire to control strategic areas. The Vietnamese government has indeed been unable to ignore such aspersions upon its sovereign dignity, and its acceptance of U.S. aid in resolving internal security problems has been hampered by the knowledge that its enemies would interpret too easy acceptance of American recommendations as symptomatic of American domination. Thus even when cooperating with an ostensible ally, the United States has seen programs undertaken in the common interest of protection against subversion seriously weakened by political difficulties.

Encouraging the government of an underdeveloped country to resist Communist subversion may also provoke resistance from vested interests within the established regime. In order to strengthen a friendly government, American representatives have recommended reorganizing police forces, adopting austerity measures or social reforms, offering greater freedom to responsible criticism, weakening the resources of dubious elements whose support would be a handicap rather than a help in the long run, and generally moving from traditional political procedures toward freer and more efficient Western practices. In these circumstances even close identification of general interests between the United States and the host government has not prevented contradictions and tensions when it came to specific issues.

Whatever the faults of the non-Communist regimes of Southeast Asia, American policy has not actually favored the downfall of any of them, for that would hardly seem the way to guard against Communist subversion. American enthusiasm for existing governments in the region has, however, varied from country to country. While we have tried to aid peoples and not just governments, we have assumed no mandate to intervene and our official blessing naturally has tended to fall on strong anti-Communist leaders. Conversely, leaders pledged to America have considered the United States obligated to their regimes rather than to their peoples. Such situations have presented some of the most difficult political problems we have had to face.

The Civil Guard Case

The history of the Civil Guard in Viet-Nam illustrates the reluctance of a beleaguered government to adopt internal security measures considered necessary by American advisers. Both political and technical reasons were involved: the Ministry of the Interior feared that loyal province chiefs might lose control of the local paramilitary organizations; the army was reluctant to permit the formation of rival national forces; there were rumors of presidential distrust of the Civil Guard; and Vietnamese officials preferred the French tradition of a heavily armed, mobile rural police force, together with use of the army, for purposes of internal security.

For a few years after the civil war of 1955 internal security in Viet-Nam improved continuously in spite of sporadic violence. The security problem that emerged, however, began to take newer and subtler forms. The unruly, vice-ridden armies of the Binh Xuyen and other disorderly sects that challenged Diem's government in 1955 were replaced by a highly trained cadre of Communist professionals, whose activities, tactically related to Viet-Minh strategies north of the 17th parallel, were far too formidable for the capabilities of an untrained rural police. Rural development was being impeded by the sabotage of valuable aid equipment; and above all, as long as officials were being assassinated in the countryside, the administration of local government remained tenuous. In 1959 the toll of such assassinations had risen to twenty each month, and in another year it increased twentyfold. Subsequently the dimensions of the security problem increased immeasurably through stepped-up Communist raids and infiltrations across the borders from the north and west.

The concern of the government of Viet-Nam over Communist violence was obviously shared by the United States, and in May 1955 President Diem invited the U.S. Operations Mission (USOM) to bring a police advisory team to Viet-Nam. Michigan State University provided the requested team, which was expected to recommend both emergency and long-range programs. Assured of ample staffing and financing, the team gradually enlarged the size and the scope of its activities until it covered the entire range of modern police administration, from fingerprinting and traffic engineering to riot control. Because the stakes were high, its recommendations were given support in high places; but performance was not always up to the agreed schedules, especially when the team's proposals threatened established interests and procedures. Few technical assistance projects were more closely related to common policy objectives in Viet-Nam, but few proved more frustrating in practice.

A month before the arrival of the team from Michigan the Vietnamese government set up a Civil Guard under the Ministry of Interior. This force was to reach a maximum strength of some 70,000 members, most of whom were remnants of paramilitary forces at loose ends after the civil war. Some had once fought against Ngo Dinh Diem and had joined him before the fighting was over; others had been his loyal followers from the beginning. Although the Civil Guard was by far the largest of the five police agencies in Viet-Nam—outnumbering the combined strength of the smaller municipal and communal police, the gendarmerie, the sûreté, and volunteer rural police organizations—its professional, social, and political standing was well below that of the army or the rest of the civil service.

The Civil Guard was transferred from the Ministry of the Interior to the Presidency in November 1955, acquiring a broadly defined mission including protection of public security and maintenance of order; enforcement of laws and administrative rules; pacification of recently liberated zones; guarding public buildings, convoys, communications, and national monuments; and ensuring public safety at times of natural disasters. The Guard's early operations were, in consequence, almost all of a military character; they occupied areas recently subdued by the army, engaged bandits and Communists, carried out patrols, seized illegal matériel, and guarded key tactical points and public places.

In spite of these important responsibilities the Civil Guard was poorly equipped and poorly trained in its first year. Many of its members were illiterate. Its pay scales were markedly inferior to those of the national army (which, however, was one of the best paid in Asia). The operations of the Civil Guard were directly controlled by the province chiefs, who were in turn responsible to the Ministry of the Interior and the President for security within their borders. An intermediate regional command was supposed to coordinate activities among provinces, but this command was later abolished, leaving the Guard to function in uncoordinated provincial groups. Units of the Civil Guard were companies of some one hundred and fifty men, normally limited to the boundaries of a single province—it was said that a company was unable to cross provincial boundaries even in hot pursuit without agreement between the chiefs of the two provinces involved. Because each company maintained its headquarters in a military encampment, the Guard's function was necessarily confined to roving patrols and guard detail.

In May 1955, the police advisory group had been invited to survey the Civil Guard's manpower and equipment needs. Its report, approved by the U.S. mission and forwarded to Washington in August, recommended that the Guard should be "a civilian police in every respect . . . apart from any military encampments, directed and instructed by the civilian personnel on civilian police matters, modified, of course, to fit the present conditions in Viet Nam. . . . It is hoped that the National Police will be so trained and distributed that they will very soon popularize themselves with the populace through extra services and courtesies. They are to work themselves into the confidence of the citizens they serve, be considered their protectors both day and night, have their homes in the villages."[1] If the Civil Guard lived permanently in villages, the report envisaged that its units could be "so organized, trained, and equipped that they can quickly become a mobile support task force . . . [coordinated] . . . with the military in cases of a civil crisis or an attack from the outside." A reduction in force to 25,000 was suggested, with the understanding that the least effective members would be eliminated first. Weapons and equipment were to be suited to civil police duties, and organizations and operations were to be designed accordingly.

Shortly after the publication of this report, a new American policy relating to internal security programs throughout the world was communicated to the aid mission in Viet-Nam. Recognizing

---

[1] Michigan State University, *Work Plan in Police Administration* (Saigon), August 29, 1955, p. 3. In later years the MSU group accepted the necessity of assigning certain paramilitary responsibilities to the Civil Guard, but its position, and that of the USOM, generally stressed the Guard's civilian character. While the position of the Military Assistance Advisory Group was less insistent on this feature, it was still perceptibly different from that of President Diem. Even in 1955–56 the training program for the Civil Guard was conducted at the Quang Trung Military Center, largely in basic military subjects, with the cooperative efforts of MSU, MAAG, and the Vietnamese army.

that the primary danger of Communist take-over in under-developed countries lay in local security deficiencies rather than weakness in conventional military defenses, American policy in areas plagued by Communist infiltration was to support the development of local police forces residing in the villages, where they could protect the farmers' lives and property and at the same time encourage their loyalty to the established government. This policy resembled the recommendations the police advisers for Viet-Nam had already offered. American policy thus strongly supported the theory that Civil Guard units stationed in isolated camps and working in the villages only on occasional military details would be, in principle, less effective than village-based civilian units, especially if they and their families could be integrated into the community life. Such a disposition of police forces was expected to weaken the effectiveness of night attacks and internal subversion, two favorite tactics of the Communist forces, by creating permanent centers of loyalty. The practice of using mobile platoons which retreated to temporary military camps or permanent barracks at nightfall was seen as an invitation to Communist activity.

Vietnamese police officials agreed basically with this approach, but pronounced themselves unable to bring the issue to a political decision. Even as late as September 1958, after more than three years of discussion, the Director General of the Civil Guard was proposing that his force should conduct a campaign "to gain the people's heart, so that they may consider us their friends, at all times ready to assist them and protect their rights and fight against rebellion. . . . Through understanding and confidence people will no longer listen to distorted words of the enemy. . . ." The Civil Guard should engage in village projects, he argued, such as building roads, opening markets, and other activities "which do not violate people's rights and property possessions, worship customs and habits."[2] A few months later, the Civil Guard prepared specific proposals for its own reorganization, recommending the elimination of rigid provincial controls over operations in order to increase the mobility of the units. Noting that the thirty-six province chiefs had thirty-six different systems for using the Civil Guard, the report proposed establishing a chain of command in

[2] From an unpublished memorandum by Colonel Dan Van Quang.

which a provincial headquarters would merely coordinate the activities of the five or more companies within its borders and supply administrative and logistical support. These headquarters would be under interprovincial and zonal headquarters for tactical purposes, and the Director General of the Civil Guard would remain responsible to the President.

In the summer of 1957 President Diem indicated, by a series of decisions rather than a general statement, that he disagreed sharply with the professional views of the American and Vietnamese police experts. When the American advisers favored giving the Civil Guard the powers of arrest, investigation, and the serving of subpoenas in addition to its wartime powers, they were supported by the Vietnamese police officials but not by the President. Recommendations for assigning civilian gendarmerie officers as Guard leaders, rather than army officers on temporary duty, were likewise accepted by the professionals and turned down by the political leaders. The Americans finally advocated a reduction in force to thirty thousand or less, resettlement of all honorably discharged members in the land development centers, and diversion of the resulting savings to an adequate equipment maintenance program.[3] The President overruled all these proposals. He determined to maintain the strength of the Guard at fifty thousand and to use it to augment his military forces, which were limited to one hundred and fifty thousand by the Geneva Accord of 1954. As the Civil Guard also appeared to be a useful device for keeping the loyalty of young and vigorous Vietnamese, Diem was all the more reluctant to see it reduced.

These serious differences of opinion were most clearly revealed in the various proposals for equipping the Civil Guard. In July 1957, the Vietnamese government requested $60 million worth of equipment, including armored vehicles, artillery, landing craft, bazookas, helicopters, and other heavy equipment. The American advisers had in the meantime drafted equipment lists based on

---

[3] Maintenance, operations, and amortization of the six hundred police vehicles given under Michigan State University advice were estimated to cost forty million piasters per year. Radio and communications equipment would cost about twenty-one million piasters annually to maintain in ten years. At "free market" exchange rates this would total about $870,000 yearly. These costs could scarcely be met by existing operating funds; but without such an allocation Americans feared the equipment would soon deteriorate.

their own assumptions regarding the role and organization of the Civil Guard; the Military Assistance Advisory Group proposed expenditures of $18 million, and the Michigan police team, $14 million. The President regarded both of these proposals as inadequate.

During these negotiations the Civil Guard continued to operate much as it had since its founding. In four years, with politics playing its accustomed role, it was commanded by five different Directors General. All training and operations continued under military command but subject to the orders of province chiefs, many of whom were army officers on temporary duty. Largely because of its expectation that the Civil Guard would remain a paramilitary organization not susceptible to the kind of advice university experts could offer, the Michigan State University group decided to withdraw from this phase of its operations. After June 30, 1959, the U.S. Operations Mission took over all advisory functions. The mission director and the ambassador were jointly to supervise policy and, it was hoped, develop a firm American position.

In the meantime, a compromise equipment list (including some of the heavy equipment requested by President Diem) was agreed at $18 million. The mission was to provide this equipment over a four-year period with the understanding that the Civil Guard was to be made into a civilian operation and reorganized along proposed village lines. By means of this compromise, the Americans hoped to work out a step-by-step conversion to a civilian basis. They planned to schedule the release of funds and equipment to insure compliance with the agreement.

Reorganizing the Civil Guard remained, however, the exclusive responsibility of the Vietnamese government. Although American technicians predicted that neither training nor improved equipment would change the Guard's essential structural weakness as a rural security organization, they knew they could go no further. Some even suspected that the Vietnamese government deliberately permitted a certain degree of insecurity to justify a high level of American aid. Whatever justification there may have been for that theory, Vietnamese officials argued that a centrally controlled, well-equipped, and specially trained Civil Guard might eventually constitute a threat to the regime, and that discharging many of its members would increase internal dissension.

Internal security, in short, meant different things to Americans and Vietnamese. Yet it was not solely unacceptable American technical advice that created these complications. Among the Vietnamese themselves there were differences of view. Above all, questions of internal security were primarily political issues to those who exercised power; the problem was too close to the vital center of sovereignty to be left in the hands of police or military technicians.

The controversy over the Civil Guard and its role in promoting internal security, a jointly accepted goal, brought out on both sides a sharp distinction between technical and political considerations. The American ambassador finally decided to support the Vietnamese President's view that the proposed village-based mobile civil police would represent a net political disadvantage that would offset any technical improvements. On such a fundamental matter the technicians might ordinarily have counted on stronger support; but the President's determination about the issue, and differences within the American community, coupled with the absence of any possible American sanctions (short of a self-defeating termination of the program), gave Ngo Dinh Diem basically what he wanted. But during the interim of wrangling, the Civil Guard was unable to perform its mission effectively.

Civic Action and the Bureaucracy

Another joint effort to build the positive elements of internal security was the Civic Action project, which was eventually all but destroyed by bureaucratic rivalries. The Vietnamese government provided $1.5 million for this three-year rural development program, while the United States contributed only $500,000 in contrast to an original request for $2.5 million. These unequal contributions accentuated the natural reluctance of Vietnamese officials to defer to foreign opinion.

The project originated in 1954–55 out of a military effort to encourage villages to rebuild war-damaged public facilities. In 1956 its activities expanded to include distributing drugs and medicines, building village information centers, and offering seeds and advice to farmers. Soon the Ministries of Health, Information, and Agriculture began to protest over alleged infringements on their responsibilities; province chiefs objected because these extensive activities were not under their control; and even the villagers who were the project's beneficiaries sometimes resented the visiting teams because they were staffed with refugees from the north—strangers who spoke a different dialect and practiced a different religion. Almost all refugees from the Communist regime in North Viet-Nam were Roman Catholics, and the government's costly program for them, together with the policy of using such strong anti-Communists as Civic Action leaders, stimulated much envy and resentment. Southern villagers felt their sufferings from the civil war equally entitled them to compensation and special welfare.

In spite of these objections, the Civic Action program continued because it was useful. The stimulation of community self-help was needed to overcome the lethargy that followed the destruction of homes, bridges, schools, and farms; and political indoctrination against communism could be better performed, both Vietnamese and American experts thought, by this special agency than through normal administrative channels. By the end of 1956 there were 1,400 Civic Action workers, organized in teams of ten, who served for two weeks in each village, dressing and living as farmers and working in the fields. Their lives were austere, their code of ethics severe. Indeed, so great was their zeal and so familiar their skill at ingratiating themselves that they were often paid the high, ironic compliment of being taken as Communist agents.

When at the end of 1956 vast supplies of goods began to arrive from the United States, Civic Action was not allowed to channel this aid into the villages. The province chiefs succeeded in gaining control of general distribution, while the Ministry of Health asserted and won jurisdiction over the distribution of pharmaceuticals. Shortly afterwards, Civic Action, in the hope of finding a legitimate, permanent role for its activities, proposed a community development program. In spite of strong support from members of the American aid mission, the proposal was defeated and Civic Action survived thereafter only as a semimilitary operation.[4]

No American funds were jeopardized by the failure of Civic Action, but a difficult lesson was again driven home. As in the case of the Civil Guard, the record of Civic Action illustrated the principle that America cannot easily influence the administrative

[4] Some of the issues involved in the defeat of this proposal are discussed in Chapter IV, in connection with the dissolution of the aid mission's Field Service Division.

organization of underdeveloped countries, even when aid funds are involved in a program designed to serve common interests. Only the advice that filtered through the network of local politics could be translated into action.

Land Development as a Security Measure

A third nonmilitary approach to internal security was the Land Development program. This project began harmoniously and with very substantial amounts of American aid, but in the months that followed there were such sharp disagreements over planning and techniques between the aid mission and the Vietnamese government that U.S. aid was eventually withdrawn altogether. Because the total amount of dollar aid to Viet-Nam had already been fixed, however, the funds withheld had to be transferred to other aid operations and thus the American withdrawal cost the Vietnamese government nothing. Diem's government simply reallocated "its own" funds to Land Development and pursued its own policies. As the Vietnamese were well aware of the total U.S. commitment, the threat of American withdrawal from this particular program was necessarily weak. Unfortunately for the prestige of American technicians, subsequent events failed to vindicate their predictions that the project would fail unless their advice was followed.

The Land Development program originated late in 1956 in a conference between the director of the U.S. aid mission and President Diem. The Americans visualized an opportunity for new applications of skills the Vietnamese had gained from the vast refugee operation of 1954-55, when more than 300,000 North Vietnamese had been settled on tracts of abandoned land.[5] After only two years on the new land some of these refugees were better off than many long-time residents living on infertile ricelands or in overcrowded cities. Millions of hectares of rich farmland were still lying idle, moreover, useful only to Communist guerrillas and dissident factions while thousands of families became disaffected because of misery and want.

The Land Development project was planned to allow the Vietnamese government, with American aid, to match those unused human and agricultural resources. President Diem saw a further

[5] See above, p. 47.

possibility of creating a "wall of humanity" along the borders and in the Communist-infiltrated areas south of Saigon: if loyal supporters were settled on these lands, they would pre-empt the supplies of Communist guerrillas and inhibit raids against isolated farmers. It is true that these lands, especially those in the highland areas, had been little used, required the raising of unfamiliar crops, and would involve new farming methods and ways of life. But although complications were to be expected, success would serve military and social purposes and at the same time contribute to the diversification of the economy.

American and Vietnamese purposes thus coincided in general, although economic, military, and political objectives were already acquiring different emphases. In April 1957 America agreed to commit over $10 million—$3,288,000 in dollar aid and 235,540,000 piasters ($6,729,742) of counterpart funds—to which the Vietnamese government pledged to add 44 million piasters (about $1,250,000 at the legal exchange rate). The American view that the project's primary purpose was agricultural development was written into the wording of the agreement as follows:

> To assist the government of Viet-Nam in the permanent resettlement of 11,000 to 12,000 indigenous families (who are now in overpopulated areas of the country) on new lands or lands that were abandoned during the war. It will result, therefore, in putting into cultivation land that is presently non-productive. An additional, and important, factor is that the resettlement of loyal Vietnamese will greatly improve the security and stability of areas now, or recently subject to, anti-government influence.

The stated economic goal was an immediate and substantial increase in agricultural production, together with eventual industrial development. But the agreement to cooperate on land development projects offered little guidance for resolving conflicts of short-term goals or for equalizing the different degrees of urgency that moved the two parties.

It was clear from the freedom and speed with which the Land Development agencies were able to operate that President Diem had awarded their work an urgent priority, basically for security reasons. Operations were begun under military management, using army equipment; and while it was anticipated that the General Commissariat for Refugees and Rehabilitation would gradually phase its refugee work and personnel into Land Development projects, the operation always retained a military flavor. In the early months all operations were scheduled at an unprecedented pace, spurred on by the enthusiasm of the President, who made frequent field inspections and exercised immediate authority. Because the urgent requirements of security outweighed economic and technical considerations, normal administrative regulations and the technical requirements of sound agricultural development were set aside. Land Development enjoyed an autonomous budget and exemption from the rigid Vietnamese civil service procedures; its staff was rapidly recruited and paid well in excess of civil service scales; finally, to accommodate fast-moving field operations, budgetary procedures were improvised and heavy equipment was requisitioned from the agricultural and public works agencies. This extreme haste caused severe hardships during the early months of the project: many villages were established during the rainy season when no housing could be built and no lands properly worked. American technicians, who feared that the government had overcommitted itself to this project, were able to point out that 238 million piasters were already budgeted in 1957 for the 11,500 families involved in Land Development, almost double the amount assigned to the entire Department of Agriculture in that year for its nation-wide activities.

In April 1957 the General Commissariat for Land Development (GCLD) was created and normal government procedures were installed. About half the personnel used in the earlier months were absorbed into the new organization, which also retained some of the technicians from the refugee program. Although all were now subject to civil service rules, some juggling of titles and regulations was necessary to accommodate the technicians possessing special skills or enduring unusual hardships in the new centers.[6] At the same time, a gradual regularization of the financial procedures took place. But in spite of having to follow these bureau-

[6] Difficulties of recruiting personnel for a temporary and crisis-ridden agency were partly resolved by the inducements of extra pay and liberalized per diem allowances, waiving of civil educational requirements, and the suspension of loyalty investigations and budgetary procedures. Where necessary, the President overruled the Civil Service Directorate. For details, see "The Commissar and the Law," in John D. Montgomery and the NIA Case Development Seminar, *Cases in Vietnamese Administration* (Saigon: National Institute of Administration, 1959), pp. 204–214.

cratic procedures, in its first 19 months of operation the agency settled 85,000 persons in 46 new communities.

When sites had been selected for the new centers, however, procedures established as a condition of U.S. aid were frequently circumvented. As required in the project agreement, Diem's government appointed joint parties of Vietnamese and American technicians to investigate and approve the proposed sites, many of which had been personally selected by the President. Although Diem usually made his selections from military maps or from aerial reconnaissance, the Vietnamese technicians who investigated the proposed sites at first hand seldom offered to criticize their President's choices. The American members of a joint party considered one proposed site altogether unsuitable because of its soil and drainage characteristics; yet the Vietnamese government planned to settle 10,000 persons there and actually succeeded in transplanting 3,600. In an effort to salvage this center the U.S. aid mission's Agriculture Division suggested growing industrial fiber crops. The government decided instead to plant sugar cane and pineapple, which were agriculturally suitable but could not be marketed because of transportation problems. Eventually the village survived only because of a continued government subsidy. At another site, also considered unsuitable because of mountainous conditions, soil erosion, and remoteness (it was 87 kilometers from the nearest town over roads impassable nearly half the year), the Vietnamese government settled 169 families, which two years later were still dependent on government subsidies for their livelihood. As a result of a last-minute change in the agreed location, another village was settled four kilometers from the nearest water supply. All water was carried by hand, until the aid mission learned of it and arranged for wells to be drilled. Many similar cases dismayed and disconcerted the participating American technicians.

Even acceptable sites were, at times, not used according to the agreed specifications. The President originally announced that land would be allotted in the new centers on the basis of one hectare to each family (a plan that may have been suggested by experience in the well-developed lands in the fertile Mekong delta). Because they considered tropical upland agriculture still in an experimental stage, American technicians suggested that each family would need for subsistence at least 3 to 5 hectares of land, the precise amount depending upon soil and water conditions. A strongly worded recommendation to this effect was privately accepted by many Vietnamese agricultural specialists, but land assignments were nevertheless made according to Diem's low figure.

Late in 1957, judging the results of the project to be uneconomic, the U.S. mission suspended all Land Development funds. A month later the issue was compromised by agreement to accept the recommendations of a three-man committee (representing the GCLD, the Ministry of Agriculture, and the mission), which would determine the acreage necessary for family subsistence by means of visits to each settlement. When, after a few months, this committee was organized, the Americans discovered that the Vietnamese representatives had been instructed not to agree to anything over one hectare. The American Agriculture Division chief was about to protest this decision and suspend the funds again when Washington instructed him to exert no further pressure.

Still more serious conflicts arose over the use of American funds and equipment. Cash was provided in each center in the form of subsidies to cover transportation costs and of grants and loans to each family. Although the Vietnamese government had agreed to "match" American contributions with some 44 million piasters, it failed to budget any funds at all until the American mission threatened to withdraw from the program—a threat which apparently caused some 25 million piasters to be earmarked for the project by the end of calendar 1957. After complete American withdrawal, Vietnamese expenditures on the new centers in 1958 amounted to a total of 350 million piasters.

In addition to these funds, American aid had also supplied well-drilling facilities and personnel, maternity and dispensary facilities in each village, medical supplies and services, elementary school buildings, and plowing and clearing equipment. Unfortunately, these facilities were seldom used as the American technicians had expected. Finding medical supplies intended for the villages still stored in warehouses after many months had passed, one technician was told: "You Americans are too sentimental. People here always get sick; they will die anyhow." The hospitals each had five rooms, two of which were permanently lost to their original purpose because the nurses and midwives insisted on living on the premises, rather than occupy other quarters (for which funds had also been provided). A finished school stood vacant for two years because village officials had not received a written order from the

Ministry of Education authorizing its opening. When pumps supplied to villagers broke down, they were thrown away because of inadequate facilities for maintenance. Work on sixteen new villages was started before the original thirty had been completed, thereby diverting needed equipment and personnel from centers still struggling for viability. The U.S. aid mission was informed of these and other deficiencies when field inspections were made by its Agriculture Division's technicians or its field representatives. When American experts in Viet-Nam contemplated future end-use audits, routine checks, or even possible congressional inquiries, their sense of cumulative frustrations brought them to the edge of despair.

Perhaps the most serious disagreement of all arose when the Vietnamese government abandoned its agreement to use an autonomous agency to manage, operate, and maintain the vast stores of agricultural equipment required for the project. This agency, known as ONEMAM, had been set up in July 1957 under the Vice-President (thus occupying the same administrative level as the GCLD itself) to serve government agencies and private landowners engaged in clearing and cultivating lands. In addition to central administrative offices and central repair and storage facilities in or near Saigon, ONEMAM had five regional offices, a series of decentralized shops and warehouses (either in operation or planned), and field units operating throughout the country. The agency had been originally financed with 10 million piasters, provided half by the United States and half by Viet-Nam, in addition to 469 tractors, 38 bulldozers, 16 winches, 129 plows, 40 vehicles, several 100-ton portable track presses, and heavy maintenance equipment already supplied by the United States. Once established, ONEMAM was intended to achieve financial independence through charging contracting fees for all services rendered, whether to government or private agencies. Its early financial reports were deemed sound.

In April 1958 political rivalries led the Vietnamese government to dissolve ONEMAM and transfer its functions to GCLD, a unilateral action which was greeted with consternation in the U.S. aid mission. Apprehension grew as the staff of 1,200 was cut in half, tractors became inoperable, the replacement of spare parts began to take weeks or months instead of hours, and training facilities were abandoned. The agency's contracting fee was elimi-

nated, leaving operations dependent on inadequate funds allocated
from the government's budget. An American technician, charged
with advising on the use of agricultural machinery, reported:
"This $45 million business is being operated as a side-line." The
chief of the Agriculture Division then suspended any further
dollar procurements for Land Development, but the suspension
was lifted by higher authority after a few months in response to
Vietnamese representations.

Certain Land Development centers were used as political re-
education camps and barracks for political prisoners under the
supervision of army forces, a matter of grave concern to the U.S.
mission. Camps at Pleiku and Banmethuot had been designated
as resettlement centers, to be supported by U.S. funds, without
any suggestion that they would be detention camps. The whole
question broke out into the open with an incident in June 1958:
the village of Cu Ty rose against its guards during a heavy rain,
attacking them as they huddled under ponchos, seized weapons
and vehicles, and fled to Cambodia. Once more the possibility
of a congressional investigation began to arouse apprehensions
among the American advisers.

Such differences of judgment and lack of understanding on the
meaning of agreements threatened to bring about a general deterioration in relations between the American mission and the Vietnamese government. Bui Van Luong, Director General of Land
Development, later gave his view of the difficulty in a public
speech:

> According to the President, . . . Land Development must be started
> first in areas having few favorable conditions for the development
> regardless of how remote they are, or whatever difficulties may exist
> in order to create attractive centers and develop them later. . . . The
> American technicians did not agree with these views; they wanted
> to work slowly but surely with careful preparation in light of purely
> economic considerations. . . . They welcomed land development in
> areas where operations were easy, sure of success, and without risking
> loss, even those losses that are known in advance but sustained for
> the sake of experience—calculated risks.[7]

An even more vigorous dissent was uttered by the President's
brother and chief political adviser, Ngo Dinh Nhu. In a published

[7] Quoted in USOM, Division of Agriculture and Natural Resources, *Land
Development* (Saigon, 1959), p. 5.

interview he launched a vigorous attack on the American aid program, speaking particularly of American hesitancy to support the Land Development scheme:

> The Americans distrust any projects they have not thoroughly studied. In agricultural affairs they want to venture only into those projects which can return 100 per cent the first year. But on the high plateaus it is obviously necessary to wait a certain time before being sure of success. USOM, which is charged at the same time with studying projects under their financial administration, is always afraid of criticism from the American Congress. . . . I could say the same thing for the development of the rice paddies of the Cochin-China. We find that the development of our economy suffers from American slowness. We should prefer to form a committee of experts from all nations, in which USOM would have nothing but financial control of the funds rather than, as now, having USOM first develop and then financially control projects. Having all responsibility in one single body paralyzes it.[8]

Because American policy continued to favor the basic economic and stabilizing objectives served by Land Development, efforts had to be made to improve working relationships with the Vietnamese as the problems arose. By the end of 1957, the Agriculture Division had started to devise procedures that would, as one technician put it, "brake the reckless speed of the project and protect U.S. funds against possible serious misuse." The original project agreement of April 1957 was expanded into 30 subprojects, specifying in detail for each new village the area to be cultivated, the number of families involved, and the financial support to be allotted. Unfortunately for this effort, the Vietnamese government began moving in families while the subproject agreements were still being discussed. Later some of the subprojects were disapproved by USOM, and funds already released to them were reassessed against the Vietnamese government. Other funds were later suspended, warning letters were written, numerous technical conferences were held, and eventually the Director of USOM decided to withhold the counterpart funds (175 million piasters or $5 million) budgeted as the U.S. contribution to Land Development during 1958, leaving only $1 million for purchase of equipment.

[8] *La Vie Française*, May 15, 1958, reprinted in *Journal d'Extrême Orient* (Saigon), June 3, 1958.

The aid mission was not attempting to impose its will upon Viet-Nam by the tactic of withdrawing funds, for the 175 million piasters involved were reprogramed with counterpart funds provided to the Vietnamese government for military purposes. This sleight-of-hand operation left the government free to finance Land Development by a single transfer of funds back from its military budget, and relieved the United States of any further direct responsibility for the project.[9] After allocating 350 million piasters for Land Development in 1958, the Vietnamese government continued to support the project with its own funds. Meanwhile, the U.S. mission continued to withhold counterpart financing, except for $281,000 set aside for spare parts, tools, replacements, and equipment.

Thus a cooperative project intended to serve common interests had brought about a serious crisis between the partners. The sense of urgency and common purpose that characterized the refugee program of 1955 and originally prompted the United States to support Land Development was no longer in evidence. By 1958, something approaching a name-calling stage had arrived.

At this point, however, a change of attitude occurred on both sides. Vietnamese officials began to feel embarrassed by the extremes to which relations had deteriorated, while American technicians accepted the fact that on the political level U.S. policy called for continued support for Land Development despite technical and administrative problems. It was apparent, moreover, that the withdrawal of U.S. counterpart funds had made Vietnamese financing much more prudent: family allowances were cut in half; technicians whose warnings had previously been ignored found that their advice was now solicited and sometimes even followed. The ambassador's obvious sympathy with President Diem's favorite project, the reduced responsibility of the mission's agricultural advisers for the economic validity of the program, and the success of a few of the more favorably located Land Development centers combined to restore more satisfactory relationships.

[9] Ambassador Durbrow, persuaded of the usefulness of the Land Development project, was unwilling to exert further pressure against the Vietnamese government. When agricultural specialists at ICA in Washington warned the ambassador, in a long cable, that he might have to answer to Congress for likely economic failures, he accepted the challenge with the classically short response: "Durbrow assumes responsibility."

Finally, a decision to experiment with fiber crops in the new centers provided a new challenge to which all could respond.

The economic turning point for many centers may have been the introduction of two such crops, kenaf and ramie, by American and Vietnamese technicians working together. Many of the villages, consisting of small marginal farms without adequate transportation, had not been able to achieve even subsistence and depended upon a continued food subsidy from the government. Moreover, poor security conditions had made it impossible to carry out long-range development plans in spite of a promising agricultural potential. Planting industrial fiber crops, it was argued, would provide a cash return three to five times that of rice, thus compensating for the low productivity of land in the central highlands. Because kenaf and ramie are not perishable, the centers would be less vulnerable to guerrilla raids and the settlers could overcome their remoteness from markets. The experimental plantings of fiber crops began late in 1957, and within two years more than 2,000 hectares had been planted with kenaf and 800 with ramie. Winning over to this new venture first the administrators, then the politicians, and finally the settlers themselves required great resolution and imagination; above all, it necessitated and achieved the closest cooperation between the American and Vietnamese technicians.[10]

Land Development continued to prosper until, as of mid-1959, some 125,000 persons had been resettled on about 90 sites, including six resettlement centers established for highland tribes.[11] More villages were planned for 1960 and later years, and in spite of the fearful predictions of earlier years some of the original centers have achieved or are approaching self-sufficiency. Most of the land has been farmed communally, against the advice of Americans who had favored individual ownership. In this case, however, experi-

[10] See "Technician's Dilemma: The Kenaf Fiber Case," in Montgomery, *Cases in Vietnamese Administration*, cited, pp. 216–224. The use of ramie had already been suggested by UN technicians several years earlier.

[11] See also figures given in Republic of Viet-Nam, Commissariat General for Land Development, *The Work of Land Development in Viet Nam* (Saigon, 1959), p. 27. For a balanced statement of problems and achievements in Land Development, see William Henderson, "Opening of New Lands and Villages: The Republic of Vietnam's Land Development Program," in Wesley R. Fishel, ed., *Problems of Freedom: South Vietnam Since Independence* (New York: Free Press, 1961).

ence validated the Vietnamese judgment; communal productivity proved greater than that of individual families, probably because improved agricultural techniques could be used more efficiently on a larger scale.

While the project could begin to claim some measure of economic success, its contributions to security were less striking. The best lands were still left unsettled, awaiting police action to make them safe. American advisers were confirmed in their belief that internal security was a police problem, not capable of solution by resettlement without adequate protection; but fear of Communist activity apparently remained the basic Vietnamese justification for Land Development.

In spite of the congruence of American and Vietnamese purposes, Land Development eventually had to continue without aid funds and with only as much technical advice as the market would bear. As in the case of aid to Burma, American ideas became more acceptable when they could be considered strictly on their technical merit, instead of as conditions for financial gifts or loans. Even the most friendly government must display sensitivity in matters touching the vital center of national sovereignty; and if the governments of underdeveloped countries sometimes fail to distinguish between the central and the ceremonial parts of sovereignty, that has to be expected and accepted as one of the hazards of foreign aid.

In the matter of internal security, neither American nor Vietnamese goals were achieved. By 1960 assassinations by Communist guerrillas were each month taking a toll of hundreds of lives, defections in the countryside had grown at an alarming rate, and criticism of the Diem government among Vietnamese intellectuals had reached serious proportions. Given the determination and skill of the Communist leaders and the growing proportions of their military campaign, it is extremely doubtful that adoption of the American technicians' proposals could have stabilized the situation. The operational flexibility of the Civil Guard and the loyalty of the farmers probably could have been strengthened, however, if the Vietnamese government had been more receptive to external technical and political advice.

In the final analysis President Diem's struggle for survival was his own. The United States could not lay down the law, no matter how great its interests and sympathies, how massive its aid program, or how urgent the needs of Viet-Nam. The Vietnamese resisted any advice accompanied by what they took to be foreign pressure. The absence of real technical certainties, the difficulty of asserting American control over aid projects possessing a powerful domestic impact, and the importance of maintaining the good will of the Vietnamese led the American ambassador to accept relatively inefficient methods of cooperation even in establishing a degree of internal security that was desired by both parties.

If compromise is inevitable in such situations, it is to be hoped that it is only the antagonisms, and not the vital common interests, that have to be compromised.

2. Problems of Economic Growth

Economic growth is second only to internal security as a symbol of common purpose and mutuality in the U.S. foreign aid programs for Southeast Asia. U.S. policy generally assumes that economic growth affords protection against Communist agitation and subversion, but supports it out of other motives as well, both compassionate and political. For their part, nearly all newly independent governments are committed to the abstraction of economic development as well as to the fulfillment of concrete promises made to their restive citizens.

In spite of agreement in principle, however, attempts to work at detailed cooperative programs have brought out troublesome differences in both policy and technique. Most Asian governments are reluctant to entrust their countries' economic future to private enterprise, while the United States for its part has been reluctant to assist highly centralized programs of virtual state capitalism or socialism, even where there is little prospect of a private alternative. There has also been disagreement on priorities and methods for promoting economic growth and on the general balance between agriculture and industry; within each of these economic spheres, moreover, there are grounds for dispute about the balance between export and subsistence crops or between large- and small-scale industry. Planning for national economic development has been the subject of endless negotiations, together with debates over the dangers and handling of inflation during periods requiring great military and capital outlays.

Economic development is increasingly regarded by supporters of foreign aid as an end in itself. Many consider that communism can be checked only by systematic economic growth, thus disparaging temporizing measures like military aid; some go so far as to believe that U.S. economic programs can provide the basis for new and more humanitarian principles and practices in international relations. There are serious questions posed by all those hopes, not least by the assumption that economic development alone will check communism, especially since the Communist powers themselves promote economic development abroad for their own purposes. A decent standard of living may be necessary to check communism, but it is surely not sufficient to do so. Moreover, although the United States appears to be committed primarily to a special kind of economic growth through private initiative, its efforts to encourage development through private enterprise are not always appropriate in the underdeveloped countries. This is especially true where, as is often the case, they imply parallel efforts to discourage government entrepreneurship even where no real political or economic alternative exists. To cite another dilemma, the country providing aid is constantly confronted with the choice of either strengthening the economic power of the central government—often with uncertain consequences to personal liberties in the receiving country—or of withholding aid and thus risking the political consequences of economic stagnation.

The host government's interest in economic development is likewise complicated by political uncertainties. There is no uniform law of economic progress that can be applied in all circumstances, and each choice—capital or consumer imports, agricultural intensification, crop diversification or industrialization—involves great possibilities for benefit or for injury. All the Southeast Asian governments aspire to economic development; but only Taiwan has assigned a high priority to industrialization, and none has been notably hospitable to private enterprise. To the American planners and advisers, on the other hand, economic development has meant both industrialization and free enterprise.

Because these differences lie on an outer perimeter of sovereignty, the governments of Southeast Asia have generally tolerated American advice in the strictly economic field with better grace than American ideas about internal security. Taken together with the widespread admiration for American economic achievements and techniques, it is not surprising that American persistence in economic matters was often rewarded.

The Consumer Issue: The Commercial Import Program in Viet-Nam

Viet-Nam's major economic needs, once agricultural production had been restored, were to satisfy nonagricultural consumer demands, to stimulate capital investment and light industrial development, and to check inflation.

The Commercial Import Program in Viet-Nam, one of the costliest and most controversial aspects of American aid there, represented an attempt to achieve those economic goals by supporting the "natural" operation of a free market. It emphasized the private distribution of imports, supported the introduction of capital goods for private use, and provided consumer goods to absorb the excess buying power generated by the military and economic aid.

Like most U.S. aid programs in Viet-Nam, the Commercial Import Program was initiated in the successive crises of war and reconstruction. It was first improvised to prevent inflation after the withdrawal of France and the introduction of American dollar aid. During the last year of fighting in Indo-China, the United States had given $785 million to support the French expeditionary corps and the new Vietnamese army. Most of this money had been spent in Viet-Nam. In December 1954 a special grant of $28.6 million was made to the Vietnamese government to buy piasters to finance the movement of refugees, to which $11.6 million was added from unexpended or reprogramed funds.[12] This was followed in January 1955 by another grant of $25 million to buy piasters for the payment of Vietnamese troops. Meanwhile, Viet-Nam was spending more than $275 million annually for imports and nearly an equal amount for invisible payments abroad, a serious drain on the supply of convertible foreign exchange. The Commercial Import Program supplied the dollar exchange necessary to import foreign goods that could be sold to the public. The injection of these goods into the market was calculated to absorb the surplus piasters generated by U.S. grant aid, supply some con-

[12] *Final Audit Report, Project 30-95-075, Aid to Refugees (Operation Exodus)*, reprinted in *Situation in Vietnam*, Hearings before a subcommittee of the Senate Committee on Foreign Relations, 86th Cong., 1st sess., July 30, 1959 (Washington: GPO, 1959), p. 43.

sumer and capital goods demands, and provide a means of converting dollars to piasters for local use without creating inflation. The total dollar aid provided through this program in 1954–55 and 1955–56 alone was $451,179,000.

Although simple in concept, the program was complex in administration. It consisted of extending dollar credits to Vietnamese importers in exchange for equivalent sums of piasters deposited in "counterpart funds" to be spent in Viet-Nam.[13] Most of the importers were accustomed to dealing with French firms, but the commercial import dollars made it possible for the Vietnamese to seek new sources of supply and to engage in forms of price and quality competition unknown in colonial times. Some French importers were at first dismayed by this turn of events; some actually threatened to strike when Japanese textile imports, cheaper and sometimes better than those supplied by the French, were brought in. The strike did not occur, however, because the tremendous demand for consumer goods absorbed both French and Japanese textiles.

In the early days of the program, the danger of inflation was considered so imminent that commercial import dollars were allowed for bringing in almost anything: any salable commodity, after all, could absorb excess purchasing power and thus help stabilize prices. At the same time, these sales rapidly built up funds of counterpart piasters that were useful in financing the local costs of aid projects. But this undiscriminating practice inevitably caused in the earlier years a larger proportion of "luxury" imports than the U.S. government considered desirable. Except for wines, liquors, jewelry, and a few other items, anything that was desired could at first be imported, including electric fans, air conditioners, automobiles (if they cost less than $2,400),[14] and other items later declared ineligible for dollar support.

[13] The Commercial Import Program was also financed in part through "triangular francs," that is, the proceeds from the sale of U.S. surplus agricultural commodities to France which were made available to the Vietnamese government for imports from the franc area. Piasters generated from these sales were also deposited in the counterpart fund.

[14] Investigation of one famous complaint that the streets of Saigon were filled with Cadillacs brought in by the Commercial Import Program revealed that there were only five Cadillacs in Viet-Nam, four of which had been brought in privately, using no commercial import dollars. The fifth was a gift from President Eisenhower to President Diem.

The presence of luxury goods in Saigon was real but somewhat deceptive. Of roughly 9 billion piasters' worth of imports entering Viet-Nam in 1955, about 20 per cent represented capital investment goods (mainly heavy machinery and equipment, although sewing machines and air conditioners were listed in this category); 19 per cent, raw materials for local manufacture (yarn, tobacco, petroleum, cement, tiles, coal, chemical products, and other materials); and 61 per cent, other commodities (food, drink, and tobacco constituting the largest items, followed by vegetables and vegetable products, animals and animal products, chemical products, and others), many of which could also be classed as raw materials for the production of consumer items by local processing industries.[15] Few items could have been eliminated without injuring some segment of the economy, for a large share of the imports (40 per cent of the total) consisted of foods (excluding beverages), pharmaceuticals, and textiles. At any rate, there was no demoralizing black market in consumer items in Viet-Nam, and inflationary tendencies in commodity prices were minimized.

The decision to include large amounts of consumer goods in the Commercial Import Program was designed not only to absorb cash quickly to prevent inflation but to keep important segments of the economy in operation. Additionally, there was a third and equally important element in the decision: to find a political instrument for generating support for the Diem regime. A plentiful supply of consumer goods would provide the middle class (army officers, civil servants, and small professional people) with goods they wanted and could afford to buy. The Commercial Import Program helped demonstrate that national independence did not mean bleak austerity.

The importation of consumer goods also forced the distribution system of Viet-Nam to accommodate itself to an unaccustomed range and intensity of consumer demands, and thus indirectly stimulated the development of a free-market psychology. Vietnamese businessmen, lacking an adequate conception of free enterprise and ignorant of the precise patterns of a buyer's market, found it hard to adjust to the new system. Their first orders were

[15] *Director of USOM, Viet Nam, to the Committee on Foreign Aid, Government of Viet Nam* (Saigon, June 14, 1956), Appendix A, Table 1–3.

often based on guesses and fads, producing a succession of shortages and surpluses. The situation was further complicated by the
application of approximately 25,000 different firms and individuals
for import licenses, including many speculators and soldiers of
fortune. The Vietnamese government assigned licenses at its own
discretion, but demanded proof of experience and, at first, a 350,-
000-piaster deposit (a requirement that was rescinded in October
1957).

Exaggerated reports of luxury imports led to recurring criticism
which was, for these reasons, not wholly justified. Because the
established French importers could carry on their operations without dollars and without special licenses from the government, it
would have been extremely difficult to limit the total amount of
nonessential imports. Any pressure from American sources in favor
of capital imports would have tended to strengthen the economic
position of the Chinese or French entrepreneurs who possessed
financial and managerial resources to use them, a course which was
then politically unacceptable.

America's long-range plan for encouraging large-scale private
expansion by means of the Commercial Import Program was hampered by an unfortunate combination of political considerations
and administrative rigidities, both American and Vietnamese.
Capital goods costing over $500,000 could not be imported under
the program without special permission from Washington, even
though a private businessman might be putting up the money in
local currency to finance the investment. A more basic problem
arose out of disagreement about the proper form of ownership
for new enterprises: the United States permitted capital equipment
to be imported under the program only for privately owned and
operated enterprises, while for its part the Vietnamese government,
unwilling to permit any basic industries to be controlled by
French or Chinese, demanded the right to a majority of stock in
all important enterprises. This conflict of principles seriously
weakened the Commercial Import Program as a device for building up the industrial sector.

In spite of these difficulties, the Commercial Import Program
effected major changes in the local economy. Materials and equipment brought in by this system filtered through to remote areas
of Viet-Nam much faster than project aid distributed through
government channels. During its first year the program resulted

in the sale of 50,000 sewing machines and thus completely re-established the traditional clothing industry. The transportation system was radically reorganized by the importation of Lambretta three-wheelers and other small trucks. Several new industries could also develop, usually on a small scale, and existing industries were expanded or made more efficient by the imported machine tools and other equipment.

Such an important program was almost bound to attract attention and local criticism, often in an anti-American context. In view of Diem's policies, it was ironic that Vietnamese complaints about the Commercial Import Program were usually triggered by American visitors' criticisms, particularly allegations that U.S. aid provided luxuries for city dwellers at the expense of the country's economic and industrial needs. Ngo Dinh Nhu, the President's brother and principal political adviser, publicly denounced American aid because it "offered much more in the form of consumer goods than for the support of our policy of increasing production." He offered as an example:

> . . . a Chinese textile group [which] is ready to invest 100 million piasters to set up a spinning mill and a weaving plant with the equipment the quality of which it had tested in Formosa. The Vietnamese government is ready to furnish its equal contribution of 100 million piasters; but the Americans criticized the equipment which the Chinese plan to supply and proposed instead another project which would cost 180 million piasters. Now the Chinese know their equipment and are not able to invest more than 100 million piasters; USOM intervention stalls this project.[16]

Nhu's criticism was taken up by Vietnamese newspapers. *Nguoi Viet Tu Do* approved his statement that U.S. aid "presented itself in consumption commodities rather than as a support of Vietnamese policy of developing production." Somewhat inconsistently the United States was simultaneously belabored for paying "more attention to reinforcing the military potential of Southeast Asia than to bettering the living standards of the population." The paper finally published a letter purporting to explain America's commercial import policy as follows: "Aid to foreign countries is

[16] *La Vie Française*, May 15, 1958, and *Journal d'Extrême Orient*, June 3, 1958.

a means of absorbing American surplus. No wonder, then, that the supplies do not really fit our needs."[17]

These attacks on American aid were never directly answered in public, although facts were misstated and the basic issue distorted. Nhu's comments ignored the fact that his own government issued all import licenses and that the American mission had no authority to review the specifications of private consumer imports. Indeed, it was to avoid complicated reviews that the U.S. mission had originally suggested using Commercial Import dollars to bring in the equipment designed by the Chinese industrialists (for whose economic health, incidentally, the Vietnamese government had never extended much solicitude). Above all, such criticism obscured America's continual efforts over several years to reserve more Commercial Import dollars for capital goods, a policy which required the Vietnamese government to restrict the use of dollars by requiring the importation of consumer goods with other foreign exchange. In June 1956, the American aid director had publicly urged the government "to increase the portion of direct capital imports in the aid program" in order to reduce the importation of consumer goods.[18] Such a measure would, however, have required austerity measures—a political risk which Diem's government did not choose to take.

The U.S. mission itself finally imposed some limits on the commercial import of nonessential goods by issuing lists of "luxury" items ineligible for dollar support. When the mission published these lists (covering, for example, 225 items on the three lists issued between 1956 and 1958), it expected that the Vietnamese government would use its own foreign currency to import desirable items now excluded from the Commodity Import Program. But the American restrictions caused certain "luxury" goods to disappear and others to be overpriced mainly because the Vietnamese government had established multiple exchange rates to protect its dollar reserves. In one case, for example, a Lambretta assembly plant was faced with ruin because it was denied the dollars necessary to import motor-scooter parts from Italy, which the Vietnamese government would make available only at the doubled "luxury" rate. At the same time a competitor, importing Vespa parts from a

[17] *Nguoi Viet Tu Do* (Saigon), July 9, 10, 12, 1958.
[18] Statement to Committee on Foreign Aid, cited, p. 17.

plant in France with unrestricted francs, was able to continue operating. Finding the Vietnamese government unwilling to sacrifice its own foreign exchange, the Lambretta assembler exerted pressure upon the aid mission to remove the needed parts from the "luxury" list.

The Commercial Import Program continued to represent the largest part of American economic aid to Viet-Nam, amounting in 1958 and 1959 to roughly 80 per cent of the total. Furthermore, the program gave rise to a large indirect subsidy in the form of customs revenue. Dollars for commercial imports entered Viet-Nam at the official exchange rate of 1:35, only about one-half their value on the open market, which meant that licensed importers could obtain Commercial Import dollars at a virtual 50 per cent discount. The importers were forced to share this bounty with the state, however, because heavy customs and import duties were imposed on goods entering Viet-Nam. Customs taxes, in fact, constituted the largest single source of public revenue and were largely derived from items brought in under the Commercial Import Program. Each Commercial Import dollar did double duty for the government of Viet-Nam: as a direct contribution from the United States, it produced thirty-five counterpart piasters, which were used to pay the local costs of military and other aid projects; in addition, customs revenue averaging eighteen piasters per dollar accrued to the government. These latter funds (the usual source of Vietnamese contributions to joint projects) were part of the revenue of a sovereign state; as such, they were in no way amenable to U.S. supervision or control. Many Americans argued that the use of an unrealistic exchange rate in the Commercial Import Program disguised the full extent of Vietnamese dependence upon American aid and encouraged Diem's government to spend "its own funds" more lavishly than economic realities warranted.

Alternatives to the Commercial Import Program seemed unacceptable to both sides for one reason or another. Any of them would have required greater austerity in the Vietnamese economy, either by raising the prices of imports, increasing taxes, adopting more realistic exchange rates, or lowering export prices. If U.S. aid had been converted to loans instead of grants, some thought, the Commercial Import Program could have been drastically cut, at least in theory, without producing a totally inflationary effect. But the Vietnamese economy could not have supported the obligations of repaying loans on a scale sufficient to carry its current military program, nor would loans for salaries and local costs have provided a means of absorbing the surplus of local currency. Moreover, loans would have represented a more rigid and bureaucratic means of introducing capital equipment than the Commercial Import Program, since they required careful delineation of projects well in advance and a demonstration of the economic feasibility of each proposal. The alternative of administering all U.S. assistance in the form of project aid would also have required a backlog of carefully prepared projects and would have benefited government enterprises almost exclusively. Even if the United States were to "give" factories to Viet-Nam by providing capital equipment under project grants, the effect would either be inflationary or it would endanger the military defenses by slowing the generation of local aid currency to the pace of project implementation.

Other alternatives were also considered unfeasible or unpalatable. Developing Vietnamese foreign trade to reduce dependence on the Commercial Import Program, for example, would almost certainly require devaluation. Many Vietnamese also feared that U.S. aid would be cut as trade increased. A proposal to establish a completely free market like that of Hong Kong would have been fantastic for Viet-Nam, a country short on native businessmen and long on suspicion of foreign traders.

Many bitter recriminations about the Commercial Import Program came from both Vietnamese and American sources, ranging from criticism that it was out of control to protests against the tight government licensing system. But many of these criticisms did not deserve very serious consideration. In spite of Nhu's protest, the Vietnamese constantly tried to relax American restrictions on nonessential dollar imports, while the American mission tried continuously to liberalize the government's attitude toward private enterprise so that entrepreneurs could import machinery and equipment. But as long as the United States supported the major portion of the Vietnamese budget directly by grant aid, and a large share of the rest came from customs revenue on dollar-financed imports, no alternative to the Commercial Import Program was possible. Only basic revisions in the national economy or drastic reductions in the military burden would have permitted the adoption of alternative means of supplying American aid.

On the whole, the Commercial Import Program achieved most

of its objectives. Genuine common interests and cooperation enabled it to survive criticism from both sides and to become an acceptable and practical method of transmitting aid. It checked inflation, supplied consumer needs, and even introduced some of the symbols of prosperity to Viet-Nam; and if it did little for industrial development, the principal reason was that the Vietnamese government assigned priority to other objectives.

The Industrialization Issue in Viet-Nam

Direct efforts to encourage industrialization in Viet-Nam were less effective than the Commercial Import Program. The need for commodity imports was clear and tangible to the Vietnamese; industrialization, on the other hand, was merely an abstraction in the first years of the republic, and free enterprise was alien both to long-standing traditions and to public policy. The conventional obstacles to industrialization—lack of capital and inadequate managerial or labor skills—were perhaps less serious than a lack of will. One official explained his government's indifference to industrial projects suggested by American advisers by pointing out that in Vietnamese eyes agricultural advancement was much more important.[19] President Diem's concern (which was often the nation's prime source of action) was with the pacification of a countryside plagued with guerrilla activities, the resettlement of refugees, and the restoration of war-damaged facilities. Although industrial development was the byword of Communist efforts north of the 17th parallel, it was less urgent in the South, where, furthermore, the foreign initiative seemingly necessary to industrial development was actually suspect.

Evidence of these attitudes was provided late in 1954, when plans to organize an industrial development bank came to nothing. A National Investment Fund was created in January 1955, but as no U.S. or French funds were forthcoming and private capital remained in hiding, the national treasury eventually had to advance 200 million piasters for its capital. The fund's loans were made on considerations other than industrial development policy, and not all were for new productive facilities. No technical or managerial assistance was provided, apart from the uncertain bene-

[19] Vu Van Thai, "Our Concept of Development," *Vital Speeches of the Day*, December 1, 1959, pp. 101–102.

fit of government equity participation which gave the bureaucracy so many managerial prerogatives that private enterprises were unwilling to participate to any significant extent. In July 1955 the U.S. mission renewed proposals to establish an industrial development bank, only to abandon the effort when it became evident that the suggested arrangements still failed to appeal to the Vietnamese. The Americans decided instead to cultivate a more favorable attitude in key Vietnamese officials by inviting them to visit programs operating in other countries.[20]

After almost two years of such quiet preparation, the aid mission judged the time was ripe to propose an Industrial Development Center (IDC) for loans and technical aid to private industry, with the understanding that project aid would still be available for government enterprises as well. Although the proposal was accepted in record time (it was made in May 1957 and accepted on June 27, just in time to obligate the funds before the end of the fiscal year), the Vietnamese did not authorize the establishment of the center until the following November, and the final agreement was not signed until June 1958. During that intervening year it became apparent that the Vietnamese government had had reservations about the proposal from the beginning, largely because of its doubts about the role of private capitalism in the country. Finally, after no less than fifteen drafts had been considered, a compromise intended to protect the state's entrepreneurial function was written into the final agreement.

The compromise that made the IDC possible was the aid mission's acceptance of the principle of government ownership, at least in part, of the cement, sugar, and glass industries, all of which would continue to be eligible for project and commodity aid. The Vietnamese government, in turn, agreed that the center itself was to confine its aid to the private sector. Yet in the months that followed, the aid mission received a number of requests for IDC aid to various government enterprises; and in spite of the agreement, before a year had passed it was responding to requests for

[20] A detailed account of these activities appears in H. Robert Slusser, "Early Steps toward an Industrial Development Bank," in Richard W. Lindholm, ed., *Viet-Nam, the First Five Years* (East Lansing: Michigan State University Press, 1959), pp. 245–254, and Nguyen Duy Xuan's Commentary on pp. 255–256. See also M. N. Trued, "South Viet-Nam's Industrial Development Center," *Pacific Affairs*, September 1960, pp. 250–267.

advice from government-owned plants. But private companies were also beginning to request loans and technical advice.

The financial resources of the IDC, which were provided entirely by the United States, consisted of $6 million reserved for importing equipment and materials, and 121.1 million piasters for local industrial loans. The center was managed as a public corporation with a board of directors, consisting of the Vice-President of the republic as chairman, two secretaries of state, an economics professor, and two bankers. Its part-time director was assisted by three engineers, and a contract for additional technical advice was made with a private American firm, which later provided four more engineers and a financial adviser.

The Industrial Development Center had been patterned after experiments in the Philippines where similar institutions were authorized to advance funds to commercial banks, which in turn were fully responsible for repayment at the end of a stated period. Since Vietnamese banks did not normally make long-term industrial loans, they wished to be guaranteed against possible business failures. Such guarantees were especially important for the foreign-owned banks, which were forbidden by law to hold property beyond a certain period and therefore could not effectively foreclose in the event of defaults. Because of earlier experiences with the National Investment Fund, the aid mission hesitated to insert any guarantee provisions that would expose the operations to political control, fearing that the IDC as a government corporation might already be disposed to favor other government agencies. In order to compensate for varying risks, the Americans eventually agreed to offer flexible guarantees to a maximum of 80 per cent of each loan. The IDC interest rates were to be increased in proportion to the size of the guarantee; commercial interest rates, on the other hand, were to be reduced in inverse proportion, since the risk borne by Vietnamese banks was reduced as the U.S. guarantee increased.

The first loan applications were processed in March 1958, and within six months one hundred had been received and nineteen approved. The first beneficiaries were light industries using mainly local products. About half of the applicants—which included two ceramics plants, a processor of fertilizer, a manufacturer of tin cans, a fish cannery, a textile plant, a weaving mill, a duck-egg powdering plant, starch and glucose manufacturers, and a match

factory—represented new industries. As a start it was not unpromising, but the government persisted in its indifferent attitude.
Although no official obstacles were placed in the way of the IDC,
the shortage of personnel assigned to it, the designation of a director on a part-time basis only, and inadequate facilities provided for
office and demonstration space continued to handicap operations.

In addition to offering professional advice to investors and
prospective industrialists, the IDC also helped them secure the
governmental permission necessary for business operations. Eventually, the Americans hoped the center would be invited to advise
the government itself on tax revision and other measures designed
to encourage domestic and foreign investment; but that step would
have to await a more favorable climate of government opinion.

In spite of the relative indifference to private industrial development, it appeared that the government's mere tolerance of American efforts to encourage free enterprise would permit an increasing
rate of progress, which in turn would have a heartening effect on
those working for the industrial development of Viet-Nam.

The Industrialization Issue: Economic Growth in Taiwan

The belief that free enterprise can accelerate industrialization if
given the opportunity also underlay American aid operations in
Taiwan. Although the Chinese Nationalists originally entertained
prejudices against free enterprise similar to those of the Vietnamese, private industrial progress was so striking that they began
to reverse their position. By 1960 ICA was able, without too much
hyperbole, to designate Taiwan as a symbolic "island of development," where substantial investments would yield spectacular economic growth.

For many reasons Taiwan's circumstances were more favorable
to industrialization than were those of Viet-Nam. A long-standing
need for military hardware had already impressed the government
with some of the economic requirements of modern statehood. At
first many of these requirements could be met because the Nationalist government inherited an industrial base in which the Japanese
had made substantial capital investments. Then, military needs,
consumer demands, and the technical skills brought over from the
Chinese mainland had led to such substantial private building on
this base that by 1959 there were over 14,000 separate manufacturing and processing enterprises, and more than half of the total

industrial production was private. The Taiwanese standard of living was second only to that of Japan in the Far East. Government corporations, formerly confined to unimaginative managerial practices, were beginning to feel a competitive urge to produce efficiently and to lower prices in the interests of gaining additional business. In some cases, government interests in public corporations were even being sold to private investors.

During the first ten years of Nationalist government in Taiwan, over 40 per cent of American project assistance was devoted to the development of industrial enterprises, including power, fertilizer, paper, chemicals, cement and ceramics industries, metal production and processing, and, to a less extent, timber and reforestation projects.[21] In consumer industries such as sugar, textiles, and food processing, American aid was small and the Chinese effort large. On the whole, Taiwan's industrial prosperity after the first decade of Nationalist rule was natural rather than planned, with Chinese efforts outweighing American contributions by a substantial margin. Nevertheless, the use of American funds for industrial development constituted an important contribution to fulfilling the basic purposes of American aid to Taiwan, whose economic stability and prosperity have been as important to the free world as its military strength.

The largest program of U.S.-backed loans in Taiwan was administered directly by the aid mission on a matching basis. As of the end of 1958, 60 loans totaling over $157.2 million had been made, mostly to government enterprises (the nascent growth potentialities of the private sector receiving less financial support than public enterprises). Most private industries were required to subscribe half of the required capital funds, except for coal mines (35 per cent) and shipbuilding other than fishing vessels (only 30 per cent). In basic government industries, like power or transportation, a lower capital subscription was required.

Private industry was served by the Small Industry Loan Program, capitalized in 1955 at U.S. $11 million (7.3 million U.S. dollars and 124 million New Taiwan dollars) to offer one- to four-year loans at a composite rate of 9.7 per cent, excluding yearly surplus charges. A special committee was appointed to service

[21] Department of State, *The Republic of China*, Publication 6844 (Washington: GPO, 1959), p. 34.

requests for about three times the available annual funds of $1.5 million and 50 million New Taiwan dollars. By the end of 1959, more than 600 requests from over 400 companies had been processed. The loans were protected by a mortgage held by the Chinese Council on U.S. Aid, but the delinquency rate was only 3.5 per cent, which even permitted a small profit from penalties and interest.

Longer-term loans were available through a private institution called the China Development Corporation. Founded in May 1959, this group was empowered to make loans of nine to twelve years, ranging in value from $50,000 to $600,000, at 12 to 15 per cent. Its Chinese capital was expected to reach $3 million, largely from private sources to which ICA planned to add 300 million New Taiwan dollars free of interest. The Development Loan Fund was committed for amounts up to $10 million and another $2.5 million was to come from the proceeds of U.S. agricultural commodity imports. Additional long-term, low-interest loans were available, directly from the DLF in large amounts and at various rates, ranging from the 3.5 per cent charged to the government to 5.5 per cent for private industry. In 1958–1959, for example, $27 million was approved for loans to government enterprises and $8 million to the private sector.

The success of these loan agencies indicated the presence of a powerful industrializing thrust in the economy. To take advantage of this force, the China Productivity Center was established in 1956 to offer various managerial and technical services to Taiwanese industry. It was here rather than in the establishment and operation of the lending agencies—although the center itself was also a lending agency in a small way—that considerations of domestic policy and some indications of disagreement between Chinese and Americans began to become apparent.

The first important decision in the organization of the center was to leave its sponsorship and management wholly in private hands. The two governments hoped thus to minimize businessmen's fears that the agency might serve surreptitiously as a tax inspector after examining company books with the ostensible purpose of giving advice. Even so, some suspicions of the center's genuinely private character remained, and speaking tours at business clubs by its distinguished private leadership had to be arranged to offset them. The fact that the government's ownership of basic heavy industries dominated the economy meant that the government—that is, the "mainlanders"—derived the greatest benefit from the center's operations. The mainlanders' greater command of English also gave them a preferred position in attending training courses which were conducted in that language.

The China Productivity Center introduced industrial engineering programs to improve plant layout, quality control, and preventive maintenance—the most obvious technical needs of Taiwanese industry. In the first three years more than 2,000 trainees took courses under the center's sponsorship. Two-week management courses were jointly offered on three occasions by Harvard Business School and Chinese professors, and regular courses were given in statistics, advanced quality control, standardization, and other fields. The activities of the center's personnel, totaling about 30, were supplemented by the assistance of many graduates of previous courses (who were assigned by their companies on a half-time basis for two years after completing the course).

In 1959 plans were made for the reorganization of the center to promote foreign trade. The 15-man board of directors (5 representatives from government, 6 from industry, and others from universities, unions, and public and private life) was to be expanded to include 6 new members from trade and commerce. The executive secretary, a mainlander, was to be designated manager, with two assistants: one for productivity (a Taiwanese, on recommendation of the aid mission) and one in trade (an English-speaking mainlander who would work in overseas public relations). The management confidently expected that this reorganization would diminish Taiwanese resentments against mainland dominance of the center and increase interest in technical and managerial improvements.

It is evident that in Taiwan private industrial development was not a political issue as it was in Viet-Nam; such political considerations as were present could be accommodated by simple administrative measures because Chiang's government had already made the basic commitment to industrialization. And because it did not become a vital political issue on the domestic scene, it presented no major problems in relations with the U.S. aid mission or conflicts with American policy.

3. Conclusions

Administrative and political friction hampered the mutual aid programs in Southeast Asia, but the basic community of purpose between the United States and the cooperating countries nevertheless afforded an ample basis for effective operations under joint sponsorship. Substantial progress was made in Viet-Nam and Taiwan, especially where important issues of domestic politics were not at stake.

The more painful aspects of cooperation were partly a result of rigidity on both sides. American technicians were confident in their specialized knowledge and skills and fearful that any departure from the canons of efficiency would lead to censure; the Asians, for their part, were reluctant to adopt merely technical approaches to what they considered to be primarily political problems. Each side blamed the other for the same fault, "rigidity." As Ngo Dinh Nhu expressed it in his famous interview of May 1958 in *La Vie Française*:

> Of course, we admire the Americans for the quality of their work and their discipline, but we object to rigidity, which renders their aid insufficiently adaptable to the specific nature of each people.

Just as insistence on technical and administrative efficiency made the Americans appear unyielding, it was domestic politics that made the Vietnamese government appear unresponsive and inflexible on the issues of the Civil Guard, land development, and commercial imports. In Viet-Nam, the President's lightest statements became policy which few dared criticize, and his convictions were immune to any pressures the Americans might try to exert.

Conflicts arising out of different views on the desirability of private capital as a means to industrialization did not produce the animosities generated by questions of security. Nhu was notoriously skeptical about the use of private capital, but the Vietnamese government was not unwilling to permit some experimentation, provided that its interests were not threatened. Yet the general Vietnamese attitude toward capitalism was somewhat hostile. "Capitalism on one side and Communism on the other side are profitable for only one class," Nhu told a group of civil servants on November 15, 1957.[22] "We do not preach nor do we want all private property suppressed as the Communists do, because we follow the theory of personalism, where every man can have basic property or man will not become man," he added. Foreign aid was a potentially dangerous instrument, he believed:

> The World Revolution began more than 100 years ago, since the Europeans conquered America, Asia, Africa. . . . The World Revolution has taken the form of colonialism, and now it appears in the forms of Communism and Aid, as well as in other forms. . . . It creates disorder in the history of the world. There never existed such a large force urging the masses of the world to demand freedom and higher standards of living. . . . In this World Revolution, Europe [sic] advocates mutual aid to underdeveloped countries. It is an attitude. The other European attitude of colonialism is the Communist attitude.

The obscure philosophical content of this speech was clearly based on a profound suspicion of capitalism, which he equated with "aid," and a monumental misunderstanding of its nature. At one point in the address he referred to the fact that "democracy without a morsel of private ownership is a false democracy," adding, "this sort of democracy is seen in the free capitalist countries of Europe, and in Communism." It is easy to see why the chief political adviser to the President of Viet-Nam rejected both capitalism and communism for his country, since in this extreme but important statement he drew no distinction between the two. But it is also significant that American doctrines of economic growth were nevertheless tolerated in Viet-Nam, while American views on internal security matters were unacceptable.

In Taiwan, similar but less violent distrust of capitalism, deriving from the socialism of Sun Yat-sen, had been modified by subsequent Chinese experience with the accomplishments and techniques of the West. Even here, however, the favored position of public over private enterprise was evident.[23] This anticapitalist attitude was more evident in Burma and Thailand, where similar suspicions of the stronger commercial elements appeared in gov-

[22] From an unpublished but authenticated transcription of the speech.
[23] See below, Chapter III, p. 120.

ernment circles and racial or nationalist sentiments strongly reinforced the traditional prejudices.

Perhaps the most serious political obstacle to achieving objectives held in common by indigenous and American leadership was
the vagueness of the decision-making locus in the administrative
apparatus of both sides. The great personal authority wielded by
Ngo Dinh Diem, by Chiang Kai-shek, and by the national leaders
in Burma and Thailand created among their ministers and principal administrators a reluctance to act aggressively and decisively;
thus at the levels where timely decisions were most needed, caution
prevailed. Similarly, for different reasons, American technicians
were responsible either to remote supervisors in Washington or to
men in the local embassies who often lacked technical understanding. At times, there was some doubt whether technicians had the
clear support of their superiors. These factors retarded decisions
and increased the opportunities for misunderstandings between
technicians of both sides. Cultural differences were accentuated
wherever slowness in executing agreements appeared to one party
to be the result of the other's suspicion or unaccountable alien
inefficiencies (Nhu once described the administrative mechanics
of American aid as *bien lourde*—very cumbersome).

Oversimplification of American motives by Asians was matched
by American tendencies to find facile explanations for natural
caution or changes of policy on the part of local officials. Nhu
explained to a Vietnamese audience that "the position of Viet-
Nam with respect to American aid is a clear-cut one: they help us
because we are not Communists, and we are not Communists not
because of American aid but because of our dislike for Communism. . . . Thus, in our relations with America, the government
always sets clearly defined limits, to avoid regrets in the future. . . .
The Americans have a particular way of life . . . and they always
adopt that way in treating with us."[24]

It is clear that common objectives will not automatically eliminate frictions and tensions in the execution of mutual aid programs. Often the United States has had to accept something less
than optimum performance, especially if its own position was
weakened by indecision or by a necessary, though in some ways

[24] From the unpublished speech of November 15, 1957, cited.

excessive, respect for the independence of the governments it supports. But it has been only on rare occasions that operating difficulties have been great enough to frustrate the attainment of basic common objectives. The main question was, and is, how to keep inevitable friction at a level tolerable to both sides.

III THE ABSENCE OF MUTUALITY: UNILATERAL POLICIES IN BILATERAL PROGRAMS

THE MAJOR achievements of American foreign aid have emerged out of genuine cooperation between the aid missions and the governments receiving aid. Community of purpose is no guarantee, however, against sharp differences of opinion over political priorities and operations techniques, as was shown in the preceding chapter. In addition to these differences, arising in spite of explicit common purpose and active cooperation, foreign aid operations must contend with another class of difficulties: at times, both the United States and the recipients of aid attempt unilaterally to impose national interests, policies, or "strings" over and above the general terms of partnership, forcing the other party to exercise a degree of tolerance sufficient to support continued operations. Such unilateral policies can be merely the result of domestic political pressures, but they can also arise from the conviction that vital interests are involved or that the integrity of an entire aid program is at stake.

The intrusion of unilateral policies is not necessarily the greatest source of difficulty in foreign aid operations. For the most part, unilateral demands arise in marginal matters where the spirit of compromise can be invoked without sacrifice of principle. Fortunately, each government understands that the most frequent cause of unilateral requirements is domestic political pressure, and this common understanding encourages tolerance and mutual forbearance. So long as the success of its own aims and preferred projects is not affected, each government enjoys a flexibility limited only

by its own patience and self-assurance, and it can yield to the
other in exchange for reciprocal favors. It is one of the many paradoxes of foreign aid that projects not equally desirable to the two
parties may produce less friction on the operating level than those
that are. This does not mean that the issue of "strings" on aid is in
any sense inconsequential, or that unilateral demands and requirements are not a real source of irritation and tension. It means only
that the rule of mutual forbearance is a useful supplement to
jointness in foreign aid.

1. UNILATERAL AMERICAN POLICIES

American preferences and conditions are variously pressed upon
the host governments: through legislation, bilateral executive
agreements, detailed project agreements, world-wide administrative
regulations, and personal communications. The issues range from
the much-mooted extension of diplomatic privileges to aid technicians to suggested administrative and political reforms. When a
necessary but unpleasant action can be blamed on American
insistence, the host country may yield and be grateful for a scapegoat, but when U.S. demands or suggestions seem both politically
undesirable and irrelevant to the immediate success of an aid
project, the response is often one of resentment or rejection.

Strings attached to the foreign aid purse cannot be drawn as
tightly as those tied to domestic appropriations. Controlling waste
and corruption through accountability requirements is a fairly
recent development even in the United States, where indeed it is
still an uncertain remedy in some state and local governments.
In underdeveloped countries there are different, and often inadequate, standards of administrative accountability as well as different, and often incomparable, standards of technical performance.
Measures of efficiency applied in foreign aid must be flexible.
American technicians learn to accept lower or different standards
out of sheer administrative necessity; even where substantial U.S.
funds may be involved, there is no alternative to yielding preced-
ence to the recipient government in the management of its own
internal affairs. American administrative resources are too limited
to carry out the far-flung development operations of foreign aid
independently in any case; but such a course (even if it were
acceptable to the host country) would leave little of permanent

value behind except new buildings and dams. The impact of foreign aid as a device for "institution building" in new nations is hardly less important than its physical contributions to development.

The institutions to be developed and strengthened by foreign aid are, of course, internal to the host country, and the changes introduced by friendly external action presumably take place with the tacit consent of that government. Thus there are limits and conditions on both sides. The host government must have the ultimate voice in determining how much American direction and control are acceptable, while the United States must limit the extent to which uncontrolled experimentation with American funds can be tolerated. Most of the arguments about the need for "strings" are related to these limits.

The most important fact about American "strings" is that the various sanctions available to U.S. aid administrators are either too severe or too trivial to be effective. Withdrawing a program or even withholding funds for a period defeats the object of the aid, a fact well known to both parties. The "post-audit" device with its "disallowing" of improper expenditures, so effectively used in American practice, has little significance in a country where the aid level is fixed: an expenditure "disallowed" by an administrative audit can simply be switched by the host government to one of its own accounts and a more acceptable item substituted. Observance of accounting and administrative procedures unilaterally required by U.S. law is therefore largely a matter of good faith, hard bargaining, and, above all, the acceptability of the requirements themselves as reasonable and perhaps even useful.

Accounting and Programing Requirements

First and most immediate among unilateral American requirements are the planning and accounting procedures designed to prevent careless administration. The most important document used in programing aid funds is the "project agreement," an elaborate contract between the U.S. mission and the appropriate ministry or agency in the host government. It consists of a financial description of the project, a definition of the respective contributions and responsibilities of the United States and the host government, and a work plan. Usually the project is stated in terms of specific goals, with an estimated time schedule generally divided into quarterly periods. The financing of the project, both in dollars and in local currency, is set forth in detail and the entire document is signed by responsible officials representing both sides. While the agreement does not actually order equipment and services, it obligates dollars for the first stage of the project and authorizes the comptroller of the aid mission to release the first installment of counterpart funds to the host government. Thereafter allotment and fund releases are usually worked out jointly.

The project agreement constitutes a legal obligation upon the U.S. government because it is a commitment to issue funds for an agreed project. But because of the absence of effective sanctions it does not in fact bind the host government, whatever its legal status may be. Recourse to threats and legal hair-splitting over the agreement itself is only an irritant to another government whose sovereignty over internal management may be invoked in response.

Further difficulties may arise from misinterpretation of the agreement, caused by poor drafting, informal arrangements, or language difficulties. During the colonial period in Indo-China, for example, each project agreement was recorded in French and English; but when French lost its status as the official language, it was decided that the English version had to suffice. Unfortunately, however, in 1954 the English language was little better known in Viet-Nam than Vietnamese is in the United States today. Understandings between technicians sufficed to develop lines of agreement and secure signatures, but they were not binding upon the higher echelons of the government (and indeed were sometimes not even communicated to them) where the basic administrative policies were established. Excessive looseness in the interpretation of project agreements could easily result in transfers of valuable equipment to an unintended use, in changes in counterpart fund allocations, and in unexpected organizational decisions and personnel assignments. Such changes had to be accepted as appropriate and normal manifestations of sovereignty, especially if the circumstances leading to the original agreement had also changed.

U.S. aid missions have temporarily suspended funds on several occasions in the hope of holding a host government to the terms of a project agreement, but these efforts have proven almost uniformly disappointing. One of the major efforts to require the

Vietnamese government to comply with purely technical provisions of an aid contract occurred late in 1957. The director of the National Agricultural College, which was founded with U.S. aid in 1954, decided to confine the college's functions to the training of government employees, and to discontinue the training of private farmers and the establishment of demonstration projects— activities included in the original agreement and considered important by American agricultural experts. After repeated and fruitless discussions between American and Vietnamese technicians, the American official responsible for the project wrote the Director of Technical Education of the Ministry of Agriculture as follows:

> We regret exceedingly to learn that some deterioration of relationships between Agriculture Ministry personnel and the USOM Advisor at Blao has taken place. . . . The real difficulty seems to lie in some misunderstanding and misapplication of the terms of the project agreement on the part of certain college authorities. . . . It appears that the College staff is receptive only to financial aid. . . . When there is little regard for our efforts and advisory recommendations, as provided by mutual agreement, we must reassess the need for our cooperation in the College Project.
>
> Since there appear to be imperfect working relationships, based on the principles of mutual assistance, we feel it desirable to suspend further financial aid to this project—both direct aid and dollars and counterpart piaster aid—until complete clarification and agreement are reached.

At a subsequent conference a new agreement was reached, and the project funding restored; nevertheless, events failed to confirm the renewed agreement. The program resumed its expected course only when the normal rotation of civil servants brought in a new director and a new American adviser.

The use or threat of fund "stoppages" may not only fail to achieve compliance; such drastic action may even undermine existing agreement. Experience in Viet-Nam and elsewhere suggests that it is wiser to eliminate projects whose implementation is seriously faulty than to attempt to force the acceptance of American policies or administrative practices.

After some experimentation with procedures designed to give American technical advisers detailed control over the periodic release of counterpart funds, the mission to Viet-Nam (like many others) made monthly or quarterly releases of these local currencies an automatic procedure. The Vietnamese Director General of Budget and Foreign Aid estimated monthly expenditures in advance, based on obligations already incurred, and these estimates were reviewed in detail by the program office of the mission and the technicians concerned. Funds were then released in accordance with the revised American version, which took into consideration any shortages or surpluses carried over from the previous month. This procedure gave American technicians a degree of control over the current operations of agreed projects; on the other hand, it seriously compromised their nominal status as "advisers" to the host government.

Although all counterpart funds are originally created by dollar grants, they are legally the property of the host government. Their use, though not under the actual control of American advisers, nevertheless requires the consent of the United States: if the funds are misspent, they can be recovered. A post-audit is used to determine whether money has been improperly used, and the host government may even be required to reimburse such losses. To avoid requests for refunds which are caused simply by inadequate records, the host governments usually establish accounting procedures that will be acceptable to American auditors—and indirectly an important reform may be introduced. In practice, a request for reimbursement is rare. Few refunds were paid in Viet-Nam until August 1958, when the government paid $480,000 to the United States (leaving about $2 million of "rejected" expenditures to be restored later). In Thailand, unsatisfactory audit reports rarely led to requests for refunds; the usual practice was to amend the project statement retroactively. On the other hand, the use of sophisticated accounting techniques is sometimes contagious: the host government has often extended the practice of post-audits into other public operations, thus voluntarily adopting a key principle of American administrative controls and inaugurating a trend toward the greater delegation of responsibility to its own technicians.

Reforms as a Condition of Aid

A second category of unilateral American requirements is our occasional insistence upon institutional, fiscal, and administrative reforms as a condition of aid. In general, the U.S. missions recommend only reforms which are intended to increase the efficiency of aid programs; certain proposals for reform, however, while closely related to aid operations, may actually be intended to advance other and more general purposes of U.S. policy. Any American suggestion for change is likely to encounter some degree of resistance, depending upon political circumstances or the attitudes of the administrators involved. If the host government is relatively indifferent to some proposed reform, it may be willing to "swap" the performance (or, at least, the promise) of the desired reform for financial aid to some project closer to its heart.

Even without specific American insistence, some kind of administrative reform nearly always results from the introduction of large amounts of U.S. aid. Increased funds and many new projects force the host government to expand certain of its operations, especially those relating to planning and programing. In many underdeveloped countries surveying, census-taking, and planning agencies have to be created and organized from scratch, sometimes with only grudging support from governments already feeling overwhelmed by more pressing demands of statehood.

American technicians attempting to design economically acceptable programs feel the need for data-gathering and planning agencies more keenly than Asian officials intuitively aware of their nation's needs. Yet the need for adequate planning has sometimes been painfully obvious to both parties as technological shortcomings dramatize its absence: in Thailand, for example, two roads recently built in Bangkok, with no provision made for water mains and storm sewers; the lack of general topographic information to insure that roads built with aid funds would have an elevation higher than that of the adjacent lands; 500 fire hydrants installed in solid concrete, at public expense, with no connection at all to the Bangkok city water supply. In such cases it was not difficult to reach an agreement on the need for better planning, at least for engineering purposes. Aid funds were used to bring city planning organization to Bangkok; in response to a World Bank recommendation relating to improvements in Thailand's economic condition as a prerequisite to future loans, an economic planner was appointed adviser to the national government; and another project made it possible to expand and improve the central statistical office.

Not all planning needs have been so easily demonstrated. American advisers have often felt forced to insist on improved planning procedures as a condition of aid. On one occasion in 1958, the director of the aid mission to Thailand, considering a replacement for a community development adviser due to leave in a few days, wrote to a Thai minister requesting some idea of future plans for community developments. The director's letter pointed out that four different government agencies were engaged in projects relating to the activity in question, adding:

> These efforts to increase the effectiveness of government services . . . are most commendable. However, it seems to us that this dispersion of community development programs in several Departments results in competition for funds, inefficient utilization of limited trained manpower, and overlapping of functions. The Mission is interested in learning whether or not the Thai Government has plans to coordinate or consolidate the administration, training, and field activities of the several community development programs.
>
> Any information you can give us on the foregoing points will be very helpful in making a decision whether to replace the present community development adviser at this time.

After five months had elapsed, the Thai minister answered that his cabinet had "decided to take a corrective measure, consolidating all project activities." One week later a new American adviser was named to fill the four-month-old vacancy. But the requested coordinating agency was subsequently organized at the divisional level in the Provincial Administration Service of the Department of Interior, an arrangement not at all satisfactory to the American staff. Ten days after the announcement of this decision, the mission director wrote again:

> It is not clear to us how this [coordinating agency] can be made effective by its administrator at this level in the Ministry, since for its success the program must achieve a reorientation and retraining of a considerable portion of the provincial and local administrative staff of the Ministry of the Interior. . . .
>
> It would seem that the official administering this [interministerial] program should reflect, on a full time basis, the status and authority of the Office of the Director General of the Interior Department, perhaps serving as Special Assistant for Community Development.
>
> We understand that final decisions about the organizational setting of the Community Development Program in the Ministry of the Interior have not yet been taken. It might be desirable for a small group of Thai Government officials to visit the neighboring

Eastern Countries of Burma and the Philippines for purposes of observation and discussion of their experiences in getting their programs underway prior to finalizing these decisions. USOM would be happy to support such arrangements. . . .

When the Americans clearly stated their intention of suspending contributions to the proposed 47.8 million-baht project until they were satisfied with the administrative arrangements, this announcement even stimulated cooperative planning. Because this project was not indispensable to American purposes in Thailand, an unusual degree of American firmness was possible and the self-confident Thai officials were free to react positively to blunt American criticisms.

In other circumstances American participation in national planning may be much less direct. The political consideration that aid to Burma should be a symbol of American good will often overrode technical objections to Burmese procedures. An official U.S. economic report on Burma, prepared late in 1959, asserted: "The general unreliability of the data is well known and cannot be overemphasized. As in most Asian countries it is grossly insufficient or just nonexistent. Magnitudes for certain sectors . . . are almost pure guesses. The activities of the private sector at least in aggregate terms are virtually a mystery."[1] In spite of the evident need for adequate Burmese planning, much less American pressure could be applied than in Thailand; indeed, the aid mission refrained from any planning recommendations in order to minimize the appearance of meddling. Most of the foreign planning assistance was for a time sponsored by the Ford Foundation, but even this private agency decided against renewing a planning contract, largely because of the unfavorable climate in Burma even for nongovernmental planning assistance. If Burma requested further aid in planning, the World Bank was expected to fill the gap.

American pressure for improved planning was also limited in Viet-Nam. Although the deficiencies of the Ministry of Planning were strikingly apparent, it was all but immune to American influence. With the ministries directly concerned with aid projects,

[1] Many of the extensive planning activities inaugurated by the U Nu government were not maintained by the Ne Win regime. See Frank N. Trager, *Building a Welfare State in Burma, 1948–1956* (New York: Institute of Pacific Relations, 1958), pp. 12–26.

however, procedures could be worked out jointly for planning the stages of projects and measuring their progress. A steady improvement was induced by the gentle pressures of annual programing and periodic reporting, and IBM accounting procedures, originally introduced for administering aid projects, were gradually extended to other government operations.[2] New statistical data concerning the public sectors of the economy also became available as a result of American innovations, although some time was to elapse before national economic planning caught up with the new information.

In addition to introducing administrative changes, there were also occasions when American pressures brought about social advances ranging from agrarian reform to new public services. Such changes have usually been proposed as a means of generating popular support for the government, creating a basis of political stability, encouraging the growth of democratic institutions, contributing to the prospects of economic growth, or maximizing the effects of technical innovations already under way. Because the changes are only indirectly related to the "legitimate" American concern for accountability and efficiency in the administration of aid funds, both the political impetus and the popular credit for reforms of this type must usually be assigned to the host government. Even suggesting such reforms is a delicate and sensitive mission in the diplomacy of American aid; but if they prove successful their benefits may be profound.

The most sensitive, and also the most important, reforms which the United States has endeavored to introduce in Southeast Asia have concerned taxes, the civil service, and currencies. Even where there have been little or no domestic pressures for improvements in these fields, American advisers have tried to presuade the host governments that such reforms were both just and prudent. Because the improvements were only indirectly related to the aid programs, American pressures have been almost entirely confined to informal advice based on general political considerations. A striking exception occurred when the reluctant government of Laos was virtually compelled to adopt a more realistic exchange rate, but this compulsion arose from objective economic conditions

[2] See "The Decision to Introduce Mechanical Accounting to the National Budget," in John D. Montgomery and the NIA Case Development Seminar, *Cases in Vietnamese Administration* (Saigon: National Institute of Administration, 1959), pp. 20–31.

which were vitiating the effect of aid funds, as well as from explicit American insistence. The following case studies are concerned with the application of American pressures in less extreme situations. Even where necessity was not the mother of reform, our advisers have achieved some measure of success.

Pressures for Tax and Fiscal Reform in Viet-Nam

Years of American criticism of Vietnamese financial arrangements had little effect until, in 1958, the government agreed to permit an American adviser to study the incidence and administration of taxes. It made no clear commitment to reform, but the adviser's findings were so startling that American officials were tempted to press for changes in spite of their concern over the possibility of embarrassing the Diem government. In 1959 and 1960, the Vietnamese government raised about one-third of its total budget from its own sources, excluding the revenue derived from import duties (which was obtained from taxes made possible by the Commercial Import Program and an artificial exchange rate). The tax adviser found that income taxes provided only 12 per cent of the internal revenue; out of a total population of 12,300,000, only 15,000 individuals declared income taxes—and 12,500 of this small group were civil servants and military personnel. Even so, only about 11 per cent of all civil servants were taxable and an infinitesimal percentage of privately employed citizens paid income taxes. Under the schedular system, the tax rates differentiated between private citizens and civil servants so that the heaviest burden rested on the former. Public policy was also reflected in the incidence of income taxes on corporations—especially foreign enterprises—which were taxed at a much higher rate than individuals. Moreover, the actual collection of taxes on corporate and individual profits for the years 1954–58 was 85.9 per cent of all assessments, compared with 54.4 per cent of taxes assessed on salaries.

Real property taxes in Viet-Nam were considered by American authorities to be in still greater need of reform, being assessed unevenly and collected indifferently. A spot check revealed that in 1959 a quarter to a third of the best buildings in Saigon-Cholon were not even on the tax rolls; and furthermore that such taxes as were collected were based only on "legal" rents, ignoring the much more important "key money" paid for the privilege of occupancy.

Taxes on vacant land were sometimes higher than those on occupied land. Only about two-thirds of the ricelands in Viet-Nam were on the tax rolls, and rural tax collections varied from 30 to 90 per cent of the assessments, according to location. Lands used for coffee production (often foreign-owned) were taxed an average of 300 piasters per hectare, as compared with 110 piasters for the best of the ricelands.[3]

American policy was to call these facts politely and objectively to the attention of the Vietnamese government, exerting no pressure or influence toward reform, but leaving no doubt as to U.S. preferences. This self-restraint resulted in part from the very extent of Viet-Nam's dependence on American aid, which could not have been significantly reduced even by the most thoroughgoing of tax reforms. The American ambassador decided that fiscal reforms should be introduced, if at all, on the advice of unofficial American groups, such as the advisory group that the Brookings Institution agreed in 1959 to establish in Saigon with the aid of a Ford Foundation grant.

Structural and procedural changes in the Treasury Directorate of the Finance Ministry had also been urged, mildly and without success, by American technicians under contract to the aid mission. This group was brought in from Michigan State University to "assist the government in developing sound organization and methods in regional administration with a view to improving relations between regional and provincial administration." As early as the summer of 1955, delays in the payment of government obligations had become such an important source of irritation between the government and the business elements of the community that American advisers began to suggest reforms. In October the Finance Minister agreed to the appointment of three joint working parties of American and Vietnamese experts on economic resources and national income, foreign exchange, and taxation. But none of these groups was authorized to consider administrative problems of fiscal management, and not until March 1957,

[3] Milton C. Taylor, *The Taxation of Real Property in Viet-Nam* (Saigon: Michigan State University, Viet-Nam Advisory Group, 1959), Appendix E. Statistics on income taxes above came from Taylor's *The Taxation of Income in Viet-Nam* (Saigon: Michigan State University, Viet-Nam Advisory Group, April 1959), p. 39.

after repeated American suggestions, did President Diem express official concern and order corrective measures.[4]

One of the American advisers concluded, in an internal memorandum, that "the situation can only be corrected by a major change in the current budget execution procedures," adding that such a change would "take months, if not years, because it involves an overhaul of the entire Vietnamese fiscal procedures. Although there appear to be many Vietnamese officials who are aware of the deficiencies in the present system, there still remains a large group of influential and important Vietnamese officials who are not convinced that changes should be made."

In April 1957, the Secretary General of the Ministry of Finance agreed to permit American advisers to study the possibility of paying government obligations by check instead of the usual cash payments. The U.S. technicians planned a comprehensive study, including surveys of facilities for preparing and cashing checks,[5] a cost comparison of check-writing as against cash payments, and a survey of general attitudes toward the use of checks. These sample surveys were to be carried out in three representative departments in Saigon and in three provinces.

There were soon signs that the management of the Finance Ministry was still hesitant about authorizing these studies. One of its highest officials refused a written request from a U.S. technician for permission to visit a province to study fiscal management, and when offered a chance to see the report when completed, he responded, "I have no interest in it." In spite of such misgivings, however, the survey was finally started. A letter from the Secretary of State at the Presidency set forth new procedures for the American consultants, indicating that they were to confine their interviews to directors and directors-general assigned by the departments. This rule would have barred access to operat-

---

[4] A nine-page circular letter from President Diem (Simplification of Financial Formalities, 21-TC) concluded with this earnest but ineffectual order to each office in the Finance Ministry: "In case responsible personnel cause delay in liquidation without due reason, you should take, following administrative regulations, disciplinary action against him as an example."

[5] Vietnamese employees of Michigan State University, the contract group in question, were paid in cash because of the difficulties of cashing checks even in Saigon. See Robert Scigliano, "They Work For Americans: A Study of the National Staff of an American Overseas Agency," *American Sociological Review*, October 1960, pp. 695–704, for a description of this system.

ing personnel and transferred the data-gathering functions to the Vietnamese departments. Obviously, information a department wished to keep confidential could easily be screened from outside scrutiny, and the consultants also feared that the information to which they had access would be prepared by unqualified personnel.

At first the Treasury Directorate study was permitted to continue because the interviews had already started, but after a few more weeks, the Secretary General requested on October 1 that the group suspend further study and withhold any prepared reports. He expressed doubt as to some of the recommendations already beginning to take shape, especially the elimination of certain pre-audit control steps ("the government can hardly prevent dishonesty as it is") and the possibility of paying by check ("even now we live under an obsession of checks drawn without sufficient funds to cover them"). By then, however, the interviews were already completed, and the Americans continued to work on their report until it was finished in March 1958. When the ranking officials in the Treasury Directorate declined to discuss it in advance of publication, the Americans decided to publish it in draft form in August.

The American report recommended wholesale changes in the structure of Vietnamese fiscal administration. The Treasury was to be stripped of several important functions: national budgetary accounting and control were to be entirely transferred to the Budget Directorate; the Treasury's private banking functions were gradually to be withdrawn; and a number of other operations were to be moved to other agencies. An interministerial committee with the task of eliminating uncoordinated or duplicate operations was to be established and a number of processing and operating techniques changed. In September the draft report was transmitted to the Director General of the Treasury and the Minister of Finance, together with an invitation to discuss the recommendations or their implementation. There was no response to this invitation.

After five months a second letter reminded the Secretary of State for Finance of the report, asking for his reactions and suggesting further steps. A few days later the Secretary of State notified the American consultants that he had asked the Director General of the Treasury to discuss the report with them. At the Americans' request, a meeting was held with the Director General.

Stating that he preferred to have his staff prepare comments on the proposals independently, without consulting with the American technicians, the Vietnamese official suggested that the report be submitted directly to the Budget Directorate and the Presidency, leaving the Treasury comments to follow in a month or so. Subsequent discussions, however, occurred only at social gatherings. The American technicians resigned themselves to a long wait until their recommendations had won their own way to acceptance, or until the necessity for reforms in Treasury operations became unmistakable and further proposals were invited. The work of an unofficial private group under contract to the aid mission received no diplomatic support, of course, and the technicians themselves, in spite of personal access to the highest levels of the government, found their advice unwelcome.

Pressures for Administrative Reforms in Thailand and Taiwan

In general, pressures for administrative reform exerted by an aid mission through diplomatic channels are much less direct than those applied by consultants and contract technicians. Few ambassadors are prepared to take a positive stand on a technical issue. An exception was John E. Peurifoy who as ambassador to Thailand adopted an exceptionally direct approach because of his personal convictions and his standing with the Thai government. In a letter to Field Marshal Pibulsonggram (March 21, 1955) he referred to "the assumptions upon which my government had expressed its willingness to make available additional assistance" as including the understanding "that the Thai government will make every effort to assure the best use of its own resources."[6] The letter then proposed specific improvements, including placing all government expenditures in a single national budget to be prepared by a new budget bureau and thereafter submitting them to annual appropriation by the National Assembly. Recommendations were also made for improving the tax system and encouraging competition and private initiative. Subsequent American studies of Thailand's public finances and fiscal management, and other attempts to improve fiscal management, were received with interest, if not enthusiasm, by Thai government agencies: many rec-

[6] This sentence was taken from a letter from Harold Stassen, then FOA Director, to General Phao Sriyanonda, December 4, 1954.

ommendations were adopted. It was principally in matters of personnel administration, where adopting American methods often implied extensive reduction in force or the elimination of age-old traditions of favoritism, that the suggested innovations were entirely unwelcome.

Even when an American ambassador chooses not to press for reforms at the top level, changes can sometimes be introduced through informal discussions between interested specialists. In Taiwan, Chinese budget technicians returning from training in the United States found themselves neglected by their conservative colleagues. In order to maintain their interest, the aid mission invited the technicians to form a "budget workshop" to discuss administrative problems. They enthusiastically accepted this opportunity to apply their observations of American techniques to operations at home, even as an abstract exercise. As minutes of these meetings circulated unofficially through government offices, the budget technicians began indirectly to encourage and influence plans for reorganization, even at administrative levels previously immune to their suggestions. The proposals of the group included changes in the organization of financial administration and procedures, together with detailed technical improvements.

In Taiwan, as in Thailand and Viet-Nam, the government displayed no active interest in improving personnel administration, again largely because political considerations prevailed over technical requirements. Government employment was a principal means of providing for mainland Chinese whom the island economy could not otherwise absorb. Belief in a return to the mainland justified the employment of many civil servants who were surplus to the immediate administrative needs of Taiwan. The subject of personnel administration was thus taboo to foreign advisers, representing perhaps the most sensitive area for technical reform in Southeast Asia.

This does not mean that American advisers were able to confine themselves to reforms that were devoid of political passion. In recommending changes in social and economic institutions the U.S. aid missions often appeared in some ways subversive to conservative elements in the host country. Few social institutions exist, however regressive, that do not benefit someone and usually someone who is powerful. American efforts to influence or reform such institutions therefore become more tentative than those involving organizational practices, except in the few cases where for technical or economic reasons a change is clearly desired by the host government. American initiative in these cases may bring about reforms in social policy even if powerful forces are in opposition, provided a sufficiently general benefit can be antici- pated from the change, the opposition can be countered or ignored, and the proposals themselves bear a reasonable relationship to the national interest.

In Taiwan, for example, uneconomic pricing practices in certain government enterprises were modified as a result of American pressure. Public power, rail, and telecommunications services had been supplied to the army and to civil agencies free or at nominal cost, the loss being covered either by disproportionately high public rates or by government subsidies. American advisers argued that this practice constituted an unnatural burden upon the pri- vate sector. Since these public utilities were receiving financial aid from the United States,[7] the aid mission felt justified in urging the government to operate them on a solvent basis. In 1957 nom- inal rate increases were agreed, but not until aid for the utilities project was actually suspended, pending a satisfactory settlement, did the Prime Minister offer to recommend corrective legislation. The Chinese position was based partly on political considerations favoring government (especially military) requirements over in- dustrialization through private enterprise. It was also based on the fact that, since most of the capital equipment had been con- fiscated from Japanese owners after World War II, it did not represent a high original investment by the Chinese and therefore did not require a high rate of return. The Americans, on the other hand, stressed eventual replacement costs and the necessity of rapidly developing an industrial base by unhampered private initiative.

The American threat to suspend aid funds for the utilities program was based on a somewhat legalistic interpretation of Section 517 of the Mutual Security Act. This section, a 1958 amendment to the 1954 Act, prohibited any agreement commit-

---

[7] The $80 million of loans extended to public power agencies up to 1959 constituted 40 per cent of all project assistance to Taiwan. Loans to Taiwan's rail system already amounted to $8 million when a DLF loan of $3.2 million was also made available. A proposed complete conversion to Diesel engines would cost another $20 million.

ting over $100,000 of aid funds "if such agreement . . . requires substantive technical or financial planning, until engineering, financial, and other plans necessary . . . have been completed." This provision was interpreted as requiring "the ICA to delay the obligation of funds until it has reached a decision that each project has been adequately planned." The aid mission in Taiwan argued that because the public utilities yielded insufficient returns to cover depreciation and future replacement of capital equipment, these programs had not been "adequately planned" and were therefore ineligible for further American support.[8]

Procedural inquiries made by the Chinese in response to earlier pressures failed to meet the mission's criticisms. A power-rate commission appointed in 1957, for example, had found no rate changes necessary under the existing accounting procedures, although American technicians had recommended a 30 per cent increase. Only substantive policy changes could remedy the problem; and since these involved new legislation to increase the valuation of power facilities, the issue became political. To overrule those who advocated subsidized power or a supposedly "anti-inflationary" stabilization of utility costs,[9] it was deemed necessary to secure the Prime Minister's promise that he would set about securing approval from the Legislative Yuan.

Pressures for Agrarian Reform in Viet-Nam

When a government has been hostile or indifferent to some basic social reform, only extreme political urgency has justified American initiative. For regardless of our ideological or humane

[8] In his report to the director of the mission (January 14, 1959) the legal officer argued: "it must be conceded that the authors of the law meant that the financial plan should be a worthwhile financial plan; not a nebulous one. In other words, a poor financial plan is no financial plan. . . . If the project recipient's financial mismanagement is apparent, there cannot be a good financial plan for the project as prescribed by Section 517. In the event that the allegations of such financial mismanagement are true in fact, it would appear that they should be corrected prior to further obligations of funds. . . . The Mission should get responsible assurances from the government of the Republic of China that [necessary] legislative action will be completed within one year from the date of the project agreement."

[9] The value of the New Taiwan dollar, in terms of the U.S. dollar, dropped from 10 to 1 in 1948 to 36.4 to 1 ten years later. The "cheap power" advocates argued that increasing the rates to accommodate cost increases would be a further encouragement to inflation.

convictions, it is the intensity of the host government's interest that ultimately determines the prospect for successful reform. In Viet-Nam, for example, the American mission had continuously urged for several years the establishment of comprehensive agrarian reforms but a program was finally inaugurated only because of the necessities of Vietnamese politics.

Agrarian reform had been advocated in Viet-Nam since 1951, but little was done about it until the Viet-Minh Communists introduced it by force in the areas they controlled. Under the Communist interregnum in rural areas of South Viet-Nam prior to the Geneva settlement of 1954, the payment of rent had almost disappeared, although farmers' "contributions" to the Viet-Minh absorbed any savings in rental. When the Communists withdrew, collection of rents by landlords was not immediately restored, and the first efforts by the Diem government to "reduce" rents were resisted; a reduction in rent below prewar levels could hardly be as appealing as no rent at all.

The early implementation of land reform under the Diem regime was somewhat apathetic by comparison with what the Communists had promised and in part carried out. As an anti-Communist government official reported, "under the Viet-Minh regime the poor farmers are in no better economic condition, but they are happy because they are more important in the village, while the landlords are becoming poorer and have lost their former prestige and importance."[10] The new government tended to regard land reform as a local affair; but at the same time it required provincial authorities to concentrate their attention upon security problems primarily. In the spring of 1955, however, an American agricultural adviser submitted a field report suggesting that land reform and security were closely connected. The adviser urged the U.S. aid mission to press for more vigorous action in land reform if it was to "save the day in the coming Battle for Viet Nam"; "apathy is the dominant note" among the Vietnamese, he reported, insisting that the government's lack of local activity—its "mere promulgation of the reform measures"—was the direct cause

[10] J. Price Gittinger, *Agrarian Reform Status Report*, ms., n.d.; see also Gittinger's "Progress in South Vietnam's Agrarian Reform, I and II," *Far Eastern Survey*, January and February 1960, and his "U.S. Policy toward Agrarian Reform in Underdeveloped Nations," *Land Economics*, August 3, 1961.

of "the political vacuum so characteristic of the countryside." After submitting this report, the adviser was invited to discuss the issues personally with President Diem.

This somber report was a climax to years of unrelenting American pressure for agrarian reform. Efforts to encourage an active program began as early as May 1951, shortly after the establishment of an MSA Technical and Economic Mission for Indo-China. At this time, "land reform" was no more than a popular slogan. Emperor Bao Dai had just promised tenancy agreements and credit control, together with regularization of some squatters' holdings, "without, of course, impairing the interests of the established landowners who are entitled to a just compensation." After President Tran Van Huu was inaugurated in March 1951, he also promised agrarian reform but failed to pass enabling legislation. His successor, Nguyen Van Tam, made a somewhat ironic pledge to maintain certain redistributions already made by the Communists during their brief occupation. A Committee for Agrarian Reform was organized in July 1952, partly at American prompting, but it did not meet until April 1953. Its first efforts to draft ordinances produced only an unenforceable statement from President Tam that rents were to be reduced to half their prewar figures, or a maximum of 15 per cent of the harvest. No enforcement machinery was created; without Emperor Bao Dai's sanction, even the legality of such a pronouncement was in doubt; and finally, the figures themselves were considered much too low to be accepted by the landlords.

Four basic land reform ordinances were finally adopted in June 1953, and provincial agrarian reform committees were organized to enforce them. The duties of these committees were only vaguely defined, however, and once more no penalties for violation were provided. American advisers had strongly urged both of these missing features, without which they regarded the rent provision as unenforceable; and in any case they considered the promises made in the ordinances far short of the actual Communist achievements in land reform. When the government of Prince Buu Loc succeeded the Tam administration late in 1953, it declared agrarian reform its "first objective," but no practical gestures in that direction had been made by the time the Diem government was installed in July 1954. Political conditions—especially the lack of

effective government over the rural areas—were not ripe for carrying out orderly and thoroughgoing agrarian reform.

The first approach of the Diem government to agrarian reform
was extremely conservative. Certain changes in tenure rights were
envisaged, as well as a number of small pilot projects to be developed by cooperative groups on land provided by the government. Asked to consider this program for American support, the
ICA mission found it "completely unacceptable to us in its present
form" and held a series of meetings with the Minister of Agriculture to push for more extensive reforms; at the same time, the
American ambassador made personal representations to President Diem. The French adviser to the Ministry of Agriculture
reinforced American arguments for restricting land holdings, regu-
larizing contracts, improving landlord-tenant relations, and
strengthening local enforcement agencies. Complete American
recommendations went still further, including expropriation with
compensation, transfer of lands to tenants, and realistic (i.e.,
enforceable) rent limitations. A study tour of Japan was arranged
in August 1954 to suggest a more fundamental approach to Vietnamese officials. The American interest in land reform included
combating Communist propaganda, stimulating the government's
interest in rural welfare (thus generating local support for the
Diem regime), and creating economic incentives for better cultivation and crop diversification. Yet the Vietnamese government,
not wishing to disturb the strong landowning classes, resisted the
proposed transfers of land and the sharper rent controls. The
Minister of Agriculture, Pham Khac Suu, even made an oblique
attack on the American proposals as merely a propaganda weapon
against the Communists, using their own "line."[11]

The turning point finally came when refugees began to pour
down from the north in such numbers that Ngo Dinh Diem was
forced to appeal to President Eisenhower for help. The possibility
of transferring abandoned land to these refugee farmers appealed
strongly to American advisers and when General J. Lawton Collins
came to Saigon as Eisenhower's personal representative, he was
already instructed to say that agrarian reform received a high
priority in American eyes. French technicians, whose influence was
then perhaps greater than that of Americans, also began to attach

[11] Government of Viet-Nam, press release of September 13, 1954.

greater importance to land transfers as the refugee problem became acute. While concerned over the effect of any reform on French landowners, they also wanted to increase productivity through co-operative efforts. In July 1954 the American advisers strongly urged a vigorous program: "An honest land reform intelligently and aggressively applied may offer one of the best means available for meeting the Viet Minh challenge. . . . Earlier land reform programs were largely talk, but if a program can be developed that is more than just sham, it will offer one of the best propaganda weapons against the Viet Minh." Conservative landowners might now be won over by the argument that "the alternative to a government-sponsored program may be a Communist one." The State Department concurred in this strong position, dispatching for reinforcement a distinguished American agricultural administrator from Taiwan.

When General Collins arrived in November 1954, he again endorsed these recommendations, and the aid mission mobilized its forces to launch the government on a "campaign to get all idle land in South Viet-Nam into cultivation in 1955," largely by transferring some titles to refugees and clarifying landlord-tenant relationships. If the Vietnamese proved their acceptance of this proposal by "early and definite action," the United States agreed to extend grants and credits to the settlers. After a number of conferences with French technicians, detailed suggestions for the revision and implementation of existing agricultural laws were jointly presented to the Vietnamese government by Ambassador Collins and General Ely, the French representative. It was expected that Vietnamese action would begin without delay, if only to prove the Diem government's good intentions before the summer of 1956, when general elections were scheduled in both North and South Viet-Nam as a prelude to national unification.

The joint presentation by French and American diplomats produced the desired effect. Almost immediately French, Vietnamese, and American technicians began to draft a new ordinance, and in three weeks the first part of the new program was promulgated. But the agrarian reform plan, although generally applauded by American officials, still disappointed technicians who had hoped that the Vietnamese government would delegate decisive authority either to local officials or to the numerous commissions that were appointed. Moreover, before the machinery of agrarian reform could be put in motion, an unexpected reorganization of the agricultural administration took place on May 10, 1955. The field organization for agrarian reform was separated from its Saigon headquarters, and the Ministry of Agriculture itself was split. By the end of the summer the two chief technicians from the Ministry who had participated in the drafting of the new program were jettisoned by the head of the newly created Agrarian Reform Ministry.[12]

No refugees were settled on the idle ricelands during the first six "demonstration" months, because overriding emergencies—the activities of armed religious sects, Communist infiltration, dangers of invasion, and the necessity of providing for refugees—demanded the attention of most high government officials, while the land reform agencies themselves were ineffectively organized. Even after security conditions had improved, the American advisers reported that "the failure of the land tenure program to move forward must still be blamed on the lack of serious interested administrators and topside command. Government officials, beginning with the Minister for Agrarian Reform, have divided loyalties, being themselves landholders." The Minister of Agrarian Reform was reported as not having "signed leases with his tenants as provided for by land reform decrees and he is most certainly not interested in land distribution which would divest him of much of his property."[13]

As the program continued to develop, the aid mission began to urge greater progress in the modest provisions for standardizing land tenure contracts even if actual transfers of ownership did not take place. The agrarian reform specialist reported: "President Diem and other officials are continuously prodded into overcoming

[12] The new minister, a political appointee, was related by marriage to the President. Nevertheless, subsequent failure resulted in his removal, and later a high-ranking administrator in the Directorate of Land Registration was dismissed because of alleged irregularities in preparing titles, which may be taken as evidence of the President's support of agrarian reform. When the program was actually started, the government abandoned previous favoritisms, and lands belonging to the Vice-President and to the Vietnamese ambassador to the United States were transferred along with the rest. On the other hand, some 150,000 hectares of land held by the Roman Catholic Church were not transferred or even surveyed.

[13] Gittinger, *Agrarian Reform Status Report*, cited, for this and other quotations.

existing handicaps. In our advisory role the idea of land redistribution has also been posed, . . . but the initiation and implementation of this or any other land reform program rests with the government and the people of Viet-Nam. We can help stimulate action in certain directions but we cannot substitute our will for their will."

By December 1955, the refugee problem had reached serious proportions. The famous Cai San land reclamation project was begun, and the aid mission's efforts to promote general agrarian reform were suspended. After December 31, 1956, the Vietnamese government was informed that no further funds would be available to support rent control and rent contract programs.[14] The resurgence of Vietnamese interest in agrarian reform did not occur until a new Minister of Agrarian Reform began a full-scale effort in January 1958, moving the project ahead so swiftly that the programs for rent and tenure security were soon extended to some three-fourths of the tenant farmers in Viet-Nam. By mid-1961 the transfer of land was expected to be complete. But it required new Vietnamese leaders and changes in domestic politics—basically, a dwindling of the landlords' influence—as well as American advice and pressure finally to translate policy into one of the most successful agrarian reform programs in the Far East.[15] The American role required, first, persistence and patience in focusing attention on a long-standing Vietnamese problem and, second, sustained financial and technical assistance.

For both governments land reform programs arose more out of political than economic objectives. American persistence grew out of profound convictions about the political necessity as well as the

[14] U.S. aid to agrarian reform by the end of the fiscal year 1960 was set at $4,000,414, largely for administrative expenses. The salaries of 180 field agents were paid out of these funds, as well as over 700 at the Ministry working on land transfers. President Diem had requested $30 million in direct aid funds to purchase land for redistribution from the large holders. This request was rejected as excessive in price and contrary to U.S. policy. The United States did, however, authorize a $3 million increase in funds for highway maintenance, which enabled the Vietnamese government to transfer this amount into funds for land purchases.

[15] See Gittinger's articles in the *Far Eastern Survey*, cited, and Wolf Ladejinsky, "Agrarian Reform in the Republic of Vietnam," in Wesley R. Fishel, ed., *Problems of Freedom: South Vietnam Since Independence* (New York: Free Press, 1961).

intrinsic value of reform. Perhaps, as some critics have suggested, our attitudes about social justice tend to be strongest when they refer to a far-off country where the U.S. involvement is indirect. Americans could overlook the manifold obstacles faced by the Vietnamese government, even indulging in some indignation when an obviously just program was poorly administered. But the basic urgency of the U.S. concern arose out of the political crisis posed by a flood of refugees and the need to give the peasants a stake in their country, rather than from abstract support for social justice. The primary American role was that of a persistent gadfly until our financial and technical resources could be brought to bear. Even given the nature and extent of the U.S. commitment to Viet-Nam, it is doubtful whether stronger American representations could have resulted in faster action until a legitimate joint program was undertaken.

Pressures Resulting from U.S. Legislative Requirements

From the standpoint of cooperation with the host governments, the most troublesome of all unilateral American policies in foreign aid are those imposed by Congress as "riders" to mutual security legislation. Whether in response to domestic pressures, ideological convictions, or efforts to influence the foreign policies of receiving countries, such provisions—when enforceable—are often inconvenient, uneconomic, or boundlessly irritating. If they exceed what is believed to be the legitimate scope of American aid, such conditions or "strings" arouse resentment far out of proportion to their importance, thus providing a fruitful source for Communist propaganda. Some provisions are literally unenforceable, being beyond the power of either government; in other cases, our administrators are forced to evade unworkable regulations by a series of subterfuges. Such results are dubious testimony to the workings of representative democracy in foreign relations.

Among the most irksome of these requirements is the so-called "50/50" shipping clause,[16] which requires use of privately owned U.S. flagships for the transportation of at least half of the gross

16 This requirement was included in Sec. 509 of the Mutual Security Act of 1954. It was deleted from the Mutual Security Act of 1957, however, because meanwhile the Merchant Marine Act (originally enacted in 1936) had been amended in 1954 to apply the 50/50 requirement to mutual security shipments. PL 664, 83d Cong., 2d sess. (August 26, 1954).

tonnage of commodities provided by American aid. Under ICA regulations this clause was applied to commercial import programs as well as to project aid, and it covered half of every category of merchandise imported, in each quarter of the year and from each region of the world. While the law arose out of the evident concern of Congress for what seemed the reasonable and necessary requirements of American merchant shipping, its economic and political effects on foreign aid ill served our important interests in Viet-Nam.

The first result of the shipping requirement when applied to Viet-Nam was a slight increase in prices. Vietnamese importers then began to seek sources of supply from ports where no American ships called and which were therefore exempt from the "50/50" clause. This evasion proved to be a complicated and uncertain gamble. In 1955, for example, the requirement was waived for shipments from Japanese ports, but after a few years American vessels began to run between Japan and Saigon. According to the law, even if the U.S. flag vessels could not service 50 per cent of the ICA-financed goods, they still had to be used to the extent available. Importers who were forced to use the costly American shipping began to protest because of their weakened competitive position, and ICA in Washington suggested that the differential in shipping costs be absorbed out of the aid mission's local funds. But the differences were so large (for example, cement carried for $3.80 on a Japanese ship cost $12 in an American bottom) that the mission in Saigon rejected Washington's suggestion, pointing out that adjustments in rates might have cost up to $800,000 a year. Because the American shipping lines discontinued service, the issue was dropped. But in July 1958 American services between Japan and Saigon were resumed, the waiver was again lifted, and the price of delivered cement from Japan rose to about $25.00 (as compared with $16.80 from India and $17.80 from Sweden, neither of which was served by American lines). No more Japanese cement was shipped to Viet-Nam after this ruling, and Japan may have lost as much as $5 million of annual business to other suppliers.

Another practical effect of the "50/50" clause was a grouping of the Vietnamese importers into crude cartels for self-protection against the somewhat unpredictable enforcement of the U.S. shipping requirements. Certain bulk commodities came to be ordered by one importer acting for all or by small associations of importers. In this way any added shipping costs could be readily passed on to consumers without disrupting the system of distribution (as might otherwise occur if one importer succeeded in getting a waiver—that is, found a port not served during that period by U.S. shipping—and his competitors did not). For these reasons and because waivers were generously and fairly granted, the competitive markets of Saigon were not seriously affected. The shipping clause nevertheless produced an inordinate amount of adverse publicity. Vietnamese critics, unsympathetic to the problems of high-cost American shipping, failed to see why the aid mission had to quibble over a matter of so little relevance to declared American purposes in Viet-Nam.

Another legislative clause that has been difficult to explain to Vietnamese importers is that designed for the protection of American small business.[17] The Mutual Security Act established procedures for notifying all American enterprises when purchases of goods produced by them were to be made from any aid funds, so that even small businessmen, typically uninformed about foreign markets, would have an opportunity to bid. This provision became all but unworkable in Saigon, where thousands of importers were using U.S. aid funds in daily operations, and many were conducting very small operations which would have foundered under the weight of specifications, competitive bidding, and licensing. Many of the advance specifications that were submitted for bids were improperly prepared or badly translated. A brief experiment in 1956 resulted in a paper inundation in Washington and thereafter the small business requirement was waived in Viet-Nam except for industrial machinery (i.e., capital goods costing more than $5,000) and the few imports brought in by the Vietnamese government's Central Procurement Agency. In March 1958 ICA proposed that the small business requirements be extended further, but the Vietnamese government objected so vigorously that the extension was indefinitely postponed.

American agricultural interests have also been successful in obtaining special advantages from foreign aid legislation. For many years ICA adhered to a policy of world-wide competitive

[17] Sec. 504 of Mutual Security Act of 1954, as amended; ICA Regulation No. 1, Sec. 201.13.

bidding for the procurement of foreign aid commodities.[18] The only exception was a provision that a fixed amount of American surplus agricultural commodities be purchased under a loose quota system established in Washington. These quotas were not rigorously enforced, however, and the aid missions were not expected to try to influence consumption habits in favor of American commodities. The PL 480 program was intended to encourage the export of surplus agricultural commodities, but this was not considered primarily foreign aid legislation. Local currency obtained from the sale of these commodities was to be used for such purposes as military budget support, local operating costs of American government agencies, information programs, loans to American firms contemplating expansion, stimulation of consumption of U.S. agricultural surpluses by means of loans for agricultural market development, and local agricultural processing industries. In some cases the funds even served to maintain consumer preferences for the produce of other countries. Since France had purchased surplus cotton from the United States, for example, a supply of francs became available in the former Indochinese states to pay for commercial imports from France.[19] ICA's decision to link development aid to American purchases to reduce the gold outflow, announced November 16, 1959, was a reversal of longstanding policy in all fields except agriculture.

American farm interests actually attempted to restrain aid activities that might unduly increase the production of items competing with U.S. surpluses. Thus for several years the Commercial Import Program could not supply dollars to import any industrial foodprocessing equipment that would increase Viet-Nam's export potential in rice or other commodities declared in "world surplus." Only after extensive special negotiations were replacements authorized for rice mills that had been destroyed in the Indochinese

[18] In April 1957, the Vietnamese government, as a gesture of friendship to the United States, had suggested that an order for government vehicles be worded to favor U.S. specifications. The suggestion was immediately vetoed in Washington as contrary to U.S. policy.

[19] Care was taken to insure that the supply of these so-called "triangular francs" did not tend to increase the consumption of French products at the expense of American. Even for their French purchases, however, the host governments preferred the more stable dollar and even succeeded in obtaining a U.S. guarantee against any losses in their holdings of triangular francs due to franc devaluation.

war, and even then only small plants located to serve domestic rather than overseas markets were permitted. Sugar-milling and noodle-processing equipment, on the other hand, was readily available because their products did not compete with U.S. surplus commodities. John B. Hollister, Director of ICA, stated U.S. policy as follows: "We should not assist directly cooperating countries to increase production of surplus agricultural commodities so as to result, over a reasonable period of time, in increased exports or decreased imports of such [i.e., American surplus] commodities." Even if projects already under way could not be immediately discontinued, they were to be reduced "with a view to discontinuing our participation entirely next year."[20]

Even producers of rice *for domestic use* were theoretically ineligible for financial or technical assistance from the aid mission. As long as rice was listed as a U.S. surplus item, aid was denied to Viet-Nam's most important domestic crop and also, second to rubber, its major export earner. Although by encouraging crop diversification U.S. aid could help make the Vietnamese economy more self-sufficient and stable, it was rice production that held the greatest possibilities for increases in the national agricultural output. The average yield—1.3 metric tons per hectare—was among the lowest in Southeast Asia, but the poor productivity came from various remediable causes: single-cropping (in some areas water-control projects could lead to two or more annual crops), inadequate fertilization, pest damage, and derelict land, all of which American aid could have helped to overcome.

Under U.S. aid legislation most activities in the interest of agricultural productivity in Viet-Nam, except crop diversification, would have been officially discountenanced: irrigation, pest control, extension services, and any other broad agricultural program would have had the forbidden effect of increasing rice production. Some of these measures were permitted in Indo-China in the reconstruction years only because they could be designated as a "restoration" rather than an "increase" of productive efficiency. Other euphemisms were used to justify activities deemed essential to the development of rural economies in Southeast Asia: water-control projects for irrigating paddies were described as "restoration of wartime damage"; extension activities in the stimulation

[20] See ICA circular A-174, February 22, 1956.

of rice production were identified as "improvements in rural living"; productivity figures were recalculated to account for increases in population or the standard of living in order to demonstrate their noncompetitive nature. Fortunately, at the time when these euphemisms were wearing thin and the production of rice for export began to increase, rice was dropped from the list of commodities in "world [i.e., U.S.] surplus."

Eventually, the American aid missions were explicitly authorized to increase rice productivity and thus contribute to economic viability in all of the rice-exporting countries of Southeast Asia. But this policy reversal came as a result of accidental changes in the American commodity market rather than out of a reappraisal of Asian needs. Many Asians naturally believed that technical assistance in agriculture would again be withheld if rice and certain other commodities produced at relatively high costs in the United States became unsalable in the world market. If in Viet-Nam the restrictive policies were softened in practice, it was only because urgent military and security needs overrode the irrelevant preoccupations of American politics. But such subterfuges merely served to demonstrate that the legislative imposition of special American interests on our foreign aid programs could be administratively ineffectual as well as politically unwise.

Conclusions

In Southeast Asia the leverage afforded by U.S. aid for introducing reforms has not been great outside the explicit requirements of the programs themselves. Proposals arising from American political aims or social values tend to be accepted only when they coincide with political requirements of the host country. Those based merely on legislation drafted to serve American domestic needs are viewed with deep suspicion, especially when they detract from the local effectiveness of the aid program.

Administrative reforms have sometimes been successfully introduced by emphasizing the host government's obligation to operate the aid program efficiently and by providing specific and detailed American recommendations to that end. This approach has often succeeded when applied to financial procedures, but personnel systems and the public relations of agencies administering aid-supported programs have been significantly less subject to foreign suggestions or influence. On the other hand, American policy has a chance of contributing to broad social progress when it can demonstrate that the benefits of aid will be lost without reasonable standards of justice and decency. But such recommendations are not always acceptable and should be accompanied by a constant awareness of the ease with which American hopes can be ignored or reversed in practice.

Mild American preferences for political or social change have had little effect when expressed by technicians in the aid programs. Exhortations by the U.S. Congress that are irrelevant or antipathetic to the host government's understanding of its nation's interests have also failed to produce the desired results. The level of American involvement is in the first instance too low, and in the second, too high. The major task of adapting general American policy to the political necessities of the four countries under consideration fell to our ambassadors, who found themselves handicapped by rigidities in U.S. laws and administrative procedures. In the practice of American aid at the country level U.S. foreign policy objectives could not always prevail over less relevant demands issuing from the chambers of domestic politics or the labyrinths of Washington administration.

American political preferences stated firmly and clearly and in terms of objectives, not techniques, can contribute to the prospects for inducing social change. The reverse, a detailed preoccupation with techniques, only adds further to the rigidities already developing in aid administration. It must be recognized that there are long-standing traditions and practices in the underdeveloped world which cannot be directly changed by American action, no matter how greatly they interfere with the purpose of foreign aid. Since these conditions vary from country to country, firmness in stating American purposes must be matched by great flexibility in carrying them out.

2. Unilateral Policies and Attitudes in the Host Country

The "revolution of rising expectations" affects governments as well as citizens subject to insatiable desires created by the rise to independent statehood and exposure to the contrast between their lot and the material wealth of advanced nations. Often symbols of prestige, power, progress, and independence are politically necessary regardless of their apparent economic futility. Hospitals, steel mills, atomic energy institutes, or electronic computers may be of great political value, whether doctors, iron ore, physicists, or statistical data are available or not. At times requests for American aid to finance favorite projects have to be rejected, but wherever possible such proposals are negotiated until they approximate American standards of economic or technical feasibility. Refusal of Egypt's request for the High Aswan dam project in 1956 illustrated the cataclysmic effects of a negative decision when the political prestige of a government has been committed. Given the fact of Soviet foreign aid, American failure to achieve a workable compromise might lead a new country to alternative sources with incalculable political consequences.

In certain cases, projects unacceptable for American aid may still be financed without recourse to the Communist bloc. In Viet-Nam the Americans reluctantly rejected the Da Nhim dam project, a "high-prestige, $40 million hydroelectric plant to be located 175 miles from Saigon and designed to produce 75,000 kilowatts of power in the first stage and additional capacity in later stages," because U.S. engineering studies of electric power requirements and supply indicated that the dam proposal was "premature" (sufficient power for the anticipated needs of the next decade could be made available through modestly priced thermal facilities in Saigon). Because of continued Vietnamese interest the Da Nhim dam was eventually financed by the Japanese under a reparations agreement.[21] Similarly a road paralleling the Cambodian border in the Plaine des Joncs, difficult to build and economically unproductive, was repeatedly proposed by the Vietnamese government and rejected by the United States. In that case the Vietnamese government itself decided to begin construction out of its own resources.

Many other "political" projects have been found unacceptable for American financing. Repeated requests for permission to import luxury and semiluxury commodities under the Commercial Import Program, amounting to $20 million for fiscal year 1959, were refused by the aid mission in Saigon, as were more plausible requests for radio-jamming equipment and a 100,000-watt short-wave transmitter to counter Communist propaganda from the

[21] *Current Situation in the Far East,* Hearings before a subcommittee of the House Committee on Foreign Affairs, 86th Cong., 1st sess., August 3, 1959 (Washington: GPO, 1959), p. 38.

north. It is necessary to add, however, that other uneconomic projects have been reluctantly accepted for the sake of good relations with the host government.

While such refusals do not imperil diplomatic relations or the continuance of aid, they may nevertheless be strongly resented, especially if a proposal has been made publicly and formally. Although many projects may have been already rejected or radically revised, this does not necessarily discourage the emergence of others, of equal dubiousness from the American standpoint, from the obscure political processes of the host country. This is especially true in the absence of a strong coordinating and planning unit, or where political rivalries may make it advisable to pass questionable projects along until the Americans are ultimately forced into the unpopular role of saying no. The U.S. missions, for their part, try to forestall such requests; for the mere presentation of a request for aid, especially if it appears to invoke strong popular support, is a powerful argument for its acceptance.

Political processes in underdeveloped countries, like those in industrial America, often yield policies lacking unity and consistency. Sometimes a project is requested by an agency and approved by the aid mission only to encounter serious opposition from other departments of the host government. An agency opposed to a project may on occasion mobilize more powerful political forces than its proponent, thus introducing delays or even canceling a project. Ordinarily the aid missions have stayed aloof from local administrative differences, but there have been instances like that in Thailand where the mission served as a liaison unit among several departments of a ministry, enabling them to carry out important tasks that never would have been done otherwise.

The same political processes that induce controversy can also bring about changes of policy, or even of government, that may nullify agreements already in force. Project agreements, as we have seen, are not always considered legally binding by the receiving government, especially if made by a discredited former leadership. It is seldom, however, that changes of policy or political leadership introduce serious controversy over aid agreements, fortunately for the United States which is in no position to insist on strict fulfillment. Political changes do not ordinarily involve basic programs, and lesser projects are surrounded by a cushion of flexibility that protects them from fatal collisions; often changes simply result in delays and renegotiations. Frequent changes of Thailand's government after 1956, for example, interrupted a joint proposal of the United States and the World Bank to establish an industrial development bank.[22] Although the prime ministers who succeeded one another in 1957 and 1958 were in basic agreement, no government remained in power long enough to see the project through. Legislation was twice made ready for submission just as the government fell, leaving it in suspension. Political instability has thus sometimes prevented or delayed steps toward economic stability.

In cases where American aid is such an important political issue that it contributes to a change of government, more serious obstacles are encountered. After U Nu retired in October 1958 in favor of the caretaker government of Ne Win, the Burmese policy of favoring loans over grants was reversed. The U Nu government, in spite of its sales agreement with the United States covering the obviously sensitive matters of police and military equipment and advice, had been strongly neutralist. The Ne Win government, which asked for outright grants, was considered more openly favorable to the West than its predecessor (largely because of anti-Communist statements made by high government officials), but its actual aid requests were for politically safe road and university projects.

While $31 million in U.S. grants to Burma were being negotiated during 1958, the Ne Win government requested an additional grant from a $15-million fund of Burmese currency derived from the sale of surplus agricultural commodities. Although these funds had been established primarily for loan purposes, Washington was willing to convert $6 million from the loan funds into a grant for the Mandalay road project with the understanding that the Burmese government would utilize the remaining money in the

[22] An earlier industrial development bank had made large loans for political purposes with scanty results. Bangkok banks specialized in short-term commercial loans, usually to importers, with interest rates nominally set at 12–15 per cent but actually inflated to twice that amount by various fees and charges. On the assumption that the new bank would have a private management free of political connections, the United States released counterpart funds for loan purposes to the extent of 15 million baht ($750,000), and the World Bank participated in drawing up the charter. The Thai government was to add assets derived from the liquidation of the old industrial bank, and private capital was to be included as well.

form of development loans. In response to urgent Burmese requests for a timely show of sympathy for the new government's needs, the United States agreed to release the grant before the final signature of the loan agreement. In the negotiations that followed, however, the Burmese cabinet decided not to accept the development loans, and the American ambassador, obliged to point out that the grant was tied to the loans, was put in the position of appearing to coerce Burma into accepting loans it did not want. Permanent civil servants expressed embarrassment over this turn of events; there was no indication that the government would fail to honor its obligations, but the process of explaining these obligations to "the colonels" surrounding Ne Win was relished by neither American nor Burmese advisers.

Interministerial Rivalries and the Farm Cooperative Project in Viet-Nam

Changes in governmental policies toward aid programs can also be caused by conflict among rival ministries. A dramatic example occurred when the Vietnamese army, anticipating a rice shortage, seized funds set aside for farm credit cooperatives and used them to purchase paddy rice to be stored in cooperative warehouses until needed. For nearly two years cooperative activities were suspended for lack of funds and storage space, and the matter was resolved only after the American aid mission had complained directly to the Presidency.

Cooperatives, which had first been introduced in Viet-Nam under the French, were generally regarded with suspicion because they were dominated by the landlords, charged high interest rates on farm loans, and enforced their collections with coercive sanctions available under colonial laws. One of the early projects of the Agriculture Division of the aid mission was, therefore, to restore public confidence in the cooperative movement by establishing twenty "pilot" rice-storage and credit cooperatives that would gradually encourage self-sustaining, nation-wide activity. The mission argued that reasonable credit facilities would protect the farmers against the usury of local money-lenders,[23] and that ade-

---

[23] Borrowing against anticipated crops often took place at 3 to 5 per cent monthly interest. Many of the money-lenders were Chinese. See "Competition at the Cai Rang Cooperative Rice Mill," in Montgomery, *Cases in Vietnamese Administration,* cited, esp. pp. 150–152.

quate warehousing would enable farmers to stabilize prices by releasing their harvest gradually and at the same time would protect the nation against periodic and regional famines. A cooperative project was introduced in December 1955, financed by $150,000 in dollar-produced commodities and 35 million piasters in American counterpart funds for use in the farm credit program. By July 1956, the twenty warehouses were ready, administrative personnel had been trained, and money was available for loans.

In the meantime, the army, anticipating possible Communist guerrilla activity in July, decided to lay in a supply of rice. Its purchasing agents were unable to obtain sufficient supplies because the farmers, mindful of the army's habit of postponing payment for its purchases, had reported poor harvests in order to avoid selling directly to the army. To counteract this tactic, the army, through the Secretary of State at the Presidency, instructed the Ministry of Agrarian Reform to release 1,140,000 piasters to each of the new cooperatives (this sum representing the total amount authorized by the aid mission for the cooperative credit program) for the purpose of buying unmilled rice at current market prices. The supplies were to be channeled into the cooperative warehouses and stored until the army was ready to use them. First given by word of mouth, these instructions were confirmed in writing a few weeks later. The American technicians became aware of this procedure when routine inspection revealed that the cooperatives were inexplicably purchasing large amounts of rice at unfavorable prices. The aid mission then sent a letter reporting "serious deviations from our agreement" to the Secretary General of the Agrarian Reform Ministry, only to receive the reply that the rice purchases had been ordered by an authority that "could not be questioned."

Purchases continued at the peak of the market until 13.9 million piasters (of cooperative funds) had been expended for 4.7 million kilos of rice. In November 1956 a typhoon severely damaged two warehouses and their contents, and the cooperatives, already embarrassed by the tying up of their funds and facilities, began to express concern over the responsibilities for this additional loss. As a final gesture, when the new crops were harvested and prices fell to one-half the earlier purchase cost, the army decided to procure fresh rice on the market. Left with warehouses filled with deteriorating rice that was, at best, worth only half its original price, the cooperatives were virtually paralyzed; bereft of storage facilities and loan funds, they were powerless to render their intended services.

At the request of the aid mission, Vietnamese agricultural officials met with American technicians to discuss the problem. It was then learned that the army had originally promised to buy the rice back again at the purchase price, plus 4 piasters per bag to pay for wear and tear (no storage charges were admitted). No explanation was given for the army's later decision to pay only the current prices and not to reimburse the cooperatives for the typhoon losses. At the meeting, the American representatives stated that in all probability future aid to farm cooperatives would be suspended until the losses had been reimbursed. On December 16, 1956, the acting director of the aid mission wrote the Secretary of State at the Presidency summarizing the facts and pointing out that "if the army used current prices as a basis of payment, several of the pilot cooperatives will become bankrupt. This would certainly discourage the expansion of the program and may cause a certain lack of trust of government business practices on the part of citizens in the affected areas." After much discussion, the army decided to repurchase the rice at the actual price paid by the cooperatives, plus the 4-piaster charge on each bag, and the Presidency indicated that it would pay for the typhoon-damaged rice stores. American aid was subsequently resumed, and after a two-year delay the cooperatives began their credit and storage operations, having sustained a net loss of only a few hundred thousand piasters. As a final postscript, the U.S. Military Assistance Advisory Group undertook to help the Vietnamese army develop new procurement procedures.

Local Politics: Aid and the Press in Burma

Domestic controversies over receiving American aid may also weaken the unity and consistency of the host government's policies. Under these conditions the American aid mission sometimes serves as a conciliator between conflicting views within the host government, but more frequently it plays the passive role of "lightning rod" or even becomes victimized by domestic political conflicts, changes in personnel, and unfavorable public attitudes in the host country in the face of local rivalries, a hypersensitive press, and a volatile public opinion.

Newspaper attacks on American aid in Burma, which reached an extraordinary level of bitterness, were related to domestic politics from the beginning. The first attacks may have been Communist-inspired, but political diatribes from other sources soon followed, both in parliament and in the press.[24] During a parliamentary exchange, Thakin Chit Maung of the opposition left-wing of the government party attacked U.S. aid as follows:

> The U.S. profited from both world wars but was yet faced with economic crises. In order to relieve this distress in America the American government has introduced the Marshall Plan, Special Aid, and the Point 4 Programme. These aids solved the economic and unemployment problems to an extent but wrought havoc in the recipient countries. These aids to Europe were followed by re-armament. In the same way, the ECA was brought by the Americans to Burma to control the country's economy and even interfere in domestic affairs. Besides, under this agreement, Burma must send raw materials to the United States.

The only substantive public response to this attack was a statement by U Ba Gyn that "the Government had given much forethought to signing of such an agreement. This agreement in no way made it obligatory for Burma to sell raw materials to the United States if there are other buyer countries offering more favourable terms. . . . Moreover the acceptance of the ECA did not influence Burma's independent outlook on foreign policy."[25]

In spite of the generally unfavorable attitude to American aid among the press, in August 1951 the Burmese Journalists' Association requested ECA aid in building its headquarters. At a meeting with the chief of the mission in October, members of the journalists' executive committee were told that requests for American aid could be considered only if made officially by the Burmese government—which, for political reasons, was unlikely to support the journalists. At this "snub," as it was called, the executive committee proposed a 30-day blackout on all news relating to the ECA. The resolution was presented to the Association on October 14, and on the same day the *Union Gazette* made a detailed attack on each of the 38 U.S. aid projects. The editor of the *Nation* (who

[24] One of the most engaging was the *Nation* headline of September 7, 1951, citing a Chicago *Tribune* editorial in these words: "Americans Don't Like ECA Either."

[25] *New Times of Burma*, September 13, 1951.

was to lead the attack on American aid) apologized on the floor of the Association meeting for having at first supported ECA, adding that the mission "was staffed with inefficient and conceited officials incapable of treating the Press of Burma with ordinary courtesy." During the months that followed, the press debated this blackout resolution together with the Burmese government's response that it awaited a request for assistance from the Association for consideration and referral to the mission. Debate was effectively terminated, however, by a Washington official of ECA who, in the Christmas season of good will, held a press conference in Rangoon at which he reportedly "took the opportunity to deliver a homily on the virtue of self-help, through the practice of which Burmese newspapers which valued their independent status would not dream of soliciting aid from the government." From which one Burmese paper concluded: "Apparently . . . a newspaper which accepts ECA aid incurs the risk at least of losing its freedom."[26]

Apparently feeding upon itself, the bitterness of press attacks on American aid increased. The proposed new blackout was forgotten as other targets were uncovered, including some unidentified American technicians who were said to "live happily and merrily in this country . . . without a stroke of single work [sic]."[27] Another journal came up with the theory that "the team of experts were just dumped in Burma to keep ECA machinery going. From the individual's point of view ECA has produced nothing yet, although all this money is spent to keep him thinking in one way. Why [should he] thank ECA because his grandson will be immune from TB or malaria? He has to live now. . . ."[28]

After the name of the Economic Cooperation Administration was changed to Mutual Security Agency, the press concluded that henceforth acceptance of U.S. aid would cost Burma its independence in formulating its own foreign policy. The charge was so widely discussed that the American Embassy issued a statement intended to clear up misunderstanding:

There is nothing in the Mutual Security Act which requires any country to accept military aid. . . . Countries which are receiving

[26] *Nation*, December 24, 1951.
[27] *Union Gazette*, October 20, 1951.
[28] *The Burman*, October 26, 1951.

only economic and technical assistance will continue to do so. The
purpose of the Mutual Security Act is to coordinate the overall
administration of a series of foreign aid programs of the U.S. government. . . .

Newspapers that printed this clarification were still not satisfied:
the *New Times of Burma* (January 22, 1952) said that the required
commitment that the receiving country "join in promoting international understanding and good will and in maintaining world
peace [and] take such action as may be mutually agreed upon to
eliminate causes of international tension" was too great; and the
Nation (January 23) spoke of the transition to MSA as "unfortunate and unnecessary."

Objections were so general that the Burmese government declined to accept the new conditions, and late in January aid was
suspended. Before long Premier U Nu, noting that India had
accepted the objectionable clauses, suggested that there was "little
harm in agreeing to them, provided the U.S. government is prepared to do something towards changing the suspicious words in
the name of the Act."[29] On February 12, the Burmese government
accepted proposed changes, in spite of a mass meeting called in
protest; the term "ECA" was continued in use until June 12, when
the *Nation*, under the headline "U.S. Bows to Burmese Opinion,"
was able to report that the local arm of MSA would call itself
simply "Technical and Economic Aid." (A subsequent reduction
in aid to Burma was regarded by some as punishment for such
obstinate behavior.)

American aid in the meantime had become involved in a personal vendetta between U Law Yone, editor of the *Nation*, and
U Hla Maung, the Burmese Secretary of State in charge of coordinating foreign aid. The *Nation* had charged that "ECA in Burma
[is] not anti-Communist nor anti-anything. It is simply pro-U Hla
Maung. Its accomplishments can be measured in terms of the
number of times it has pulled U Hla Maung's chestnuts out of the
fire . . . ," an apparent reference to the prompt ECA shipment of
cotton to Burma in response to a government request, allegedly to
conceal the fact that U Hla Maung had authorized or ordered the
construction of a cotton mill which could not use Burmese cotton.
The aid mission was therefore accused of "playing politics in

[29] *Nation*, January 29, 1952.

Burma, by trying to please one or two people and ignoring the rest."[30] U Hla Maung sued U Law Yone for defamation, reportedly "not on his initiative but on instructions from the government";[31] and after several days of hearings and arguments, the government official won a token award. His suit did not, however, enhance local sympathy for American aid.

Perhaps the most serious attack to appear in the Burmese press was that mounted against a dredge named *Irrawaddy*. Shortly after the Law Yone-Hla Maung affair had been spread before the readers of the *Nation*, the aid mission announced that a giant dredge, to be named the *Irrawaddy* after Burma's famous river, was being presented to Burma to widen and deepen Akyab Harbor and fill in the surrounding swamps for a housing development. The head of the Far East Division of MSA, visiting Burma at the time the dredge was being presented, said in a widely quoted speech that:

> . . . much of the aid coming from the United States is not so apparent as this dredge. . . . [Other programs of health, education, and technical assistance] will not bring any overnight changes in the country. . . . Today, however, we have the exciting and assuring evidence here of the direct results of American-Burman cooperation. This dredge will soon be at work. Another dredge is being built in Scotland. The two will not only be of great value to Burma, but they will symbolize the friendship of two great countries and two great peoples.[32]

This dramatic symbol of American aid and friendship had been brought to Burma in record time. Rather than wait for two years for a new dredge a reconditioned vessel (originally built in 1930) was purchased and refitted in Japan[33] and then hurried to Akyab in twenty-eight days, a voyage described as the longest ocean-going tow in history. The total cost was close to three-quarters of a million dollars, about the price of a new vessel that would be subject to delivery a year or so later.

[30] Same, April 9, 1952.
[31] *The Burman*, December 4, 1952.
[32] Quoted in *New Times of Burma*, May 23, 1952.
[33] In addition to the consideration of a speedy delivery, the decision to buy the Japanese dredge may have been supported by current policy favoring offshore procurements from that country.

A few days after the gift of the *Irrawaddy* was announced, the *Nation* began a series of attacks on the vessel, charging that the reconditioned dredge cost twice the price of a new one; that the dredging apparatus could have been rigged on any pontoon already available in Rangoon; that other designs would have been more suitable; and that dredges that had been scuttled during the war could have been salvaged more economically. One half-page article, which criticized the design and lack of "foresight and capable planning," gave the appearance of having been written by an expert. Stung by such a formidable assault, the chief of the aid mission issued a rebuttal (which the *Nation* published on June 1), charging that "this article is replete with misinformation, shows a limited knowledge of the subject, and concludes with erroneous deductions." After dealing with the article point by point, the release concluded: "The *Irrawaddy* represents an efficient and satisfactory solution to the urgent need for dredging equipment for Burma." On June 4, the expert writing for the *Nation* countered that there was no urgent need for the giant dredge because use could have made of existing smaller dredges, already idle for long periods; that Holland, which built the best and cheapest dredges, had not been approached in the bidding; and that although the *Irrawaddy* had been rushed to Akyab at great expense, the monsoons would delay the project. A supporting editorial stated on June 5 that the aid mission's news release represented "the typical American attitude, blatantly displayed all over the world, of 'we know everything so if there is anyone who disagrees with us he must necessarily be wrong.'"

To all this the mission made no reply, but after one month the *Nation* resumed the battle: "This dredge should not merely be criticized, it should be condemned. The deck is so badly corroded that cement has to be used in many places to make it safe to work on. . . . Spare parts . . . will have to be specially made. . . . Pipe connections . . . are leaking badly. . . . We are paying for the nine Japanese engineers on board. . . . There is only a poor interpreter to assist them. . . . We are afraid we have been sold a pup." Once more the aid mission decided not to reply, confining itself to submitting reports on dredging operations to Washington and occasionally to the Burmese government. In these reports it was intimated that the nautical adviser to the Burmese government had been skeptical of the Japanese dredge ever since it was first proposed, because he, as a loyal British subject, had hoped the award would go to a British shipyard. It was also noted that whereas the crew and maintenance arrangements for the *Irrawaddy* had been negligent ("reprehensible" was the term used in one report), great care was taken to provide an adequate crew and facilities for the S.S. *Pyidawtha*, the second dredge which the mission had ordered from Britain.

A bad press had so persistently dogged ECA activities in Burma that the withdrawal of American aid in 1953 came, in many ways, as a relief. When aid was resumed in 1957 and continued after the coming to power of Ne Win's government, the problem of press relations was left entirely to the Burmese authorities. The interlude appeared to have healed the breach.

Aid and the Press in Viet-Nam

The censored Vietnamese press, although much more circumspect than that of Burma, nevertheless occasionally revealed similar tensions. Vietnamese criticisms of the Commercial Import Program have already been noted; other minor criticisms of American aid also appeared in Vietnamese newspapers, often in "letters-to-the-editor" columns. While the aid mission rarely made a public reply to these criticisms, all received careful attention and—where appropriate—action. On July 22, 1958, for example, the *Nguoi Viet Tu Do* and *Tieng Chuong* published a letter from a Buddhist bonze protesting against the fact that "a few days ago the Capitol Engineering Company [an American firm] had sent surveyors to stake out a new road. These informed us that certain tombs and pagodas will be destroyed in order to clear ground for the road." The letter ignored the fact that the original plans drawn up by the company had not infringed upon the sacred grounds in question, and later changes in the route had been made at the suggestion of President Diem himself; moreover, that the Capitol Engineering Company was under orders from the Vietnamese Directorate General of Public Works rather than the aid mission. Thus any implication that Americans were engaged in despoiling Asian graves was altogether misleading. The American response to the complaint was a private letter from the ambassador to the author of the letter assuring him that he would personally "look into" the matter; shortly thereafter, the Director General of Public Works wrote another private letter to the bonze explaining that several alternative routes had had to be prepared for technical reasons, and that no tombs or pagodas would be removed. No public statement was made in response to the complaint.

The general policy of the aid mission was to encourage the Vietnamese government to publicize American aid projects, so that it could use them where possible as a means of strengthening its popular support. Since no fundamental opposition to the government was permitted in the newspapers of Saigon, the aid program was spared the accusations which usually issued from domestic political maneuvers. The Ministry of Information, whose dual purpose was to attack communism and support the regime, reported American aid only as it would serve either of these objectives. When programs of mass information were necessary in a given aid project (malaria control, public sanitation, improved agricultural techniques, etc.), the mission worked directly through the ministries involved, supplying audio-visual materials and the means for disseminating them.

Leaving the public relations of American aid programs entirely to the host government is likely to prove satisfactory only when there is basic agreement on major foreign policy objectives. In neutralist Cambodia, for example, where the American aid mission also relied on the Ministry of Information, the aid program suffered alternately from violent attacks and utter neglect in spite of the fact that the ministry had itself received $1.5 million of U.S. aid for equipment and operations. This support was discontinued in 1959 after a survey showed that while all high school students could describe Communist aid projects, only four out of twelve were aware of American aid.

The overseas public relations of American foreign aid are a series of perplexities. If an embassy or aid mission avoids trying to explain or to justify itself, leaving public relations entirely to the host government, it may minimize the dangers of appearing to intervene in domestic politics; but this delegation of functions can be reliably employed only when substantial agreement exists between the two governments. On the other hand, using public relations devices for the sake of achieving popularity does not necessarily advance American interests. Whenever American policy or that of the host government is changed unilaterally, there is always a grave risk of charges of misrepresentation. Finally, the general American policy of aloofness from domestic struggles cannot protect the aid program—even when an innocent bystander —from being used as a scapegoat.

Conclusions

The success of unilateral American requirements and proposed reforms in countries receiving aid is primarily determined by two political considerations: first, how far the host government can be convinced that the efficient operation of aid programs depends upon the adoption of American proposals; and second, how much American conviction can be mobilized behind specific proposals to overcome reluctance shown by host governments. It is also important to distinguish between essential and expendable programs, for the United States can run more risks and exert greater pressure in marginal projects than in those central to its interests or the host government's survival. The art of exerting (and reacting to) unilateral pressures is perhaps the supreme challenge to the diplomacy of foreign aid, especially since the measure of American convictions about some proposed reform is not the enthusiasm of technicians on the job but the firmness of the ambassador.

The true independence of countries receiving U.S. aid is nowhere better shown than when the United States tries to insist upon some well-meant reform. There are no means of forcing governments into efficiency and few means of persuading them. Withdrawing aid from any basic joint program is self-defeating, and below the level of withdrawal sanctions scarcely exist. Well aware of this situation, a host government is in a strong position to insist upon carrying out highly complex programs according to its own administrative ideas, even if they are somewhat rudimentary. If the host government's procedures clearly endanger the very survival of some program, the United States can then threaten to withdraw support, but this extreme sanction may come too late.

Aid may safely be withdrawn from programs of lesser importance, however, if they are not being implemented according to reasonable standards. If the host government has committed itself to these programs, the United States has a powerful leverage for introducing administrative improvements; it may also be able to introduce social or economic improvements related to such programs. Yet even a strong bargaining position must not be overplayed. Apart from the damage to a relationship on which the success of more important common programs may depend and the inevitable limit to the host government's commitment to any single program, there may well be possibilities of alternative sponsorship that could undermine the entire American position in the country.

Aid projects desired more strongly by the United States than by the host government are in an extremely vulnerable position unless they are tied to other projects in which the reverse is true. This balance is difficult to achieve, however, where the relationship between the two sets of projects is assumed merely for bargaining purposes. Such liaisons may be usefully employed in furthering American objectives in the host country, provided the objectives are clearly enunciated and are sufficiently relevant to the political needs and interests of the local authorities. When policies emanating from American special interest groups are forced upon the host country in such a liaison, the flexibility of the aid mission in achieving foreign policy goals may be severely restricted.

Governments of all underdeveloped countries receiving aid may readily agree that two of America's ultimate foreign policy objectives, stability and economic growth, are elementary necessities. But the meaning and the timeliness of America's other concerns—whether they be legislative and administrative requirements or vaguer aspirations for a freer and more democratic society and world order—may be less widely accepted and only casually served by the instruments of foreign aid. The American practice of haggling over minor matters discourages any sense of mutuality. The occasions for agreement on the important issues cannot be broadened if the parties are forced to negotiate endlessly on points not essential to common or major American purposes.

Our technicians in the field are best able to judge what can be done to improve the administration of aid programs, especially when they are able to cooperate effectively with their opposite numbers; but they cannot be expected to succeed in inducing such improvements unless they or their counterparts possess substantial political support. This is the task of conventional diplomacy, through which the American ambassadors in countries receiving aid must attempt to work from our unilateral requirements toward fully mutual undertakings; for mutuality, descriptive as the term often is in concealing or in crystallizing policy differences, remains the essential ingredient. Because the political and not the technical considerations are controlling, it is imperative that the American embassy, well versed in the unique needs of each country and sensitive to changes of political mood, be made a focus of diplomatic planning for American foreign aid.

IV THE POLITICS OF PROLIFERATION:
ORGANIZING FOREIGN AID*

THE HISTORY of foreign aid administration has faithfully reflected both basic American political values and the uncertainties of recent American foreign policy. At the same time, it has inevitably reflected conflicting cultural and political values as well as shifts in foreign policy in the nearly one hundred countries where foreign aid has been offered since World War II. Maintaining a balance among these contrary forces has produced in practice a functioning "country" orientation that has persisted in spite of repeated efforts to centralize responsibility for important decisions in Washington.

American values such as efficiency, responsibility, and professionalism have dominated all efforts to improve foreign aid procedures, although they are values which are at times irrelevant or even run counter to those of most traditional societies. "Efficiency," a Western and especially American value, calls for the abandonment of many taboos and social traditions, including forms of favoritism that are essential to the family and elite systems of most of the underdeveloped world; "responsibility" implies a delegation of authority and specialization of function that are impossible in much of the world; "professionalism" requires forms of training, the development of a career service, and the introduction of standards that few nonindustrial societies can support.

* Portions of this chapter appeared under the title "Field Organization, Administrative Relationships, and Foreign Aid Policies," in Carl J. Friedrich and Seymour E. Harris, eds., *Public Policy*, v. 10 (Cambridge: Graduate School of Public Administration, Harvard University, 1960), pp. 297–331.

Foreign aid has also reflected American purposes that have ranged, over the decades, from winning major and minor wars to restoring civil order and industrial capacity, and from relieving immediate human suffering to building up the capacity for long-term economic growth. Isolationism and internationalism have variously influenced the aid program's inconstant policy and its organization, and the needs and special circumstances of scores of countries have determined the shifting direction of its actions.

It is small wonder that, given its high political vulnerability and the conflicts of values and purposes internally and between the United States and the receiving countries, foreign aid has undergone continuous reorganization. The wonder is that the abstract virtues of administration—and especially that of efficiency—have applied to foreign aid at all, and that enough of the dynamic of foreign aid has persisted in the country operations to warrant its continued existence. If the concept of efficiency has ill served American interests abroad, similarly the efforts to control and centralize foreign aid programing and operations in terms of world-wide standards have produced some illusions at home about the source and nature of the essentially country-dominated policy decisions. The abstractions of administrative efficiency and world-wide policy-making encounter reality at the point where the essential negotiations and operations take place: at the country level.

1. Proliferation in Washington

The Washington agencies engaging in foreign aid during the 1950s were variously international and national; departmental, interdepartmental, and subdepartmental; semiautonomous, independent, and subordinate; and interlocking, competitive, and coordinated. They were financed by voluntary contributions, annual and long-term congressional appropriations, and the general borrowing power of the Treasury. Each agency was created to serve a special purpose which it jealously protected. Each was the product of a crisis, political compromise, a change in dominant foreign aid doctrine, or recognition of a new potential in economic or technical assistance. Overseas each responded to policy directives from headquarters and tried to integrate its activities with the needs and demands of the country in which it operated.

The politics of interagency competition is, of course, a well-known phenomenon in Washington. Even among agencies charged with different administrative functions there is enough indirect competition in the search for funds, personnel, and political support to provide distraction from operational routines. But in foreign aid the principal agencies have been in direct competition for funds, for operating and policy responsibility, and even for specific projects. Here the distractions tend to overwhelm the operations.

The Problem of Coordination

Although legally charged with the coordination of the scattered foreign aid efforts, the Department of State was never authorized to create an adequate apparatus for that purpose. It had no control over the activities of the Defense Department, except through the forcefulness the Secretary of State might display in the higher councils of the government; nor did it have jurisdiction over the foreign aid activities of the Departments of Agriculture, Labor, Commerce, or Health, Education and Welfare. The State Department was not even permitted to act as congressional liaison on foreign matters for interested departments and agencies, a separation which Congress intensified by assigning different committees and subcommittees to each. Even in strictly diplomatic matters, American representatives on international bodies engaged in discussing and negotiating loans and technical assistance had no organizational link with the International Cooperation Administration.

Conversely, not all foreign aid operations were correlated with American diplomacy. Some congressmen argued that the Development Loan Fund (DLF) was meant to operate abroad without any reference at all to American foreign policy considerations. Although the Fund was established under a board chaired by an Under-Secretary of State in order to afford some degree of coordination, its subsequent efforts to relate its activities to American foreign policy objectives resulted in sharp congressional criticism. "The distinctiveness of the DLF has been lost," according to one House committee report; because of foreign policy considerations, certain loans "failed to bring . . . the 'businesslike' approach" that a banking agency should have. The committee severely scored the

DLF for becoming an agency of American foreign policy instead of serving the abstract purposes of economic development.[1]

For want of a coordinating apparatus in foreign aid, the agencies concerned attempted to work out informal means of distinguishing and redistributing their functions. The Development Loan Fund was said to look with disfavor on loans to the fishing, textile, coal, agricultural products, and petroleum industries, or to any publicly owned enterprise, such as municipal water works or welfare projects. ICA, which also made development loans, tended to specialize in projects that could not meet the banking requirements of the other agencies. As a matter of policy, all the lending agencies usually rejected loan applications for the exploration of oil and natural gas. Statutes also determined some specialization in the use of funds available to lending agencies: Export-Import Bank loans were for dollar purchases of items (usually machinery) produced in the United States; originally, dollars lent by the DLF might be spent anywhere and repayment could be made in local currency. International lending agencies located in Washington also entered the competition with their own specialties: the World Bank usually dealt in large loans to or through governments, more than half of them for electric power and transportation; the International Finance Corporation made loans up to a $2-million maximum, mostly to private projects with good dollar-earning prospects; and the International Monetary Fund lent only to member governments, usually on a short-term basis, to deal with balance-of-payments difficulties. Such limitations tended to reduce competition among the various agencies, but did not lead to a high degree of coordination either of policy or of operating procedures.

Even where only a few agencies undertook apparently simple

[1] *Operations of the Development Loan Fund*, 14th Report by the House Committee on Government Operations, H. Report 1526, 86th Cong., 2d sess. (Washington: GPO, 1960), pp. 3, 4, and 5, and elsewhere. The Foreign Operations and Monetary Affairs Subcommittee prepared the report. Representative Porter Hardy, the chairman, singled out for special comment loans which had been earmarked for India with no "project" designations, creating in effect an unofficial "line of credit." He also objected to similar commitments to Israel to finance commodity imports. One such $50-million loan earmarked for the Philippines "interfered with negotiations by the Export-Import Bank to accomplish similar purposes through 'hard' (dollar-repayable) loans." (Same, pp. 4, 5.)

tasks, the complexities of foreign aid administration usually required extensive coordination in order to avoid collisions. The Department of Agriculture's disposal of surplus American agricultural products, for example, posed problems both of organization and of political manipulation. Apart from relief distribution, most of the agricultural commodities available under PL 480[2] were sold in the underdeveloped countries, the local currency proceeds being used thereafter for development loans and other purposes. A total of $8,358,000,000 was programed on this basis for the first five years of operations under the act.[3]

Authority over the program was dispersed among many agencies. Primary responsibility for establishing the loan policies was assigned to the Department of Agriculture, which also took the lead in determining the countries, quantities, and commodity composition of U.S. surplus sales, in coordinating the instructions sent to the field for negotiating agreements, and in arranging for the procurement and shipment of commodities and the deposit of local currencies. The State Department was brought in to coordinate the programs with U.S. foreign policy and to negotiate with foreign governments. The Export-Import Bank prepared loan agreements which had been authorized by ICA.[4] Coordination of the various foreign aid programs financed out of sales proceeds, drafts, and loan agreements was also ICA's responsibility, and it actually handled the local currency proceeds that were to be used for economic development. The Defense Department was authorized to use part of these local currencies to procure military items; the Office of Defense Mobilization could use funds to purchase strategic materials; the Treasury Department was empowered to regulate the management of foreign currencies; the Budget Bureau allocated and apportioned local currency proceeds; appropriate

[2] "Agricultural Trade Development and Assistance Act of 1954," 83d Cong., 2d sess. (July 10, 1954), esp. Title I.

[3] Operations began in July 1954. See *The Tenth Semiannual Report of Activities Carried on Under Public Law 480, 83d Congress, as Amended,* H. Doc. No. 206, 86th Cong., 1st sess. (Washington: GPO, 1959).

[4] The Cooley Amendment to PL 480 (passed in 1957) assigned to the Export-Import Bank the full responsibility for loans (up to 25 per cent of the total) to U.S. firms for expansion abroad or to other firms for expanding markets for U.S. agricultural products. All agencies were enjoined from making loans for the manufacture of products that would be in competition with U.S. commodities.

disbursing officers and agencies paid U.S. foreign currency obligations; and the United States Information Agency was expected
to publicize these activities.

The Staff Committee on Agricultural Surplus Disposal, which
was assigned the formidable task of coordinating the activities of
these overlapping agencies, included representatives from the eight
agencies most involved: the Departments of Agriculture, State,
Treasury, Defense, Commerce; ICA, ODM, and the Bureau of the
Budget. It had responsibility for overseeing administrative operations and resolving policy differences on sales agreements (which
could also be referred to an Interagency Committee on Surplus
Disposal). Such a complicated mechanism functioned only because so much of the decision-making and operating responsibility
was delegated to the diplomatic missions in the field. Even so, the
elaborate procedural requirements led to delays that jeopardized
understanding and acceptance of the agricultural surplus program
abroad, especially in countries that already feared the competition
of American surplus commodities with their own farm production. In some recipient countries the amounts of money available
for loan funds from the agricultural surplus program were much
larger than those available under the mutual security program
itself, necessitating close coordination with ICA's country program.
For these reasons the heads of the U.S. operations missions, under
ambassadorial direction, were given increasing, although still insufficient, latitude in developing and reviewing the programs. The
procedures, however, remained more complex than those developed under the Mutual Security Act itself.[5]

Aid Forms and Procedures

American aid operations in Southeast Asia and throughout the
underdeveloped world took three principal forms: direct dollar aid
to supply foreign exchange for imports; loans or grants for economic development; and technical assistance. The first form of aid
required close and continuous relationships with the recipient
government, which could be maintained only by a resident staff;

[5] In addition to the provisions of the Act, PL 480 responsibilities are
also assigned by Executive Order No. 10880, September 9, 1954; President's
letter of September 9, 1954 (in *The Department of State Bulletin*, October
4, 1954, pp. 500–501), and Executive Order 10575, November 6, 1954. The
Department of State has also issued administrative instructions.

the second, a determination of needs based on surveys and technical studies; and the third, skilled technicians in residence for varying periods of time. ICA country missions administered all three in a variety of arrangements. Both loans and technical assistance were offered by other countries or by international agencies, as well as by the United States; but only the ICA missions could offer grants in direct support of national budgets, supply foreign currency for imports, or make use of large counterpart funds.

Among the various national and international agencies offering aid to underdeveloped countries, the most complex administrative procedures were those of the ICA missions, not only because they employed the widest variety of aid techniques, but also because in Southeast Asia they operated under the most difficult and unpromising conditions. Frequently they accepted projects from which international agencies would have been barred by their charters or where few alternative bilateral arrangements existed. Indeed, gradually some specialization of function developed among the half-dozen agencies offering foreign aid in Southeast Asia: the ICA missions undertook the broadest, most expensive, and most flexible operations; the international banking agencies were effective where economic considerations could prevail over political and strategic issues; and, finally, the United Nations and the Colombo Plan offered technical assistance where the services of individual experts could be most effectively applied. The pragmatic development of the various aid resources was an evolutionary process, corresponding to a hard-gained understanding of the importance of flexibility in dealing with the needs of each receiving country. Only thorough integration of field operations at the country level could achieve such flexibility, and this integration depended in turn upon a clear and unified conception of American interests and methods in the provision of foreign aid.

The organization of the field missions and the variety of resources available to them largely determined the potential impact of their programs. In Viet-Nam, where U.S. aid represented a substantial portion of the total national resources and included support to commercial imports, ICA achieved a substantial impact. Even where the amounts of aid were small, as in Burma, a concentration of administrative and financial effort was possible because the American program was directed toward immediate political objectives. But in the many countries where American aid was oriented toward technical assistance across the board, accompanied by loans from other agencies and by relatively insignificant mutual security funds, the tendency was to develop many small and unrelated projects loosely coordinated in the field and under the technical direction of various subdivisions of ICA in Washington. The expectation of an important political impact under such conditions was small. In such cases the specific country approach was largely confined to allocating funds and priorities among somewhat isolated individual projects.

Experience has shown that even where either the amounts involved or the specific projects themselves were comparable, the American "impact" projects seldom had the effects achieved by Communist aid, largely because of procedural requirements of the American system for precise accountability and responsibility. The gradual withdrawal of American aid from impact projects, together with increased congressional hope for more "businesslike" loans accompanied by limited technical assistance programs, seemed to reflect American acceptance of Communist superiority in the taking of large economic risks in the hope of political gain. In 1960, however, the executive branch discovered a new justification for indulging in a limited number of large impact programs. This approach accepted the thesis that countries ready for economic "take-off" could be decisively influenced at the appropriate point by massive aid. It also offered the prospect of achieving a psychological as well as an economic impact. Apart from such efforts, American country programs under ICA were by this time supposed to be limited to technical assistance unless "defense support" or "special assistance" funds were available (that is, unless plausible military reasons for aid existed).

In strictly technical assistance (which includes the activities of most personnel engaged in foreign aid operations) there are many private, governmental, and international agencies at work. In Southeast Asia various UN agencies, the Colombo Plan nations, and private and public American institutions have all supplied technical advisers, usually on the request of the countries in which they served. The organizational flexibility of these agencies and their political acceptability were probably more important to the host government than questions of strict technical competence. The United States, aware of these factors, seldom entered into direct competition with international agencies for the honor of supplying technicians. On the contrary, at times American specialists and technical assistance funds were available to the United Nations or within the framework of the Colombo Plan as well as through ICA and sometimes in a loosely integrated combination of all of these. Fundamental American objectives were not endangered by this proliferation of agencies offering technical assistance, although it did not always make for efficiency. In most cases the burden of inviting, assigning, and coordinating competitive or incompatible foreign aid activities had to be borne by the receiving country, whether or not it possessed adequate planning facilities.

Because of the difficulty of coordinating from Washington the American agencies (not to speak of the international ones) while at the same time permitting flexible operation, whatever integration of American technical assistance there was took place informally in the field, or at least on the basis of recommendations and reports supplied from the country missions. And because ICA was the only agency possessing a large staff of technicians who worked continuously overseas on long-term assignments, most of the burden fell upon its individual operations missions in the field. Despite ICA's waning prestige and growing inertia, the agency provided in practice the only means for coordinating many of the disparate American foreign aid operations.

2. PROLIFERATION IN THE FIELD: AMERICAN AID MISSIONS

The administrative patterns recently used in ICA operations were authorized by bilateral agreements with forty-nine countries and nine dependent territories and carried out, in the technical assistance program overseas, by some 6,000 U.S. technicians and other officials.[6] These technicians were assigned to U.S. aid or "operations" missions (USOM's) cooperating as closely with the host government as political circumstances permitted. The director of a typical country mission was assisted by a number of technical divisions, organized along lines parallel to the headquarters technical services of ICA in Washington. These divisions administered both economic and technical assistance for agreed projects. When grant aid was available, the ICA mission could also engage in

[6] *The Mutual Security Program*, Fiscal Year 1960, a summary presentation by the Department of State, Department of Defense, and ICA (Washington: GPO, 1959), p. xvi.

"nonproject" aid by supplying dollars for the import of commodities required for commercial and industrial uses. Local currency in amounts equivalent to these dollar imports, known as counterpart funds, could then be used either as a direct contribution to the host government in support of agreed undertakings, or as a supplement to other aid activities.

General coordination of the program for each country receiving aid was the responsibility of the "country team"—the ambassador, the chiefs of the operations mission, the military advisory group, and the information service—in conjunction with appropriate Washington agencies. Most technical matters, however, were decided in the technical chain of command unless they conflicted clearly with important policy objectives established locally. Policy differences could be much more readily resolved in the country team than in Washington because of the obviously greater difficulty of coordinating independent agencies at the headquarters level. Both the initiation of country policies and the reconciliation of conflicts among different agencies, therefore, tended to occur in the field rather than in Washington. Washington's role in foreign aid was one of clearance rather than of creativeness in establishing country policies.

Most ICA aid programs in Southeast Asia were actually carried out by agencies of the host government. American technicians performed both advisory and supervisory (control) functions, the normal "technical assistance" relationship being compounded by a somewhat inconsistent administrative responsibility for projects supported by American funds. This relationship carried at least three implications of political importance: first, that administrative decisions and operations on both sides, whether joint or separate, reflected and influenced other relationships between Americans and Asians; second, that the processes of administering aid tended to have a centralizing effect upon the governmental structures in the host country, even though in some cases the program itself required the national government to establish local services or branch offices; and finally, that there was a constantly increasing number of American technicians and their families in capitals of underdeveloped countries, where they influenced public opinion toward the United States, the West, the capitalistic system, and democracy. An examination of these three implications will assist in defining the roles played by American aid.

The administrative relationships between the host government and the ICA mission fell into three general patterns: "joint" relationships, the "counterpart" system, and the "liaison" approach. To some extent, all of these relationships existed in most given situations, but for purposes of generalization it is possible to characterize certain relationships in Taiwan as joint, those in Viet-Nam and Thailand as counterpart, and those in Burma as liaison.

Joint Relationships

Joint planning and administration represent the closest possible relationship in mutual aid. Such intimate cooperation can rise only out of clear common interests and mutual confidence, both of which are reinforced by the experience of joint decision making. The classic example of this approach is the Joint Commission on Rural Reconstruction in Taiwan (JCRR), whose authority has been exercised since its formation in 1948 by three Chinese (including the chairman) and one or two Americans, each of whom casts one vote on the disposition of funds and the design of programs for rural development. It has been considered part of both the Chinese government (under the Executive Yuan) and the U.S. government (the American commissioners being appointed by the President and responsible to ICA). The entire technical staff is merged, no distinction being made in rank or function between Chinese and Americans. A mingling of Americans and Chinese has occurred at the upper levels of the Commission Secretariat as well: of its ten divisions, four were headed in 1959 by Americans. Most of the technicians were Chinese mainlanders, the Taiwanese staff usually serving as field investigators and unskilled workers.[7] Often the Chinese technicians were better educated than their American colleagues, whose somewhat unexpected virtue was a greater familiarity with practical aspects of farming. Neither Chinese nor Americans appeared to hesitate

[7] This situation is gradually changing. As of July 1, 1960, JCRR personnel totaled 305. Seventy-five were office boys, drivers, mechanics, and unskilled workers; 35 of these were Taiwanese. Of the remaining 230, 41 were Taiwanese, including 33 technicians and 8 clerks and secretaries. There were 12 Americans on the payrolls, including 10 technicians, a commissioner, and a secretary. Earlier, Arthur F. Raper had reported that only 3 out of the 72 non-U.S. technicians, other than the 15 field investigators, were Taiwanese. *Rural Taiwan: Problem and Promise* (Taipei, 1953), pp. 69, 72.

about working under the direction of members of the other national group.

The JCRR had a strong but flexible structure which was frequently modified to meet prevailing needs and circumstances. Operating divisions were added, removed, or regrouped to accommodate the dramatic changes in a rural society undergoing rapid industrialization. When the Land Reform Division had completed its major task, for example, it was abolished and the final regrouping of fragmented holdings was transferred to the Farmers' Organization Division. This enabled the JCRR to transfer attention and personnel to new activities, and to assign added functions to the 340 multi-purpose cooperatives throughout Taiwan. The flexibility with which the Commission was able to respond to local needs greatly enhanced its reputation in the countryside, if not with ICA. A random survey of Taiwanese villages in the early 1950s showed that almost 90 per cent of the population knew of some specific JCRR project.[8]

Counterpart Relationships

The counterpart relationship[9] is the one most frequently encountered in ICA overseas operations. It involves the appointment of local partners to work with each American technician for purposes of intergovernmental project coordination and exchange of technical data. Under the system, aid projects are carried out by parallel organizations in the aid mission and the host government, each with its own technicians working separately but exchanging information, advice, and criticism. At higher levels, policy and program decisions are made independently by one party and ratified or amended by the other.

Apart from agricultural activities, most of the aid program on

[8] Same, p. 279. ICA's reluctance to apply the JCRR principle to other parts of Asia was shown when a Philippines minister of agriculture reported that his desire to establish a joint agricultural mission in his own country was discouraged by ICA. In Taiwan ICA had attempted for a time to absorb JCRR programing into its own procedures, but its attitude appeared to change in 1959 after Karl Brandt's visit to Taiwan on behalf of the Council of Economic Advisers.

[9] The official appointed by the host government to work with an American technician is called a counterpart. "Counterpart" technicians, like "counterpart" funds, are considered as part of the host government's contribution to aid projects.

Taiwan was organized on the counterpart basis. Projects were drafted, screened, and supervised by the Chinese Council for U.S. Aid (CUSA), whose membership included the premier, his deputies, four ministers (of finance, communications, economic affairs, and foreign affairs), the chairman of the Bank of Taiwan, and four other members appointed by the premier. All ministries, including the JCRR, submitted proposed projects to it for study and assignment of priorities, and CUSA held monthly coordinating meetings with representatives of the U.S. mission. Its local currency funds were released periodically with the consent of appropriate American technicians, and it conducted audits of end uses and of expenditures supplementing those performed by the aid mission.

In Thailand, counterpart relationships placed greater responsibility upon the mission than in Taiwan, although the basic organization was similar. The Thai Technical and Economic Commission (TTEC), the equivalent of Taiwan's CUSA, was organized as a committee of the cabinet but was not given administrative powers and an independent staff. In 1959 its personnel was still largely on loan from other agencies; unlike CUSA, it had no responsibility for audits and no authority to assess national programing priorities. Its principal function was to review requests submitted by the ministries, nominally in consultation with the mission; but final decisions were often left to the Americans when TTEC was unable to choose among competing agencies. In 1959 a National Economic Council was created to advise the cabinet and TTEC, but the decision-making inclinations of the latter remained unchanged.

Members of the U.S. mission who acted as counterparts to officials in the Thai ministries had to play a dual role: first, as individuals they assisted their opposite members in the design of individual projects; then, as representatives of USOM concerned with the entire country program, they often had to make final choices where a TTEC priority schedule had not been established. The aid mission was therefore in the position of advising on a project through its individual counterparts, then sometimes having to alter or even reject it after the TTEC and the cabinet had added their approval. On a personal level relationships were generally close and cordial, but an official separation between counterparts created tension at both planning and decision-making stages.

Sometimes an American preparing a project as part of the normal ICA planning cycle could not discuss the work officially with his Thai counterpart because it was supposed to be confidential until approved by Washington. In one case a project was kept under wraps awaiting headquarters' approval until the recruiting of technicians had actually begun. When finally informed, the Thai government was glad to approve, but in an extraordinary burst of bureaucratic energy American technicians arrived before the project agreement had even been signed. In such cases, as might be expected, the counterparts were something less than colleagues.

The counterpart arrangement also prevailed in Viet-Nam, where project proposals were at first designed largely by American technicians with Vietnamese officials offering general advice. As more Vietnamese technicians became available, greater technical collaboration was possible, and priorities began to be jointly assigned by Viet-Nam's Director General of Foreign Aid and the program office of the mission. By 1959 these counterpart agencies were holding joint hearings to review and justify each project, although these reviews still served the purpose of exchanging information rather than reaching joint decisions. Working relations among counterpart technicians in Viet-Nam were substantially closer than those found at the highest echelons of decision-making responsibility, where political factors were more strongly at work. Viet-Nam presented a particularly difficult situation because of the concentration of authority in the Presidency. In several cases already discussed, notably those involving the Civil Guard and the Land Development projects, the technicians on both sides were in substantial agreement but domestic politics forced the Vietnamese government into an open split with the U.S. mission.

Counterpart arrangements also became complicated when the administrative structure of the host government did not parallel the functional patterns prescribed for ICA missions—a case of inflexibility compounding bad organization. In Viet-Nam, for example, there were six agencies concerned with agricultural activities: the Ministry of Agriculture, the Agrarian Ministry, the Ministry of Public Works, the Ministry of National Economy, the General Directorate of Land Development, and the General Directorate of Cooperatives and Agricultural Credit. The difficulty of working out a coordinated program among these agencies and establishing priorities on a counterpart basis (i.e., by working separately with each agency) was at times insurmountable.

It may be said that the counterpart approach tends to strengthen relations between individual technicians and officials, but it often places great strains on the diplomacy of foreign aid: counterparts seem to thrive at every level but the highest.

The Liaison Approach

The liaison approach implies a separation between the two parties in both technical and policy-making functions. The host government plans and executes foreign aid projects carried out on its soil, permitting the donor only to approve the general design of projects to be carried out with its aid. In Burma after 1956, for example, the Burmese worked out proposals and submitted them to the American Embassy, which evaluated them by bringing technicians in on temporary duty for the purpose. Any American proposals would be prepared unilaterally or, at most, with unofficial advice from Burmese authorities and submitted to the planning agencies of the host government. All programs became subject to *ad hoc* negotiation; no joint establishment of priorities took place; and the sovereignty of Burma was thus preserved—at some indeterminate cost in program efficiency. This administrative pattern was frustrating to technicians interested in enriching project implementation by a genuine exchange of information and advice; it also discouraged any American contributions to the development of a national planning apparatus that might have emerged out of joint work on the projects. But its political necessity in a country determined to be neutral apparently justified the relative inefficiency of the arms-length negotiations.

The ICA Pattern

The three organizational relationships just described were not, of course, purely administrative phenomena. Their basic characteristics probably cannot be changed by law or decree, since they reflect varying degrees of mutual confidence and depend on changing political and cultural factors. The suspicions and tensions that produced the remote, liaison pattern in Burma were further stimulated by misunderstandings and by the inadequacy of exchanges in the design and implementation of the aid program. Conversely, mutuality in the planning process in Taiwan contributed to still deeper confidence and understanding between the two parties. A maximum effort on the part of the donor to encourage mutuality in administrative relationships also minimized the dangers of stimulating anti-Americanism as a result of ill-advised or badly administered aid projects.

These and other variations in field organization should properly be considered administrative responses to political relationships. Yet beneath all variations there lay important administrative constants amounting to a virtual ICA "master pattern," found almost everywhere U.S. aid was offered. In spite of American efforts to encourage local initiative and outlook in the host government, these standardized forms of organization tended to augment the centralizing tendencies at work in the newly developing world.

Technical assistance operations in most ICA missions were grouped into a standard field organization which reproduced in miniature the technical service divisions of the Washington headquarters. There were persuasive reasons for this standardization, since headquarters offered a reserve of expert knowledge to technicians who were rendering advice in specialized phases of agriculture, public health, and many other fields in which no expert is omniscient; moreover, standardization made possible the exchange of technicians among neighboring country missions. And finally, since most missions of any size had technicians representing most of the functional offices in Washington, this approach provided a "balanced" or "representative" organization in the field, minimizing the chances of overspecialization or neglect.

The major disadvantage of such standardization is one that characterizes any administrative centralization: a rigidity that inhibits adjustment to local circumstances. A mission might organize a special office to deal with emergencies or unusual local situations only to find its technicians hampered by their separation from normal administrative channels. When emergencies caused technicians to work on unconventional assignments, their activities were still subjected to conventional criticism from the technical services of ICA in Washington. Nor could this problem be resolved satisfactorily by entrusting new or extraordinary functions to regular divisions, since the over-all performance of each division was judged by normal technical standards which did not allow for extraordinary functions. Yet deviations from the ICA "model" were at times inevitable, and irregular procedures were followed in spite of all inconveniences and penalties. The refugee operations in Viet-Nam, for example, were deprived of technical advice from Washington until absorbed into the Agriculture Division of the aid mission; on the other hand, some sectors of a country aid program, such as nonproject aid or various financial and planning functions, had no corresponding service at all in Washington. Given such gaps in the parallel structure which generally linked Washington to the country mission, it was difficult to arrive at timely policy decisions, rationalize personnel recruitment, or maximize technical support.

Organizational standardization was not the only centralizing factor in American foreign aid. The ICA personnel system also attenuated local control over operations because careers were usually made in Washington, not in the field. A technician's advancement depended more upon assignments made in the technical services in Washington than on any mission director's judgment of his performance in response to local needs. In the interest of a stable career pattern, the ICA personnel system attached pay grades to individuals rather than allowing a specific job classification in the field to determine the rank of its occupant. This meant that professional standards would have to govern appointments and promotions. Panels engaged in converting ICA personnel to the permanent foreign service also made selections on a somewhat abstract basis of professional accomplishment. Performance under the crisis conditions frequently encountered in the field was seldom given maximum emphasis in these selections or in ICA's annual technical ratings.

To the extent that technicians looked to Washington for project guidance and approval,[10] the authority of the mission director and the program office was further weakened. Most delays in

10 In Taiwan a project for Importation of Breeding Livestock, Eggs, and Semen (58–J–200) was approved by JCRR on June 13, 1957. It took ICA six months to accept the project (PPA 84–11–453, December 17, 1957). After another six months, on July 1, 1958, JCRR urgently requested that the purchase orders be issued. About four months later, on October 27, 1958, ICA replied that the project was being reviewed by the Animal Research Institute. A follow-up cable from JCRR on July 20, 1959, brought forth no evidence of progress. Here the delay was caused as much by a decision in Washington to review technical judgments made in the field as by programing requirements.

project approval actually resulted from inadequate understanding of local circumstances rather than disagreements over techniques, but the time lost in responding to numerous requests from headquarters for additional information or documentation handicapped effective operations, even if the original project was finally accepted in Washington.

The stamp of ICA could be seen clearly in the organization of the country programs. Where there were no urgent political and military purposes, American aid suffered from a kind of organizational myopia with respect to varying "country" needs. Functions not included in the ICA model, no matter how important to the needs of particular countries, suffered chronically from a shortage of staff. Specialists in economic and social planning or in statistics were difficult for ICA to recruit, for example, because in the Washington office there were no services responsible for these functions. Planning was improved by the adoption of broader concepts in aid programing, but this was no substitute for country-based, joint economic and social planning. In most missions the program offices were continuously preoccupied with the details of projects which, when fully planned, had then to be forced into some relationship with a country's basic needs and priorities.

In technical assistance operations and grant or loan programs, ICA's organizing principle was a "project approach" similar to that of the international banking agencies. Total aid allocations to a country were subdivided by both "functions" and projects, which permitted at once an assessment of priorities in terms of a "balance" or "mix" of functions for each country, and an appraisal of the relative importance of suggested projects. Both of these appraisals took place during the programing process.

Planning a country program within the confines of the ICA "master pattern" was usually left to the resident mission; but even here, competition among technicians of varying capacity and persuasiveness, each committed to some favorite project and each looking beyond the mission for advancement, tended to make many country programs diffuse and sporadic. Technical or political decisions made in Washington also reduced the mission director's freedom to select projects in accordance with his understanding of the country's needs and subjected individual technicians to severe moral and professional pressures. A mission's capacity to develop country programs was also limited by the general shortage of men trained in economic and social planning. The technically oriented project approach afforded a good basis for developing the individual segments of a program, but not for integrating them.

The annual programing cycle was the principal vehicle by which the missions reviewed and coordinated their projects. Although slight variations in procedure occurred in the various missions, programing in ICA was essentially world-wide in character and timing. The phenomenon of dual congressional review and appropriations strongly conditioned its timing, and real ingenuity was required to fit together different fiscal years throughout the world. Southeast Asia's tropical climate, whose torrential rains occur during Washington's preferred season for setting projects in motion, added to the difficulty of matching the rhythms of American and Asian administration.

Programing can be considered as a continuous process from the first proposal of an idea to the design and acceptance of a project, and from the project agreement, the implementation orders, and the contracts to the arrival of technicians and equipment. This process seldom took less than a year, unless the desired technicians and the equipment were already located and available. Often a much longer period was required if negotiations revealed disagreements between the mission and the host government or the Washington technical service. The annual fiscal cycle obviously placed heavy pressure on the program office during peak seasons, but in a large mission it also necessitated continuous planning and negotiation. Planning on a longer-range basis was not, of course, actually prevented, although experience in underdeveloped countries suggested that planning specific projects more than three or four years ahead was somewhat unrealistic, given the political context in which ICA functioned. Recent programing procedures incorporated general plans for two years in advance of the operational year, which was probably the maximum realistically attainable. The greatest danger of projections into an unpredictable future lay in binding a fairly inflexible organization to detailed plans, some of which were bound to be visionary. Long-term planning was needed more for total programs than for individual project designs.

Identical preparations for programing were required for all ICA projects in order to standardize procedures in every part of the world. Even the JCRR, which legally enjoyed greater autonomy over its funds than the ordinary agricultural division in an American aid mission, was required to participate in the annual programing "exercise." At first all JCRR operations were financed by lump-sum releases on a quarterly basis, justified by brief descriptions of proposed activities. If unexpended funds were available, emergency projects could be initiated immediately. In 1955 a banana weevil pestilence of serious proportions was wiped out because JCRR was able to allocate 1.2 million New Taiwan dollars to it within a few days, so that provincial authorities could immediately begin work through farmers' associations and cooperatives. The crop (involving a yearly export of over U.S.$5 million to Japan alone) was saved. Later in the same year, however, ICA required the JCRR functions to be programed as four general projects, each with a separate account. A considerable amount of flexibility remained, but in 1956 a further subdivision of its functions into 19 projects was ordered, among which funds could be transferred only with ICA approval. Since the required subdivisions did not parallel JCRR operations, this change meant an almost unworkable degree of rigidity. The Forestry Division, for example, was financed by PPA 84–17–339 (forestry general), 84–17–376 (forestry surveys), and 87–17–334 (soil conservation), each of which contributed limited amounts of untransferable funds. If the weevil pestilence had occurred in 1956, JCRR could probably not have acted in time to save the crop, unless the necessary unexpended funds had by chance been left unused in the pest-control account.

A JCRR critique described the new program, which required formidable documentation, as "so involved, inappropriately scheduled and inflexible that timely and effective extension of technical and especially financial assistance . . . are greatly hampered and even substantially precluded. Programs dealing with life processes . . . must be geared to natural cycles and not to arbitrarily fixed periods. . . . Two weeks' delay in the availability of funds may well mean the loss of the entire crop season. . . . Agricultural programs are conditioned by natural phenomena. Unexpected floods, droughts, fires, etc., can require immediate and drastic changes in program implementation. . . . With the requirements that 80 per cent of approved funds must be obligated by April 30, and not over 25 per cent may be made available until ICA [Washington] approval, this leaves hardly more than four months to implement most of a full year's program. Unless great waste is to be countenanced, such a practice is impossible. . . ."[11] On the basis of such findings, in 1959 and 1960 the JCRR operations were again concentrated in five projects; but the simplicity of the first JCRR operations was gone, and, in Taiwan at least, deeply lamented.

The programing cycle and administrative difficulties in Washington have seriously delayed some projects. Construction of the Yanhee Dam in Thailand, a World Bank-DLF project, was originally carried through with power from ICA's thermal project at Mae Moh, but for an entire year the project was forced to depend on other power sources because of technical and procedural objections raised by ICA headquarters. Engineers appointed as virtual arbitrators by the General Services Administration finally decided for the ICA mission in Thailand and against Washington, but not until a year's time was lost. American attempts to design "impact" projects for maximum effect, a characteristic practice in all Soviet aid, have been seriously hampered by such procedural difficulties, sometimes compounded by careless optimism in predicting the completion dates of important projects. An emergency water project was created for Bangkok in 1958 to reduce the threat of cholera caused by polluted water (an epidemic had started in the spring of 1958 and was expected to be more serious in 1959). In spite of close cooperation from Washington, unexpected delays in obtaining equipment placed the well-digging operations four months behind schedule. The impact of the project suffered the more because of the hopes expressed when the project was begun.

Even in Taiwan, where many large-scale projects had been undertaken under emergency conditions, ICA contract procedures were still so complex and time-consuming that the Nationalist government preferred on occasion to enter directly into contracts with American engineers, even when this meant using its own scarce foreign exchange. After ICA clearance procedures caused delays totaling two years in contract negotiations for the Shihmen Dam, the government decided to negotiate itself for the engineering of the Tachien Hydro Project and the Kukuan Project, saving at least ten months in each case. In Thailand, on the other hand, in one case government funds for payment of malaria eradication

[11] JCRR–55–8001, December 10, 1955.

teams were tied up in bureaucratic procedures, and the Ministry of Public Health preferred to mingle its funds with those of the U.S. aid mission, which had developed a more efficient apparatus for such payments. This was, of course, a local operation requiring no Washington concurrence. But in Laos, alleged delays in paying the 3,200-man police with ICA funds led to "disaffection toward America . . . because they are paid by American aid. . . . In the face of exorbitant demands of control organizations of the United States cooperation mission and its inquisitorial and vexatious investigation methods" the police were reported as refusing "to discuss matters informally with United States officials," preferring "that all contracts be official and in writing."[12]

Such elaborate administrative precautions reflected the concerns of an agency that was highly vulnerable to criticism. ICA's operations in the underdeveloped world were often undertaken in crisis conditions and for reasons of great political urgency, which prevented the deliberation and precision that might seem desirable in retrospect. The system of restraints on local discretion and planning authority—the "ICA pattern"—was designed to avoid errors of judgment. Exceptions were permitted only in clearly defined crises in which normal procedures would be justifiably suspended. With the passing of the crisis conditions in much of Southeast Asia in the late 1950s, ICA programing still remained subject to restraints that, in view of the elaborate post-audit requirements imposed upon the program, seemed anything but necessary. The rationale for the persistence of these restraints was clear enough: they offered protection against the appearance of hasty, ill-considered judgments. But an overriding concern with protection can scarcely be the key to clear and effective action.

3. The "American Presence"

The presence of large numbers of American technicians and administrators in underdeveloped countries was one important consequence of the ICA system. (See Table 1.) Calculating local responses to the size, perquisites, and behavior of the American

---

[12] *Voix du Peuple*, quoted in *The New York Times*, October 20, 1959. It should be noted that in this instance U.S. officials stated that adequate funds were given for the pay period in question, leaving the suspicion that the delays occurred in Laotian administrative channels.

Table 1

Size of American Aid Missions [a]

	1950	1951	1952	1953	1954	1955	1956	1957	1958	1959
TOTAL	2799	2785	2782	2530	2740	3216	3444	3620	3888	4215
Admin.	2498	2148	1930	695	706	739	744	740	830	915
Tech.	301	637	852	1835	2034	2477	2700	2880	3058	3300
Burma	16	61	66 [b]	44	3	... [c]	...	8	12	17
Admin.	16	25	19	8	1	...	...	8	11	14
Tech.	...	36	47	36	2	...	...	...	1	3
Thailand	15	80	87	72	91	112	119	134	145	160
Admin.	15	31	30	17	17	22	24	25	28	29
Tech.	...	49	57	55	74	90	95	109	117	131
Viet-Nam	21	60	81	78	125	153	182	174	187	199
Admin.	21	36	32	23	32	34	41	38	35	35
Tech.	...	24	49	55	93	119	141	136	152	164
Taiwan	20	53	75	66	84	91	91	86	79	83
Admin.	17	31	31	21	25	27	23	24	24	25
Tech.	3	22	44	45	59	64	68	62	55	58

[a] Total ICA personnel overseas. Figures are as of December 31 of each year. On December 31, 1959, there were 2,012 ICA employees in Washington, including unassigned complement.

[b] Data as of January 31, 1953.

[c] In 1953 Burma requested the United States to withdraw its aid mission as projects then in operation were completed. The resumption of U.S. aid in 1957 was primarily in the form of economic rather than technical assistance.

Source: International Cooperation Administration.

community introduced a difficult and uncontrollable element into the politics of foreign aid. The staffing of aid missions became inevitably conditioned by imagined popular reactions to the American "presence," as well as by purely technical and administrative requirements. In some instances, the sheer size of the official American community could not help but induce some kind of local reaction. In Viet-Nam it was 2,400 strong in 1959, including official personnel, contractors, and dependents; and of these, about 1,950 were concentrated in Saigon.[13]

Asians' resentment at the presence of large, self-contained groups of Americans in their midst may result from factors unrelated to the behavior of the technicians themselves. Self-consciousness over being in an "inferior" position as receivers of advice and funds, an overreaction against the colonial traditions of Western nations, or even the disturbing economic and social effects of a newly arrived, sizable American community would account for much of it, quite apart from Communist and traditionalist anti-Western propaganda. There were often natural resentments against Americans as a source of increased rentals and higher servants' wages and consumer prices, or as a group enjoying or even flaunting special privileges. Whatever the cause—and certain American national traits undoubtedly contributed to it—such attitudes undoubtedly influenced both American policy and those of the host governments.

One approach to the problem was a simple attempt to reduce the numbers of technicians and other officials assigned to sensitive areas. After Vice-President Nixon had visited the Far East and Africa in 1957, he was reported as "convinced that there were too many Americans overseas, that they were too conspicuous and that they consequently often created resentment toward the United States."[14] Ceilings on ICA personnel overseas had already been in effect, but renewed pressure for staff reduction threatened to make serious inroads in many of the programs already under way. ICA had been processing requests for some 1,400 technicians to be sent to thirteen nations in the Middle East and South Asia in the period January 1958 to June 1959. Because of the difficulty

[13] *Situation in Vietnam*, Hearings before a subcommittee of the Senate Committee on Foreign Relations, 86th Cong., 1st sess., July 30 and 31, 1959 (Washington: GPO, 1959), pp. 48, 188.
[14] *The New York Times*, December 29, 1957.

of recruiting certain of these (especially sanitary engineers and physicians), ICA had already proposed sending only 1,200. After the Vice-President's visit the authorized figures were reduced to 800, less than two-thirds of the number requested and approved in the field. But this reduction only tended to create new problems without solving the old ones. Imposing arbitrary staff ceilings could not significantly reduce any resentments arising from the employment of large numbers of Americans abroad. On the contrary, such a drastic reduction may even have aggravated such resentments by withholding the very personnel who were actually in demand. Although no ceilings were imposed on local personnel employed by overseas missions—in Viet-Nam this figure rose from 363 in November 1955 to 770 in August 1958—this was no substitute for the skilled experts needed.

Three main countermoves were devised by the missions overseas in order to evade these numerical limitations upon their technical staffs. The first of these was to increase the number of qualified native technicians by sending trainees to the United States and elsewhere. Although a wise solution in the long run, this tactic unfortunately deprived the host country of the services of some already scarce technicians during a critical period of development. A second device was to hire technicians from third countries in place of Americans. In fields where third-country techniques were relatively close to those of the host country, this measure proved useful and it may have served to improve relations between the two countries involved (although it seems contradictory to argue that a Japanese technician working in Viet-Nam or Thailand tends to improve the standing of his country while an American serving in the same post produces the opposite effect). There were many difficulties in the use of third-country technicians, however, ranging from problems of adequate recruitment and screening to the lower prestige attached to Asian technicians in other Asian countries as compared with Westerners. The difficulty of supervising and coordinating the work of technicians from third countries also discouraged a more extensive use of this approach.

The third and most convenient device for keeping the official American community within an arbitrary ceiling was to enlarge the *unofficial* American community by letting contracts to universities and private firms. The use of contract groups often imposed further burdens upon ICA's administrative resources, since contract personnel were more difficult to control than directly hired employees. ICA's management of such contracts was notoriously inefficient.[15] Moreover, logistical support, authorized salaries, and other considerations varied so markedly from one contract to another (even within the same mission) that serious morale problems sometimes resulted. The Michigan State University group in Saigon, for example, received virtually all of the privileges afforded ICA personnel (including dispensary, theater, and commissary), while the University of Michigan group there did not even receive housing. The latter was working under a regional contract, but that was scant consolation to the technicians involved. Moving, housing, storage, overseas or hardship allowances, and salary scales were all negotiated by the contractor with ICA in Washington, and the accident of being attached to a university or firm that drove a "hard bargain" had much to do with the morale and effectiveness of contract technicians in the field. By the end of 1959, ICA was moving toward standardized contracts for university groups, but even then many conditions were still subject to negotiation.[16] Certain of the more important privileges, such as the use of dispensaries, commissaries, and military theaters, were still unevenly bestowed because, being under the jurisdiction of the Department of Defense, they could not be conferred by ICA.

It is estimated that by 1959 a third to a half of American technical assistance was carried on by contract.[17] The largest U.S. aid

[15] Even in Thailand, where the contracting system has been very successfully employed, contractors themselves were not satisfied; entirely apart from problems of substance, contract negotiations were subject to severe frustrations because of delays and uncertainties. The Public Administration Service contract in Thailand, which expired June 30, 1959, was not renewed until the afternoon of June 29, in spite of the mission's satisfaction with the contractor; and then only after protracted negotiations and a strong cable from the U.S. ambassador. A city-planning contract renewal in Bangkok with private American firms was delayed until four days before the group was scheduled to leave the country.

[16] In 1961 ICA had 103 contracts with 75 universities operating in 34 countries. Studies in the use of universities as purveyors of technical assistance have been made by the Institute of Research on Overseas Programs, Michigan State University, *The International Programs of American Universities* (East Lansing: Author, 1958), and Walter Adams and John Garraty, *Is the World Our Campus?* (East Lansing: Michigan State University Press, 1960).

[17] Henry Reining, Jr., "The Government Contract as an Administrative Device," *The Annals of the American Academy of Political and Social Science,* May 1959, p. 69.

missions, taken together, employed as many contract technicians as direct employees, or even more.[18] In Viet-Nam, with an ICA staff ceiling of 178 technicians and 36 administrative personnel, there were nearly 400 contract employees performing under the general supervision of the mission in 1959. The use of university contractors was especially highly developed in Thailand where nine different university and other nonprofit contracts were in effect. A further reduction of permanent technical staff was under consideration in Thailand, not to evade personnel ceilings but because the use of short-term, specialized technicians for specific projects was proving more effective, in spite of depressing administrative difficulties, than the traditional staffing approaches.

Importing university personnel had no effect on the problem of a large American "presence," of course, if the academic personnel merely augmented and were indistinguishable from the official staff. Yet university people are relatively free from official restraints, they are more acceptable to certain elements of the native intelligentsia, and they lend themselves to greater flexibility in the use of experts and institutional resources. The trend toward greater university participation may lighten and diversify the impact of an "American presence" in underdeveloped countries, although universities need to choose their personnel and plan their projects as carefully as any other organization.[19] The real question is not how many Americans there are, but how a group of any number— from ten to a thousand—is regarded by the local government and people.

[18] As of May 31, 1958, the largest missions in terms of personnel were as follows:

Country	Number of ICA employees on duty	Number of contract employees
Korea	305	168
Iran	229	93
Viet-Nam	183	372
Pakistan	177	204

[19] Adams and Garraty, cited, point out that past experience does not encourage overconfidence about university performance. Their appraisal is welcome as a balance to excessive enthusiasm over university contracts, but neither the observations made by the present author in the Far East nor the judgments of ICA and the contracting foundations support their pessimistic conclusions.

The Issue of Decentralization

One way of spreading the benefits of technical assistance while minimizing the liabilities of a self-contained, aloof foreign community was to assign many technicians to rural areas. Besides emphasizing the "people-to-people" approach, decentralization of the ICA missions was bound to cut down the size of the conspicuous "American colonies" in the capitals and to reinforce our efforts to minimize the centralizing effects of American aid. Since aid funds and activities were necessarily channeled through the host government, they normally tended to increase or consolidate the centralization that was already taking place in the underdeveloped countries of Asia. To offset this effect, to strengthen local initiative, to demonstrate American interest in the people in addition to support of the regime in power, and to increase the efficiency of aid projects, many ICA missions conscientiously attempted to decentralize their own activities while urging the host government to do the same. Decentralization was most consistently pursued in such fields as agricultural extension, community development, provincial health programs, and rural education.

Yet efforts to post ICA technicians in the rural areas often encountered resistance from the host government. Unpopular as Americans may have been in the large cities because of PX privileges, lavish spending, and other envy-provoking behavior, the host government usually wanted them there. In Viet-Nam this may have been, as some have argued, a result of bureaucratic fears of what inquisitive Americans operating in the field might uncover and report. It is more likely that other causes were responsible: the centralized nature of the regime itself, the desire of civil servants to remain in the cities and keep their American advisers handy, and the hesitance to risk American activities in the countryside that might discredit the regime or outpace its own services to the rural population.

The work of the Field Service Division of the U.S. mission in Viet-Nam was an important attempt to decentralize American aid. First organized in December 1954, during the height of the refugee flood, its principal function was "to provide the mission with direct and continuing liaison and representation with" regional and provincial governments of Viet-Nam, especially those engaged in refugee resettlement projects.[20] Most of these projects were adjacent to Saigon, but Field Service representatives were also to be stationed in eight regions, including central Viet-Nam and the mountain plateaus of the north. In these remoter regions the representatives were also charged with general liaison and reporting on local aid projects. Field reports on needs and conditions in the provinces, as well as on the progress of various projects, were forwarded to Field Service headquarters in Saigon and distributed to the appropriate technical divisions of the mission. After the refugee program was completed in January 1958, field offices continued to operate in six towns, with three substations and a mobile office (a converted landing craft that moved through canals and rivers in order to report on land development projects south and west of Saigon). Field Service agents were permitted to suggest new projects, to promote local self-help, and to offer small amounts of aid. They also furnished supplies and administrative support for USOM technicians in the field and served as informal liaison between the technical divisions and local government officials.

During the first three years of Field Service operations its agents helped coordinate American and Vietnamese efforts in 162 resettlement projects, involving 600,000 refugees and 316 villages. Some 2,800 field reports were sent to the mission in Saigon during this period, almost exactly half of which dealt with suggested aid projects, progress on actual projects, or general local information; 1,170 concerned refugees and resettlement; and 253, political trends and security problems. Because the commercial telegraph service was slow and uncertain, the field offices maintained radio communications with Saigon; in fact, communications between USOM and the field offices were much faster than those between the national government and provincial officials.

The Field Service Division also supported Civic Action, a political program designed originally to offset Communist influence in rural areas. Initiated by the Vietnamese government in 1954, the program grew until 1,800 Civic Action "cadres" were visiting or living in villages where they conducted adult education classes, set up and supplied first-aid centers, reorganized village councils,

[20] USOM, Vietnam, *Report of Field Service Division*, v. 1, December 31, 1957, p. 9.

established information centers, and assisted in developing village self-improvement projects. In 1956 USOM agreed to support these activities with $500,000 for equipment and supplies, and Field Service provided liaison and assistance to Civic Action, especially in the self-help projects.

As the refugees were absorbed in the provinces and rural security conditions improved, resettlement and Civic Action became less important, and the Field Service Division was left with few responsibilities except reporting on local projects and assisting technicians visiting from Saigon. In 1958 the Field Service Division offered its facilities for a community development program being considered by the Vietnamese government. The original program had assumed that USOM aid would be channeled entirely through the province chiefs, but the Director General of Budget and Foreign Aid suggested that the aid be administered through Civic Action. The Civic Action Commissariat agreed, suggesting that pilot projects be started in the southern provinces close to its headquarters in Saigon. The Commissioner General of Civic Action could then keep the first experiments under his personal supervision and even "guarantee" that the aid funds and equipment were used as intended.[21]

After discussions with the Director General of Planning and the Commissioner General, Field Service presented its proposal. The plan was for direct financial assistance to twenty-four provinces over a period of four years. The aid funds were to be used for "quick and immediate relief where needed" in order to gain "a creditable impact as well as bring a clearer interpretation of foreign aid to the people of the provinces."[22] Local participation was to take the form of providing land, labor, and building materials. Field Service representatives would work directly with the province chiefs in preparing project descriptions, which would be submitted to the aid mission and the Minister of Interior for coordination and approval, after which funds were to be released directly to the province chiefs. As finally prepared in May 1958, the Field Service's proposal was budgeted at only $410,714 for the first year. The stated basic objective was "to assist peoples in provincial areas

[21] Report to Chief of Field Service Division, "Proposed Project, Development Services for Provincial Administration," April 30, 1958, ms.

[22] Same, p. 28.

in improving their means of making a livelihood . . . [and in] their general living standards. . . . Another objective . . . is to furnish immediate assistance when and where needed and to give a clear and tangible evidence of national government and U.S. assistance and interest to indigenous populations in the provinces."[23] When this proposal was finally presented to the Vietnamese government, it was rejected on the ground that province chiefs were too busy to undertake the new responsibilities involved.

Rejection of the community development proposals restricted the Field Service Division to the role of a reporting agency, but even this function became difficult to perform. Technical divisions in the mission made infrequent use of Field Service reports, preferring for the sake of rapport to rely on Vietnamese government channels supplemented by occasional inspections by their own technicians. Field Service criticisms of project designs were beginning to arouse resentment among the technical divisions, just as criticisms of provincial implementation were resented by the Vietnamese government. In the summer of 1958 the Presidency ordered provincial authorities to give no information to American technicians except upon special authorization. This injunction applied not only to Field Service representatives but also to technicians from Saigon, who, indeed, were not authorized to make official visits at all except by arrangement with the central government.

In September 1958 the Field Service Division was dissolved. Its whole experience had shown that permanent local offices of American aid could not check a trend toward strongly centralized government unless the host government itself so desired. It proved difficult for the United States to demonstrate interest in the welfare of people living under an authoritarian regime without appearing to challenge the established order.

One of the greatest potentials in ICA's approach to foreign aid in Southeast Asia was the "country" orientation in relating the amounts, policies, and procedures of American operations to the special needs and circumstances of the receiving country. Yet the technical lines of authority between Washington and the field did not always permit the missions to develop the integrated, coherent program required in each country. Careful review of technical

[23] USOM, Field Service Division, *Project Proposal for Development Services to Provincial Administration* (Saigon, 1958), p. 3.

programs in Washington took place only at the price of losses in speed, flexibility, and sensitivity to country needs. Bureaucratic old age was beginning to harden flexibility into arthritic stiffness as aid missions began to look and act more and more alike in different countries, although the needs they served differed substantially. Some critics of foreign aid administration even began to consider the possibility of assigning all or most aid operations to international agencies where different traditions, methods, and political considerations might permit greater flexibility.

4. THE PROSPECTS OF MULTILATERALISM

Most international economic agencies established their programs during the 1950s through consideration of individual project proposals, evaluated by survey teams. Negotiations with governments requesting aid occurred principally at the Washington or New York headquarters of the agencies, to which high-ranking representatives of underdeveloped countries had to commute with appalling frequency. The impersonality of the survey teams and the isolation of individual projects from a coordinated country program gave to the lending operations at first a somewhat pragmatic turn and encouraged a piecemeal, hit-and-run, project-by-project approach to economic development. But the international agencies provided sound technical services and avoided some of the subtle embarrassments created by "gifts" passed between sovereign governments.

Credit and Banking Operations

Loans of the International Bank for Reconstruction and Development (World Bank) were guaranteed by the host government, based on surveys by special missions drawn from the Bank's permanent staff and short-term consultants. In general, loans were granted on the conventional banker's criterion of credit-worthiness, defined as the ability to repay loans in the hard currencies in which the money was disbursed. These missions assisted not only in preparing proposals for member countries but in drawing up statements of long-range economic growth requirements as well. By 1960 fifteen national development programs had been completed, often becoming the basis for official planning activities.[24]

Joint sponsorship of a project by a number of agencies could occasionally be arranged on the basis of the Bank's survey and proposals. The Yanhee multi-purpose dam project in Thailand, for example, received $66 million from the World Bank for foreign exchange costs for the dam, the power house, the switch yard, and the transmission system, with $34 million in local currency to be covered by budget appropriations; $44 million from the Export-Import Bank for the interim power plant; and $20 million, repayable in local currency, from the Development Loan Fund for the Bangkok distribution system, to which $5 million in local currency was to be added from the borrower's own resources or government appropriations. ICA helped in the preparation and execution of the Yanhee scheme, paid consulting engineers, and contributed indirectly through its road construction programs.

Although the World Bank's support was often complemented by that of other agencies, sometimes its position was weakened when competition set in. In one case World Bank credit to a steel mill in the Philippines was suspended because local authorities declined to agree to its development under private sponsorship. The Bank's attempt to insist upon private ownership was undermined when the steel mill secured an Export-Import Bank loan for a publicly owned mill. Efforts by the World Bank to promote fiscal reforms by withholding loans were also weakened by the ready availability of credit from other sources. On the other hand, the prestige and international character of the Bank were at times brought to bear against policies suggested by other lending agencies. One famous example was the billion-dollar Indus River Basin development program prepared by the World Bank. Since about half the funds were to be supplied in Indian and Pakistani currencies and a major portion of the loans were to be soft, any hard currencies lent to the program would be at a premium. The Bank suggested that Development Loan Fund credits be added to a general hard-currency pool which could finance purchases anywhere in the world, rather than on the "tied"

---

[24] A recent program is described in International Bank for Reconstruction and Development, A *Public Development Program for Thailand* (Baltimore: Johns Hopkins Press, 1959). This study, like all the survey reports, represents the work of a special mission and is not an official publication of the Bank itself.

or "Buy American" basis used by the Development Loan Fund. Under this pressure from the Bank, which had secured agreement from the other hard-currency investors, the United States agreed, against clearly stated congressional preferences. On the whole, the Bank's conservatism, its use of general development surveys, and its character as a member-serving institution combined to remove most of its operations from the sphere of international or domestic politics.

Like the World Bank, the DLF and the Export-Import Bank lacked a permanent field organization. The borrower was made responsible for preparing development projects and providing its own engineering surveys, while the lending agencies passed on requests after receiving reports from special missions made up of representatives from their own staffs. All banking operations tended to rely upon such survey teams or the services of the ICA field missions.

The loans made by U.S. government agencies were open to "political risks" as well as those inherent in overseas operations. Unlike the World Bank, the Export-Import Bank could be asked to extend credit in support of American foreign policy objectives even though the loans could not meet strict banking standards. Such political loans were sometimes combined with "soft loans" from the DLF, which could accept local currencies in repayment. Loans to Turkey are often cited as an example.[25]

The differing approaches and resources of these various lending agencies offered a wide variety of credit to Southeast Asia and other parts of the underdeveloped world. But the very multiplicity of agencies weakened the capacity of any of them to get its own fiscal or administrative requirements accepted. Reliance upon a small, mobile survey staff to screen proposed loan projects also tended to reduce the prospects for making local adjustments in such requirements or for bringing about compliance in day-to-day operations. The technical assistance made available by the World Bank offered an important means for developing national economic programs, however, both because of the high caliber of its staff and because of the general belief that the Bank was politically disinterested. The larger technical resources of the ICA, on the

[25] See Wilson L. Townsend, *Organization and Operations of the Export-Import Bank of Washington* (Washington: GPO, 1959), pp. 8, 9.

other hand, offered the best opportunity for continuous economic development where experts were needed for a long period; and the loans and grants ICA could offer, freed from banking criteria, continued to be indispensable. In underdeveloped countries not yet considered credit-worthy, and especially those in which technical advice was continuously necessary, neither the multilateral nor the bilateral banking agencies could perform services requiring the permanent facilities available to the multi-purpose ICA projects, hampered though the latter were by political considerations.

Import Programs: The Need for Bilateral Operations

The second principal form of foreign aid—dollar support to nonproject commercial imports—involved domestic politics in both giving and receiving countries. It was invariably carried out bilaterally for the simple reason that international organizations did not have the authority or the resources for it. The system, already described in the Viet-Nam context, ingeniously combined private forces and public resources in ways that served both the domestic economy and the aid program. Private importers were authorized to buy dollars at the official rate of exchange, and the local currency they paid out could be used to finance local costs of the aid program.

American dollars were thus used in three ways: to purchase essential imports brought into a country receiving aid; to give to some local currency a purchasing value that it would not otherwise have had in view of its depressed value in world money markets; and to generate local currency for use in U.S. aid projects. Because these dollars often appeared in the American economy through payments to U.S. producers, American businessmen benefited directly from the programs (although because of world-wide competitive factors they sometimes lost business to foreign producers); at the same time, because many American businessmen erroneously regarded the dollars as subject to direct American control, they were at times tempted to bring political pressure regarding their use.[26] In the host country, on the other hand, there was the danger of bribery or favoritism in the issuing of import licenses, including

[26] The Colegrove articles described in Chapter V and Appendix III devoted a considerable amount of attention to one such complaint, with important political consequences.

the possibility that powerful figures would assign the valuable licenses to relatives or friends.

Apart from a common interest in minimizing such political pressures, the United States and the host government also had to consider together the nature and amount of imports to be introduced, to establish control procedures, and to discuss exchange rates. These persistent problems suggested the desirability of maintaining a resident staff in the interest of close and continuing relations between the two governments, and might explain the fact that, except for occasional ill-fated entries into this field by the Development Loan Fund,[27] the Commercial Import Program remained an exclusive function of ICA.

International Technical Assistance

The third main foreign aid function, technical assistance, involves a larger staff and a wider variety of approaches than any other aspect of international cooperation. Like project loans and grants, technical assistance has been carried out under both bilateral and multilateral sponsorship.

The functions of government, community, and economic enterprise may all be influenced by technical assistance. Even the performance of basic functions of a sovereign state—providing for national defense and internal security, collecting taxes, or safeguarding and distributing the national wealth—can be technically improved, and often enough the force of circumstances impels the improvement at a pace beyond the resources of the available staff. Any agency which undertakes to contribute to such technical improvements enters into a very delicate relationship, which may involve both frustration over delays and failures and a paradoxical resentment over technical success that outruns the political pace of a new regime. The technicians engaged under such circumstances are performing a more intricate and demanding role than that played by most diplomats; and they are working in a field where little experience has been systematically assembled. They are handicapped by the absence of both public appreciation and, often enough, understanding on their own part of the nature and delicacy of their relationships. The great and growing variety of

---

[27] *Operations of the Development Loan Fund*, 14th Report by the House Committee on Government Operations, 1960, cited, p. 5.

multilateral and bilateral agencies offering specialized assistance is evidence of the immensity of the technical, economic, and diplomatic tasks of modernization, and hence of the desirability of encouraging pluralism in technical assistance.

International agencies offering technical aid have one decided advantage: they can mitigate the political liabilities of receiving foreign advice by sustaining the comfortable fiction that aid comes from an international community in which all states are by right equally entitled to assistance. International agencies may also encourage greater regional cooperation in economic matters free of cold war considerations, although this is becoming more and more difficult. The personnel resources of international agencies are widely recruited from a wide variety of cultural backgrounds and technical skills, although during the 1950s the absence of a career service and of a continuous tradition of rendering technical assistance presented obvious disadvantages. Many appointments made for the multilateral technical assistance programs were on a short-term, *ad hoc* basis, because concentration on specific projects characterized all of the multilateral programs.

The two principal international agencies offering technical assistance in Southeast Asia were the United Nations and the Colombo Plan. The former operated as an international unit, the latter through a series of bilateral agreements among member governments. Technicians for the United Nations were recruited on a world-wide basis after specific requests for their services had been approved.[28] This process involved lengthy delays reminiscent of ICA performance and occasionally led to embarrassment when a UN technician would discover on arrival that administrators who had first requested his services had since lost their positions. Of the more than 8,000 technicians who have served the United Nations in underdeveloped countries, most were on one-year or shorter contracts. Long-term UN contracts for particularly success-

[28] The UN Program of Technical Assistance was created in Resolution 222 (IX) of the Economic and Social Council of the UN, August 15, 1949. Its activities are carried out by technicians recruited and assigned by nine UN specialized agencies. Over 8,000 experts have been sent out on missions, in over one hundred "major fields of development." Voluntary contributions from 85 governments totaled $235 million for the Expanded Program of Special Assistance. The assessed amounts of the special agencies, UNICEF, Special Fund, and other UN funds are not included. David Owen, "After a Decade," *Technical Assistance Newsletter*, No. 56, October 1959, p. 1.

ful technicians were introduced as a substitute for a career service, but they were relatively few in number. In the field UN technicians were assigned to work directly with appropriate government agencies, all logistical and administrative support being provided by the host country.[29]

The United Nations made no over-all policy review of the activities of its technicians, nor did it attempt to harmonize the recommendations of different UN agencies in single country programs. Coordination of various UN activities in a country was a general responsibility of the UN resident representative, but he was given no jurisdiction over substantive programs. The absence of a coordinated approach tended to weaken the impact of an individual technician's recommendations, which appeared as the judgment of an individual rather than of an organization operating under a general country policy. In many cases, however, trust in the United Nations outweighed these considerations, especially in neutral countries when suspicion of the great powers was an important political factor. Henry Cabot Lodge was reported to believe that African leaders "look for help to the United Nations and other international agencies and do not want help that they suspect is offered for selfish motives."[30] Yet this favorable view of the UN was by no means universal. In Burma the Ne Win government was apparently no more friendly to UN technicians than to others. And in Pakistan even government officials often made no distinction between American aid and UN aid.[31]

The Colombo Plan Technical Co-operation Scheme for South and Southeast Asia, in contrast to the UN operations, operated by means of a series of bilateral agreements bound together somewhat loosely. The work of teams of technicians was reviewed at annual conferences held to compare and criticize results. The Colombo

[29] The problems of delay and dependence on the host government for support are discussed in Huntington Gilchrist, "Technical Assistance from the United Nations—As Seen in Pakistan," *International Organization*, Autumn 1959, p. 508; Harry L. Spence, Jr., "A Resident Representative's View of Technical Cooperation," *The Annals of the American Academy of Political and Social Science*, May 1959, pp. 13–14.

[30] Kathleen Teltsch, in *The New York Times*, January 12, 1960. A fuller statement of his view appeared in his address to the Tenth Annual Conference of National Organizations, American Association for the United Nations, Washington, March 7, 1960.

[31] *The New York Times*, February 11, 1960; Gilchrist, cited, p. 506.

Plan nations (originally Australia, Canada, Ceylon, India, New Zealand, Pakistan, and the United Kingdom, together with Singapore, Sarawak, and North Borneo) first met in January 1950 to "provide a framework within which an international co-operative effort could be promoted to assist the countries of [South and Southeast Asia] to raise their living standards."[32] Burma, Nepal, Cambodia, Laos, Viet-Nam, Indonesia, Thailand, Malaya, the Philippines, Japan, and the United States later became members. Only six of these (Canada, the United States, Japan, Australia, New Zealand, and the United Kingdom) had received no appreciable assistance by 1960, and only four (Cambodia, Laos, Viet-Nam, and Nepal) had given none.

Like UN technical assistance, the plan was activated only in response to requests for technical advice or services from one member to another. Technicians worked as employees of the host government, which provided their logistical and administrative support, but their pay was supplied by donor governments at their own civil service scales. Financial incentives in recruiting technicians for the Colombo Plan outside the civil service provided a more difficult problem than in the UN approach (UN salaries, though not very attractive to American technicians, were high by European standards). The Colombo Plan approach also offered a degree of flexibility not available under either the UN or the American systems: there was no annual budgeting problem, and equipment could be made available, with or without the services of a technician, by agreement between governments. But Colombo Plan technicians reported the same frustrating neglect of technical recommendations for political reasons that hampered UN and American advisers, and their living standards, though usually higher than those of the host officials, were often marginal in their own terms. Colombo Plan nations did not evaluate or screen requests for technical aid; an effort was made to meet all proposals. Aid offered under the Technical Co-operation Scheme was originally expected to be screened by the Bureau for Technical Co-operation and the Council for Technical Co-operation at Colombo, but the ease of working directly in bilateral negotiations made this

[32] *Preface to Eighth Annual Report of the Consultative Committee*, the Colombo Plan for Co-operative Economic Development in South and South-East Asia (London: H.M. Stationery Office, 1959), p. iii.

step unnecessary. Capital aid, the other half of the Colombo Plan program, was also arranged bilaterally.[33]

Colombo Plan aid suffered from the same lack of coordination in country programing that weakened UN technical assistance, with the additional problem that there was no resident representative to offer advice and attempt informal liaison among projects. The Colombo Plan did, however, hold annual conferences at which each country reported on the previous year's experience and the coming year's program. The criticisms and suggestions that were exchanged during the annual conferences usually offered greater challenges to national programs and operations than any government would have been willing to accept in bilateral discussions. Most important of all, despite difficulties the programs grew. The total resources devoted to Colombo Plan activities, whether in equipment, training programs, or the services of technicians, increased with each succeeding year, although the growth was not even and individual country contributions varied widely from year to year, depending upon the nature and volume of requests.

The international agencies offered programs with greater political flexibility than the efforts of any single nation, although they were sometimes difficult for the host government to combine and coordinate. A variety of credit resources, recommendations for development programs, and technical advice and assistance on almost any subject were available to the countries of Southeast Asia and of other underdeveloped areas. Most of the services offered multilaterally could be performed by a few foreign technicians, serving unobtrusively in the ranks of the host government's employees or visiting for a few weeks, requiring no supporting staff, making no logistical or administrative demands, and committed to no fixed pattern of administration. Governments could feel assured they were avoiding both conflicts of national purposes and embarrassing burdens of gratitude by accepting multilateral aid. On the other hand, in requesting technical assistance from multilateral sources they had to consider the disadvantages of uncoordinated, short-term arrangements that might bring sporadic and inconsistent technical advice. Above all, the absence of an

[33] Council for Technical Co-operation in South and South-East Asia, *Report for 1957–1958* (London: H.M. Stationery Office, 1958), pp. 4, 6.

adequate resident staff charged with preparing and overseeing a coherent country program placed the burdens of planning and coordination upon the host government itself.

American resources for that kind of advice and staff work were greater than those offered by the United Nations or the Colombo Plan. The ICA, theoretically a temporary agency operating on a project-by-project basis, actually possessed a career staff whose tours of duty were not confined to the accomplishment of specific tasks. Indeed, one weakness of ICA operations—the relatively rapid rotation of staff as compared with domestic civil service—was probably less serious than in either of the international agencies offering technical assistance. If ICA tours of duty could have been left open on a voluntary basis for stays of more than four years, a still greater technical impact could well have been made.

American aid programs also had the advantage of large stocks of counterpart funds that would permit experimentation on a large scale. Agriculture, community development, and resettlement operations benefited from these funds, which usually could not be repatriated in dollars or used for development activities involving imported equipment. The continuance of agricultural surplus and commercial import programs could be expected to result in the accumulation of large reservoirs of local currencies over the coming decades, especially as "soft" loans were repaid and new U.S. currency was introduced in further extensions of credit. Limitations on their use (most of the PL 480 funds have not been available for project support, for example) have heretofore discouraged experiments because of the project approach preferred by American agencies. Projects that were to be evaluated later by high professional standards of administration could not risk much experimentation. In almost all fields, however, the merging of Western and Asian techniques could be more effectively achieved if constructive experimentation were encouraged as a matter of policy. Several interesting experiments have already been made almost by accident when American and Asian technicians have worked out practical compromises between different methods.

It seems clear from a decade of experience that bilateral and multilateral programs each possess distinct advantages and disadvantages. Neither is likely to replace the other, and the growth in their activities suggests that both have served useful and perhaps increasingly important purposes. But the possibility of directing these different programs into complementary channels depends mainly upon the prospects for national planning and coordinated administration in the underdeveloped countries.

The Problem of Coordination

As the ultimate sovereign power, the host government remains responsible for all aid programs developed on its soil. This responsibility imposes serious burdens of planning and coordination, of establishing priorities, and of superimposing complicated operations upon what is usually a rudimentary state apparatus. One cannot expect anything approaching perfect performance in most cases. Technical assistance programs that rely upon the requesting government to formulate its technical requirements with precision run the risk of technical errors, but often the government prefers that risk, serious as it is, to acknowledging any dependence upon foreign agencies in matters that appear to touch its sovereignty.

It is also true that the host government may have a wide range of choice among competitive offers of assistance. Planning resources for economic development are available through the short-term missions of the World Bank; UN Special Fund financing is available for general surveys and certain types of engineering; Colombo Plan conferences afford an opportunity for each country in Southeast Asia to present data and programs and to review progress in a friendly, critical forum; and the programing facilities of U.S. aid missions are available for developing projects requiring financing or technical assistance from American government agencies. These resources are all flexible enough to permit some adjustment to the needs and policies of the host government in spite of the inherent limitations of the functions of each.

It is also probable that the planning functions of each of these agencies could be expanded without extreme effort. The United Nations, although possessing no permanent country staff, could at least give its resident representative authority to coordinate the work of technicians assigned to his country. And in countries where the U.S. operations missions are the largest foreign aid organizations, they could extend their planning staffs in order to assist the host governments in planning economic development, and they could decentralize their supervisory technical staff in order to assist in coordinating the local activities of multilateral or other bilateral agencies.

Adequate coordination and country programing involve something more than merely preventing individual technicians from neutralizing each other. The detailed country plan which guides a U.S. operations mission represents at least one affirmative effort to integrate all activities in a coherent policy. These plans, although primarily related to U.S. objectives and seldom available to other governments, could serve with adaptations as the basis for wider plans and general country programs covering both foreign assistance and local efforts. It is almost certain, however, that except in special cases the governments of the host countries must continue to bear the greatest responsibility for economic coordination. The most useful foreign contributions to national planning will be informal advice, coupled with a readiness to assist in building up adequate planning facilities within the host government itself. The permanent presence of a large, comprehensive U.S. operations mission may make it the most useful agency for such purposes, although it may also be advisable in many situations to give international agencies some part in planning a country's economic future.

As the decade of the 1960s opened, ICA was not well organized for country planning. Effective coordination of the several sources of foreign aid will require greater attention in the future to the operations mission's responsibility for developing goals and programs at the country level. Changes were needed both in the staff and in the responsibilities of the typical ICA mission. The experiment introduced in India of assigning to the American ambassador an economic aid coordinator with authority over the economic policies of all U.S. agencies might be extended and expanded. Consideration should be given to providing a highly trained American staff under the ambassador to plan and coordinate all American aid operations under the jurisdiction and control of the host government.

In the last analysis, there remains little prospect for a reduction in the number of agencies or countries engaged in offering foreign aid to the underdeveloped world. The purposes of the donors are too disparate to permit the merging of all their activities into a single agency, or even to yield to a very high degree of coordination. The highest qualification for success—jointness between the donor and host government—cannot be achieved in all cases by the same approach. Joint operations of various forms, such as that of JCRR in Taiwan, the former Iraq Development Board (which included British and American members with full voting power), or the *servicios* of Latin America, could doubtless be extended further if the United States, other donors, and host governments were willing to simplify certain administrative procedures. But the objectives of donors of aid also include operations where joint control would be impossible, and certain foreign aid activities, especially for military purposes, will continue to be separated from the national development plans.

5. CONCLUSIONS

Because foreign aid has served so many national and international objectives—political, military, economic, social, and cultural—it must be seen and managed in its particulars. Administrative coordination of its manifold activities can scarcely be achieved by agencies located outside the receiving country, especially those relying upon temporary inspections or routine exchanges of information. It is especially doubtful if coordination can be achieved in the large technical or administrative groups in Washington or New York whose role is arranging clearances rather than creative participation. Placing authority for coordinating aid within each recipient country offers the most promising means of integrating the various forms which it takes. Assuming that such authority must be partially entrusted to foreign planning experts, the fundamental question is what effect upon sovereign prerogatives a truly integrated aid program would have.

Sovereignty is held to be an indivisible attribute of statehood. Understressed in recent Western political thinking, it has become for the newly emerging states a political reality, the prize of national independence. Although technically requiring no more than the making and enforcing of ultimate political decisions, its symbolic manifestations may demand constantly fresh demonstrations of the new nation's authority and competence. In such circumstances the process of allocating scarce economic resources, even those derived from external aid, may well be unfavorable to planning for maximum productivity. Token gestures toward national tradition, seemingly arbitrary decisions, and irrelevant personal considerations may grate against the economic rationale of Westerners; certain Western values such as free enterprise, individual productivity, and public efficiency may be rejected in principle or ignored in practice. When external planners find these attitudes combined with a defensive reluctance to concede any inadequacies of technique or knowledge, they are seldom in a position to insist upon their own economic standards and technical criteria. They have to concede the need for compromise.

One great principle is clear: aid must be offered with equal respect for the requirements of economic development and for the politics of sovereignty. The proposed country approach to aid planning does not imply a substitution of one sovereign will for another. But the donor is obliged, both by morality and by prudence, to offer his aid in its most useful form, even if it is not accepted. Frequently, in fact, this obligation may require a deliberate and sustained effort at persuasion. The country approach includes not only a determining of needs and priorities but also the definition of a coherent American position.

The country approach may also become an administrative necessity in dealing with cold war politics in "the African decade." Greater authority and more adequate staffing will be necessary to assist ambassadors in coordinating the overlapping and competing U.S. aid agencies at work in many countries. In fact, even before a nation achieves independence, preliminary country aid planning in Washington may be necessary if the United States is to move quickly and effectively when the opportunity is presented.

Attempting to utilize conventional diplomatic approaches to the complex challenges of foreign aid has not yielded encouraging results. Prompt, effective responses to the economic needs of emerging states can seldom be made through the limited and often rigid processes of traditional foreign relations. Events in Guinea and the Congo have dramatically shown that the groundwork of foreign aid may need to be laid well before a state has come into existence. And thereafter the speed and effectiveness of aid programing may also be impaired by the attempts to administer foreign aid through a cumbersome bureaucracy operating uniformly on a world-wide basis. The country approach to aid policy and programing offers a means of predicting emergencies, responding to unusual needs, and using development diplomacy consistently to further the national interests of all nations involved.

If acceptable to the host governments, the economic services the United States could render by coordinating American aid with contributions of other governments and international agencies could be of enormous value; and if sovereign sensibilities ruled otherwise, the country approach could nevertheless purge American foreign aid efforts of excessive remote control and incoherent planning that have plagued the country programs under the bureaucratic requirements of the 1950s. But these reforms will not be possible unless future domestic support for American foreign aid reflects a national consensus at home heretofore denied our operations in countries on the edge of the modern world.

V AMERICAN POLITICS AND
FOREIGN AID

In few areas of American public life is there so little national consensus on purposes as in foreign aid. Few governmental functions, consequently, are subject to greater political vicissitudes and vagaries. In view of these facts, the continued existence of large-scale, planned programs of military and economic aid at all is a tribute to leadership and courage in the executive branch and in both houses of Congress.

The survival of foreign aid is the result of a series of uncertain political compromises. Many enthusiastic advocates have accepted it merely as a clear international duty, without making any serious contribution toward consolidating domestic political support. Well-meant humanitarianism can rarely offer any concrete support for the program against even irrelevant and uninformed criticism; abstract moral sentiments provide no standard for choosing among a multitude of charitable and useful projects. Many humane speeches "favoring" aid have urged no remedies for its shortcomings except the expenditure of more money; others, uncritically confusing two distinct international duties, have suggested that all U.S. aid be channeled through the United Nations, without regard to the practical consequences of such national self-denial.

The absence of a consistent *political* rationale for foreign aid has created great difficulties for those of its supporters who are too prudent to rely on humane considerations alone. They have been forced to justify its continued existence by appealing to a shifting series of formulas of national security, reflecting the most

urgent political and economic necessities of the day. The executive branch has developed a number of arguments upon which its
annual defense of the program rests—help to allies, strengthening
the independence of free nations, contributions to political stability and economic development, and building resistance to
communism; but these have become stereotyped phrases, often
too debased by excessive usage to justify specific programs. Thus in
spite of annually renewed support from the President and from
congressional leaders, the continuity of the program has often been
in doubt, and congressional trimming and buffeting has reduced it
to an unstable, anxious, and highly vulnerable arm of American
diplomacy.

Some have explained the unstable political history of foreign
aid by pointing to its lack of a voting constituency. As President
Eisenhower once told the League of Women Voters: "Let us
remember, foreign aid doesn't have any pressure groups in any
Congressman's district. It is something that has to depend on the
intelligence of the American people and not on selfish interest."[1]
In politics, however, the line between intelligence and selfish
interest is not easily drawn. Foreign aid has attracted support from
many sources, including a variety of interest groups as well as the
disinterested views of citizens. The farm bloc, labor unions, the
shipping lobby, certain businessmen, universities and scholarly
groups interested in cultural exchanges, and the Federal Council
of Churches have offered support to various aspects of foreign aid.[2]
There is also general acceptance of aid as a necessary defense
against Communist expansion—even to the extent of obliging its
adversaries to temper their opposition with disclaimers alleging
support for the "principle." The arch critic of foreign aid in Con-

[1] Reprinted in *The Department of State Bulletin*, May 27, 1957, p. 848.

[2] ICA estimates that 90 per cent of the military assistance program funds
and about half of the economic assistance funds are spent in the United
States. About 500,000 people are presently employed in the United States
producing goods and services, generated by mutual security funds. ICA,
Questions and Answers on the Mutual Security Program, Department of State
Publication 7027 (Washington: GPO, 1960), p. 17. Organizations support-
ing foreign aid include the AFL-CIO, U.S. Chamber of Commerce, Friends'
Committee on National Legislation, Committee for International Economic
Growth, National Conference on International Economic and Social Develop-
ment, and various professional organizations. Cabell Phillips, in *The New
York Times*, June 11, 1961.

gress, Representative Otto Passman, once regretted that he had "been placed in the wrong light," explaining that his mission was not to cripple foreign aid but merely to end "this crazy system of spending more money every year than we take in."[3] As chairman of the Subcommittee on Foreign Operations of the House Appropriations Committee since 1955, Mr. Passman claims to have "saved" the taxpayers some $1.4 billion slashed from the annual mutual security appropriations bills. Prior to his appointment over the heads of several senior members, he had voted against every single foreign aid authorization or appropriation presented in Congress since the original Greek-Turkish act of 1947; but he still did not find it expedient to identify himself as opposed to foreign aid as a principle.

If foreign aid has had no consistent body of supporters in Congress, it has also had few self-acknowledged enemies.[4] It has not been "foreign aid" that has lacked support, but rather its specific programs. These have largely been left to survive by compromise, and the agencies that have administered them have made their way by strategic retreats, reorganizations, and judicious concealment behind clouds of obscure statistics and a specialized vocabulary.

The various campaigns of abuse heaped upon ICA and its forerunners have helped to bring about a continuing succession of new administrative brooms, all intended to sweep up the debris left by previous foreign aid operations. But each new leadership in its turn has succumbed to the forces responsible for the demise of its predecessors. Neither presidential nor congressional support has been sufficient to protect the administrative essentials of foreign aid against political attack. Each allocation of funds to one country or project may invite criticism on behalf of those that are slighted. The inefficiency and corruption often marking

[3] *The New York Times*, June 14, 1960.

[4] There are, however, some. The Citizens Foreign Aid Committee, a conservative businessman's organization and principal lobbyist against aid, describes the entire Mutual Security Act as "one of the greatest pieces of 'pork barrel' legislation ever conceived" and considers it "illegal" and used "for palpably un-American purposes and projects." *The New York Times*, April 26, 1960, and June 11, 1961. Books like James W. Wiggins and Helmut Shoeck, eds., *Foreign Aid Reexamined* (Washington: Public Affairs Press, 1958), and Eugene W. Castle, *The Great Giveaway* (Chicago: Regnery, 1957), testify to the vigor of the opposition.

the conduct of poor and undermanned new governments have exposed the program to inevitable carping and blame; and so have the financial losses that flow from the need to operate in fields rejected by private investors. Planning for invasions that may not come, projects that may not be accepted, or cooperation that may not be forthcoming has produced multiple frustrations. Finally, decisions on contracts involving choices among various competing American and foreign firms open the door to strong protests against favoritism. Such virtual invitations to criticism and opposition have not been ignored.

Nor can the domestic political cost of supporting aid always be offset by dramatic diplomatic victories. The international achievements attributed to foreign aid have been, for the most part, preventive. Rarely can clear positive gains be found to balance the occasional fall of some government supported by American aid or the turning of others to totalitarian methods or to a hostile neutralism. Hindsight illuminates all too clearly mistakes and weaknesses in the emergency programs the United States entered into hastily in order to avert military or political disasters.

Because it has so rarely been constructive, criticism has had a generally adverse effect on foreign aid administration. The sharper the attack, the more the agencies of foreign aid have tried to guard against repeating past errors. They have imposed long bureaucratic delays, refused to make timely decisions, and avoided taking risky actions. In short, the bureaucracy of foreign aid has sought protection by the means most calculated to weaken the impact of its programs. By imposing added restrictions and procedures to guard against a recurrence of past errors, the comptrollers and managers of foreign aid have introduced rigidities incompatible with many of the unpredictable requirements of foreign aid. Fear of congressional and public criticism has pursued each successive agency relentlessly until it has become imprisoned by its own caution.

It is remarkable testimony to the flexibility and common sense embodied in the American political system that, in spite of unrelenting and sometimes mortal attacks on individual programs, foreign aid has survived. Congressional support, though still tempered with doubt, has been stabilized at an adequate level. Votes on authorizing legislation have leveled off at an average of some 70 per cent in favor (below this figure for Democrats and House

Republicans, above it for Senate Republicans),[5] although this generally favorable climate is occasionally disturbed by wrangles over particular items in the appropriation bills. Numerous country programs have been successfully designed and implemented in spite of changes in American policy, in the international situation, and in the host government's attitudes. Under continued exposure to the vagaries of domestic politics, administrators have fought to maintain relatively consistent policies during the past decade. Support for their efforts must be credited jointly to the leaders of Congress and of the executive branch who have co-operated in the face of unprecedented political difficulties.

The question is whether this pattern of achievement will be adequate to the accumulating challenges of the 1960s and beyond.

1. THE BUILDING OF CONSENSUS

The lack of constituent support for foreign aid has one redeeming feature: congressmen have shown themselves more amenable to a powerful presentation of the national interest in this matter than in other fields where local groups of voters bring to bear strong beliefs or powerful interests. Few passionate congressional convictions have been involved, few injured constituents have written strenuous letters, and few elections have been at stake when mutual security legislation was being debated. The absence of a minimum consensus on the purpose of aid, on the other hand, has left congressmen free to deprecate programs and other governments, propose and insist on new approaches, and even attack individual administrators. The absence of political support has created an air of uncertainty and discontinuity. The weight of this atmosphere on both executive and congressional leaders is the measure of the need for building jointly a national consensus on foreign aid.

The Congress

Distrust of foreign aid has been deepened by the annual inquisitions held in rival and sometimes unfriendly congressional committees, where each year the very survival of foreign aid is

[5] Holbert N. Carroll, "Congressional Politics and Foreign Policy in the 1960's," paper delivered at 1960 meeting of the American Political Science Association, University of Pittsburgh, processed (September 1960).

challenged. If these attacks are in fact less damaging than they
seem, and the threats to survival somewhat emptier, the repeated
turning of the congressional mills nevertheless has a serious enough
impact on the effectiveness of foreign aid operations.

Nor did conditions significantly improve during the 1950s, even
though support for the general principle of foreign aid was gradually stabilized.[6] Funds continued to flow in substantial amounts,
but the shape of the program was always in doubt. When Representative Passman succeeded in getting committee approval for
what had come to be the usual 20 per cent cut ($800 million) from
the 1960 Mutual Security Appropriations Act, *The New York
Times* (as it always does) called the action as potentially dangerous to our foreign policy as it was clearly irresponsible.[7] But it was
not the financial reductions that disturbed the program most, for
there are bureaucratic ways of surviving budget cuts; the *Times*
correctly diagnosed as the "knife in the back . . . the crippling
nonmonetary restrictions written into the bill [that would] . . .
make important parts of the program rigid, unrealistic and unworkable, thereby defeating its purpose and virtually guaranteeing
disaster." Included among these "absurd restrictions" was a requirement that each technical assistance project be individually
approved by Congress, a procedure that would make it necessary
for ICA to arouse the interests and expectation of the host government, only to run the risk of having to beat a lame retreat if
Congress was unimpressed.[8] Representative Passman also succeeded in getting committee approval to prohibit the use of any
part of the $20 million allocated to technical assistance in Africa

[6] For an analysis of this support, see Roger Hilsman, "Congressional-
Executive Relations and the Foreign Policy Consensus," *The American
Political Science Review*, September 1958, pp. 725–744; and "The Foreign-
Policy Consensus: An Interim Research Report," *The Journal of Conflict
Resolution*, December 1959, pp. 361–382. See also Holbert N. Carroll, "Con-
gressional Politics and Foreign Policy in the 1960's," cited; Richard F. Fenno,
Jr., "The House Appropriations Committee as a Political System" (Rochester:
University of Rochester, processed); and James N. Rosenau, *National Leader-
ship and Foreign Policy: A Case Study in the Mobilization of Public Support*
(Princeton: Princeton University Press, forthcoming).

[7] June 15, 1960.

[8] A similar effort to tie Mutual Security Director Harold Stassen's hands
occurred on June 6, 1953, when the Senate Appropriations Committee
ordered him "not to start any new aid programs until Congress had provided
specific funds for them." *The New York Times*, June 7, 1953.

for purposes of construction, a provision which, if enacted, would have left the special program for tropical Africa financially muscle-bound. The committee itself gratuitously denied all aid to the Indus River project, a laboriously negotiated arrangement for water-sharing between India and Pakistan, for which the United States was planning to make both loans and grants. It was a project of the greatest importance to American foreign policy as well as to India and Pakistan, and in addition one to which the United States, together with five other countries, was morally committed.

None of these restrictions survived the House debate to become part of the law, but defeating them and their equivalents year after year has required unremitting efforts from the executive branch, a combination of political forces that has to be assembled each year, and occasional good luck in the form of Soviet intransigence. In 1960, for example, Democratic liberals and Republican conservatives were brought together by accidental and unrelated political events. House Republicans were unexpectedly united in support of the President by the U-2 incident, the cancellation of his visit to Russia, and the anti-American demonstrations in Japan; while the liberal Democrats, stung by the attack on the Indus River project, joined with them to deny Representative Passman the $1.5-billion foreign aid cut he had promised and to destroy the most damaging of his amendments. The final House result, a $590.5-million cut, was only 15 per cent less than the administration request.[9] It was no tribute to national consensus on foreign aid that Mr. Passman suffered his first major defeat since being appointed chairman of the Subcommittee on Foreign Operations.

Passing annual foreign aid legislation over such determined opposition is something of an achievement toward a working consensus, but it has not laid permanent foundations for a continuing policy. Each year a few individual vendettas against foreign aid flare up, resulting in unpredictable, intemperate, and sometimes profane attacks delivered in a highly personal fashion against representatives of the executive branch appearing before congressional subcommittees. Chairmen of some key committees adroitly use "public" hearings (often with no other member pres-

[9] The average cut from 1953 to 1958 was 23.8 per cent. (See Table 2, p. 211.)

ent) to cut short explanations, prevent the introduction of material favorable to the program, and dismiss knowledgeable witnesses, so that the record will indicate little but admissions of weakness.[10] The forbearance displayed by administration witnesses before such committees, together with careful efforts by other congressmen to redeem their colleagues' irresponsible tactics, has left the program each year just about as it was before—an uneasy compromise. It is not surprising that Senator Fulbright and others have stated that foreign aid can survive few more of the yearly authorization-appropriation ordeals.

The problem is not entirely one of "crippling" amendments passed in Congress. Congressional support for foreign aid proved sufficient to defeat most of these; indeed, their intent to injure the principal objectives of American foreign policy was usually enough in itself to discredit them. Other amendments offered over the years out of honorable intentions also had to be eliminated in order to arrive at a workable program. In 1951 a proposal to deny aid to countries permitting illicit narcotics traffic was defeated in the House, as were other proposals that no nation receive aid "that did not accept technical aid from this country in the collection of taxes," and that military aid be withheld from countries failing to support the claims of colonial peoples for self-government. In 1956 the Senate defeated a series of proposals to use the aid program for reducing agricultural imports that competed with American products. Many such amendments do not survive the committee in which they are made, but their ultimate fate is not easily predictable; a committee decision can always be overridden by the full house. A proposal to bar U.S. aid to any country that exercised criminal jurisdiction over American troops was defeated

[10] One of these devices has been aptly called a "numbers game": vast amounts of "unexpended funds," even though they may have been in part already committed, are cited as evidence that new appropriations are unnecessary. One report "proclaimed that $6,195 million of unexpended funds were outstanding as of June 30 [1957] which, it was alleged, could support the program 'well beyond January 1959' without any additional appropriations. What was not stressed was that only $614 million of [these] funds were actually unobligated. . . . And, of [this] . . . $574 million had been appropriated for military assistance and defense support." H. Field Haviland, Jr., "Foreign Aid and the Policy Process: 1957," *The American Political Science Review*, September 1958, p. 711.

in the House Foreign Affairs Committee, only to be revived for floor discussion.

What is most disconcerting to the administration and to supporters of foreign aid is that some damaging amendments will almost certainly penetrate their defenses. The final protection against an irresponsible vote in either house is the atmosphere of compromise in the conference committee of the Senate and House; but in spite of that, the administration of foreign aid is increasingly bound by rigid restrictions year by year. Some ideas die hard. A conference committee defeated the Kem Amendment to deny aid to nations carrying on any business with Communist-dominated countries, heeding the administration's argument that it would force countries already trading with the Soviet bloc into still further dependence upon it, only to find the amendment restored in somewhat milder form as a rider to the Third Supplemental Appropriation Act of 1951.[11] Where the two houses have differed widely, the conference committee has usually succeeded in softening some of the harsher proposals, but the complete elimination of irrelevant or injurious amendments has not always been possible. In such cases the only recourse left to the executive has been to interpret them so as to minimize their adverse effects. When an Act of Congress declared certain countries eligible to receive specified amounts of aid, President Eisenhower interpreted the restrictions as follows: "I regard these provisions as authorizations, and also as limitations on the availability of the amounts specified, rather than as directives. To construe them otherwise would raise substantial Constitutional questions."[12] The most celebrated case of an apparently harmless but misguided compromise was a requirement that a country receiving mutual security aid should promise to use "the full contribution permitted by its manpower, resources, facilities and general economic conditions" for the development and maintenance of its own defensive strength *and the defensive strength of the free world.* The italicized require-

[11] The President thereafter appealed to Congress, and on October 26, 1951, it passed the Mutual Defense Assistance Control Act (Battle Act), which was somewhat more flexible in its application. See William Adams Brown and Redvers Opie, *American Foreign Assistance* (Washington: Brookings, 1953), pp. 165, 233, 565.

[12] White House press releases, August 2, 1955, July 31, 1956.

ment led ten countries to refuse American aid and achieved no compensating improvements in foreign aid policy or administration at all. In Indonesia, Premier Sukiman's cabinet fell because it had made gestures indicating acceptance of this requirement.[13]

Congress has represented with extreme sensitivity America's hopes and doubts, relevant and irrelevant opinions, and convictions and prejudices on the subject of foreign aid. Leaders of the Senate Foreign Relations Committee and the House Foreign Affairs Committee have consistently rallied congressional support for foreign aid, but their annual efforts on behalf of the authorizing legislation have not protected the program from ruinous cuts and hampering amendments during the appropriations process. Within their own membership, the leaders of each of these committees must struggle annually to produce a sufficient agreement to finance one more year of foreign aid operations. Each year the building of consensus is resumed; at times, it seems as if every new effort has to start again from the beginning.

The Executive

During the past decade the executive branch has made heroic (if somewhat sporadic) efforts to defend foreign aid programs considered necessary to American foreign policy. The range and intensity of these efforts indicate how seriously both Democratic and Republican presidents have taken this responsibility: General Eisenhower was summoned from his NATO command to testify against drastic cuts in European aid; bipartisan leaders such as Senators Vandenberg and Wiley were induced to restrain the economy-minded Senator Taft; President Truman personally threatened a whistle-stop tour to mobilize public opinion against congressional cuts; and the new Eisenhower administration made desperate efforts to defend the first foreign aid program it presented in 1953, after only three months to prepare estimates and before it could recruit persuasive new mission chiefs and aid executives to send before Congress. In the all but desperate search for "new ideas" to justify foreign aid, special executive study committees of distinguished citizens have been recruited to provide non-

[13] R. L. Strout, in *The Christian Science Monitor*, February 25, 1952; *The New York Times* editorial, February 27, 1952.

political support for foreign aid.[14] In order to increase public concern, business and other leaders have been called to bipartisan conferences, State of the Union and budget messages have been used to highlight the importance of foreign aid, and special appeals to bipartisanship have been issued by the President and Vice-President. After the Korean War, new terms like "defense support" were coined to dramatize the relevance of economic assistance to military needs,[15] and annual presentations bristled with references to military necessities and regional crises.[16]

Whenever the executive branch has been successful in rallying Congress, its efforts have borne the characteristic odor of crisis. Carefully considered arguments designed to gain support for longer-term commitments to foreign aid, either in funding or programing, have met with monotonous failure. In part, this has been due to a persistent view that foreign aid was an emergency program rather than a long-term government operation, and that when the Axis had been defeated, the war damage repaired, European productivity restored, and regional defenses installed, the United States could withdraw and allow normal processes to do the rest. Although lend-lease, military government, civil relief, and the Marshall Plan cost enormous sums, their goals were fixed and attainable. The indefinite necessity for American aid occasioned by the continued dynamic of Communist expansionism and the revolutionary drive of the economically underprivileged nations has revealed itself only gradually. In 1951, Mr. William C. Foster, speaking for the Truman administration, suggested that technical assistance would "continue for a long time" and was "a permanent

[14] The Randall Report (Commission on Foreign Economic Policy, January 1954) was the first Eisenhower effort in this direction. Eric Johnston's report (International Development Advisory Board, January 1957) followed with recommendations for increased appropriations for economic aid; the Fairless Report (Committee of President's Citizen Advisers on the Mutual Security Program, March 1957) called attention to the problems of long-term economic development; finally, the Draper Report (President's Committee to Study the U.S. Military Assistance Program, August 1959) was issued seriatim to attract more attention to its recommendations for improved administration and changes in program emphasis.

[15] See Harlan Cleveland, "Fits and Starts of Foreign Aid," *The Reporter*, April 16, 1959, for an account of the origin of this term.

[16] See the careful, year-by-year history of congressional presentations and allocations in Charles Wolf, *Foreign Aid: Theory and Practice in Southern Asia* (Princeton: Princeton University Press, 1960), pp. 75–248.

and long-term and lasting activity."[17] But he was referring to Point 4, only a small part of the total foreign aid program.

All efforts during the 1950s to extend the financial authorization of aid programs beyond one year were unsuccessful. In 1954 the Eisenhower administration, abandoning its early hopes that the United States could gradually withdraw from foreign aid altogether, recommended a four-year extension of the Mutual Security Act to circumvent annual re-enactments. It was defeated.[18] Secretary of State Dulles hoped mutual security would "continue indefinitely," and pointed out that it would "continually require some appropriation to support it."[19] Even Harold Stassen, who anticipated that over-all requirements would decline after 1955, said that technical cooperation at least "should be a continuing, long-term program . . . as long as there are in the world large numbers of people who are suffering seriously from the lack of technical knowledge in the fundamental necessities of human life."[20]

In 1957 the President proposed a new approach to "long-term development assistance" through a Development Loan Fund, which was to be financed independently of the appropriations cycle. Congress granted a two-year authorization with great reluctance, refusing to go any further in the direction of permanence.[21] In other respects as well, the congressional response to Eisenhower's efforts for foreign aid in 1957 was discouraging. For the first year of DLF operations, the administration requested $500 million and received $300 million; for the second and third year of DLF operations, it asked for a three-year authorization and

[17] *Mutual Security Program*, Hearings before the House Committee on Foreign Affairs, 82d Cong., 1st sess., July 10 and 11, 1951 (Washington: GPO, 1951), pp. 179, 203.

[18] *Mutual Security Program for Fiscal Year 1954*, analysis prepared by the executive branch for use of the House Committee on Foreign Affairs, 83d Cong., 1st sess. (Washington: GPO, 1953), p. 6; *Mutual Security Act of 1954*, Report 1799 of the Senate Committee on Foreign Relations, 83d Cong., 2d sess. (Washington: GPO, 1954), p. 83.

[19] *Mutual Security Act of 1954*, Hearings before the House Committee on Foreign Affairs, 83d Cong., 2d sess., April 5, 1954 (Washington: GPO, 1954), p. 21.

[20] Same, pp. 33, 359, 365.

[21] See *Mutual Security Act of 1957*, 85th Cong., 1st sess. (Washington: GPO, 1957), Report 417 of the Senate Committee on Foreign Relations, p. 11; Report 776 of the House Committee on Foreign Affairs, p. 22; Conference Report 1042, p. 4.

appropriation of $750 million and received only an annual authorization of $625 million. The administration also asked Congress, in vain, to make permanent authorizations for military aid and defense support, so that yearly appropriations requests could be included in the regular budget. Finally, the administration requested that funds earmarked for specific approved projects would remain available until used, instead of being reappropriated seriatim; and when this so-called "no-year" basis was granted, it applied only to DLF funds, although military aid appropriations were permitted to remain available for eighteen months, instead of twelve.

Senator Fulbright revived the issue of long-term financing in 1959, but the administration had already lost interest in what the Treasury Department regarded as a "backdoor" approach.[22] By the final year of the Eisenhower administration, official spokesmen were no longer even arguing for long-term authorization or commitments, having resigned themselves to the annual congressional review with all its hazards to long-term planning and career development.[23] Even a major effort by the Kennedy administration during the "honeymoon" period to achieve the same result was unsuccessful.

The passage of foreign aid legislation during the 1950s was complicated by the absence of a unified position on foreign aid in either Congress or the administration. The legislative branch had to contend with the economy bloc and the residue of the isolationists; even supporters of foreign aid were divided by peripheral issues, such as the disposal of agricultural surpluses or the use of aid funds to promote private enterprises abroad or support small business at home.[24] The administration was beset with internal

[22] *Mutual Security Act of 1959*, Hearings before the Senate Committee on Foreign Relations, 86th Cong., 1st sess., May 25, 1959 (Washington: GPO, 1959), pp. 1238–1248.

[23] See remarks of Leonard Saccio, speaking for ICA, in *Mutual Security Act of 1959*, Hearings before the Senate Committee on Foreign Relations, cited, May 20, 1959, pp. 800–801. C. Douglas Dillon, however, declined to foresee an end to mutual security even though no plans for long-term financing were proposed. *Mutual Security Appropriations for 1960*, Hearings before the Senate Committee on Appropriations, 86th Cong., 1st sess., August 5, 1959 (Washington: GPO, 1959), pp. 113, 119–120. For a more complete account of this problem, see "The Unsuccessful History of Economic Disengagement," Appendix II.

[24] See Haviland, cited, especially pp. 718–719.

conflict between the economizing forces, centered in the Treasury and the Bureau of the Budget, and the overseas operational groups, mainly supported by the Defense Department, the State Department, and ICA, which struggled for funds they believed to be essential for national security. In the mid-fifties the so-called "4-H Club" (Secretary of the Treasury Humphrey, Under-Secretary of State Hoover, ICA Director Hollister, and Budget Director Hughes) were easily identified leaders of the economizing bloc, against which were ranged the "Young Turks" (Stassen, Nelson Rockefeller, and Nixon) who favored a greater foreign aid effort. Whenever economy forces in the administration joined with congressional blocs in opposing large foreign aid appropriations, this massed political power outweighed the supporters of foreign aid, unless the President himself entered the struggle on their side; and even then, vigorous presidential intervention was often resented. During one week in 1957, for example, President Eisenhower appealed for restoration of aid funds on three separate occasions, including a TV chat and the threat of a special session; but the congressional reaction became increasingly negative.[25]

Wide fluctuations between the sometimes deliberately inflated appropriation requests and actual congressional appropriations (see Table 2) reveal the effect of crisis periods; during the first year of the Korean War requests were cut only 8.4 per cent as contrasted with "normal" years when the economy forces prevailed, at times slashing more than 25 per cent from the amount requested. The figures imply that in the absence of powerful military arguments, the financing of foreign aid has been highly unstable and essentially unpredictable.

The greatest uncertainties have usually accompanied requests for economic aid, whether described as defense support, special assistance, or funds for development. Other elements of foreign aid, however, have received consistent support, including $2 billion for the Export-Import Bank[26] provided in 1958 with little argument and less public notice, $1.4 billion for the International Monetary Fund passed in 1959 with little debate, $1.5 billion for

[25] *The Christian Science Monitor*, August 15, 1957; *New York Herald Tribune*, August 16, 1957. See also *The New York Times*, July 3, 1958.
[26] Capital for the Export-Import Bank is obtained by drawing on the Treasury, not from Congressional appropriations.

Table 2

Financial History of Mutual Security Appropriations (1948–60)

(in millions of dollars)

Fiscal Year	Executive Branch Authorization Request	Authorization by Congress	Executive Branch Appropriation Request	Appropriation of New Funds	Reduction Comparing Appropriation with Authorization Requested	Percentage Reduction, Appropriation with Authorization Requested
1948-49	8,520.0	6,913.0	6,837.0	6,446.3	2,073.7	24.3
1950	5,830.0	5,594.0	5,512.2	5,092.4	737.6	12.7
1951	8,172.5	7,922.5	7,835.7	7,485.0	687.5	8.4
1952	8,500.0	7,583.4	7,483.0	7,284.4	1,215.6	14.3
1953	7,900.0	6,492.7	6,492.7	6,001.9	1,898.1	24.0
1954	5,972.1	5,255.6	5,124.5	4,531.5	1,395.6	23.5
1955	3,448.1	3,024.6	3,438.5	2,781.5	666.6	19.3
1956	3,530.0	3,407.8	3,266.6	2,703.3	826.7	23.4
1957	4,760.0	4,115.1	4,860.0	3,766.6	993.4	20.9
1958	3,864.4	3,386.9	3,386.9	2,768.8	1,095.6	28.4
1959	3,942.1	3,675.6	3,950.1	3,448.9	493.2	12.5
1960	4,430.1a	4,676.8	4,430.0	3,225.8	1,204.3	27.2

a Includes $500 million DLF funds for fiscal year 1961.

Source: Reports of Congressional Committees.

surplus agricultural commodity aid, and $500 million for the Inter-American Development Bank. By way of contrast, a $125-million change in DLF appropriations became a major issue. The program of grant aid was regularly challenged, and regularly cut. Technical assistance cost only 5 per cent of the total foreign aid allocation, but occupied three-fourths of the Americans employed abroad on foreign aid, and, incidentally, most of the hearings and criticisms.

The drama of predicted disasters and actual disappointments in the stability of foreign aid legislation produced a variety of proposals for lifting foreign aid out of American politics altogether. Some would elevate the Congress itself above politics by an unexplained process of sublimation, while others would take the program out of American hands or at least transfer it to nonpolitical agencies. Changing the congressional role to one of general oversight is suggested in the proposals for "long-term financing," the substitution of independent public corporations for agencies of the government, and the use of the borrowing power of the Treasury instead of congressional appropriation as a means of financing aid operations. Proposals that would remove foreign aid from the American context altogether included the assignment of responsibilities to United Nations agencies, the new Organization for Economic Cooperation and Development, or other special multilateral agencies. None of these suggestions could be adopted as law, however, without reaching a degree of congressional consensus about foreign aid that has not yet been achieved for far more modest proposals.

Elements of Continuity

In spite of these alarums and excursions, it must be conceded that the administration of foreign aid has achieved a tolerable continuity—a testimony to bureaucratic durability rather than to deliberate national policy and a factor that may have discouraged Congress from taking the necessary remedies for its own unstable behavior. It is a fact that people engaged in administering aid since 1947 have survived about a dozen legislative enactments of the program (in addition to re-enactment of authorizing legislation, annual appropriations, and agricultural surplus laws), five administrative reorganizations, and seven changes of leadership.

The International Cooperation Administration functioned as only one of dozens of public agencies engaged in foreign aid;[27] and even the Agency for International Development, organized in November 1961, absorbed only the DLF, leaving the Kennedy administration's Peace Corps a separate entity. Yet the organizational deficiencies of this complex and overlapping apparatus have not been corrected by legislative inquiries or by legislation; and the need for radical changes in congressional procedures has been more evident to administrators than to lawmakers.

The political processes have permitted the survival of specific country programs and the growth of something approaching a career service in spite of the chaotic appearance of foreign aid organization. Bureaucratic survival reveals a greater degree of tolerance in the facts than in the language of congressional-executive relationships. It would seem that the only consensus visibly produced over the past decade was an agreement for Congress to review annually the advisability of continuing foreign aid, and then to decide how much money to appropriate for it. But an implied consensus has permitted continuance on a reasonable financial basis and a degree of planning and staff development for survival. Where the absence of agreement has been most serious within both Congress and the administration during the past decade has been in discouraging the creation of a doctrine of foreign aid as a continuing, forward-looking operation of the U.S. government. The need for such a doctrine is demonstrated by the amount of effort that is required merely to stand still at a time when the rest of the world has been moving so fast.

[27] Governmental agencies engaged in foreign aid, according to the report of the U.S. Commission on Organization of the Executive Branch of the Government, Task Force on Overseas Economic Operations (Washington: GPO, 1955), comprised—in addition to FOA (ICA)—the State, Defense, Treasury, Commerce, Agriculture, Labor, Interior, and Health, Education and Welfare Departments, the U.S. Information Agency, the Export-Import Bank, the Office of Defense Mobilization, General Services Administration, and others (including Atomic Energy Commission, Central Intelligence Agency, Department of Justice, and Federal Communications Commission). The Development Loan Fund was created later. Although the International Finance Corporation, International Monetary Fund, and International Bank for Reconstruction and Development (World Bank) all operated under the general aegis of the United Nations, their headquarters are in Washington.

2. Congressional Roles in Foreign Aid

During the past decade some form of congressional activity on foreign aid has occurred in almost every month of each session. Every year a new law has had to pass through both houses authorizing the administration to engage in foreign aid, to maintain a staff of personnel for that purpose, and to prepare plans and programs within a budgetary maximum. A second act has then had to pass both houses appropriating funds for the approved programs. The four key committees involved in this lengthy process—the Senate Committee on Foreign Relations, the House Committee on Foreign Affairs, and the Appropriations Committee in each house—have held hearings, sponsored special studies, and occasionally investigated country programs in person. Other committees have made continuing studies (sometimes with the assistance of the General Accounting Office) of the fiscal responsibility and efficiency of foreign aid operations. Congress has authorized, appropriated, criticized, supervised all major aspects of foreign aid policy and operations, and it has been responsible for important innovations as well. It has certainly not been a lack of congressional interest or participation that has retarded general consensus on foreign aid.

Informing the Congress and the Public

Congressional information on foreign aid derives first of all from annual hearings that are lengthy, repetitious, and usually dull. During the formal statements presented by selected witnesses, and the questions and answers that follow, various committee members file in and out. They may devote part or all of their attention to the discussion and pursue the questioning themselves in turn, although many sit silently engaged in other business. No one who has read transcripts of these hearings can fail to note the frequency with which certain questions reappear in different forms or the uneven vulnerability of different witnesses or assumptions to critical questioning. Because few committee decisions have been drastically affected by the testimony of a single individual, administration witnesses usually work to achieve a favorable effect by the cumulation of similar, reinforcing statements. Thus both parties engaged in the hearings contribute to their ponderous inefficiency.

A second source of congressional information is provided by the occasional tours of inspection which, though usually brief, are more direct and more convincing than the respectful words of Washington officials. Some inspections of foreign aid missions are carefully planned in advance with the aid of congressional staff members, while others consist of relatively uncritical formal briefings or superficial impromptu visits. Congressional and staff visitors may devote their attention to anything from matters of high policy to their own PX privileges and prospects for indulging in black-market activities. Some have been circumspect; others have shown a genius for impairing relations with both American personnel and the host government.

Staff work is an indispensable supplement to congressional surveillance over executive performance, and a valuable source of information in all fields of congressional activity. Unfortunately, however, the staff resources in foreign affairs are severely limited. In 1959 the staff of foreign policy specialists numbered only eight for the Senate Foreign Relations Committee, five for the House Foreign Affairs Committee, sixteen in the Legislative Reference Service, and thirty-five serving the two Armed Services Committees. This number would have been scarcely sufficient for the Committees on Foreign Relations and Foreign Affairs alone; and there was no staff at all serving the Appropriations Committees which exercised the power of life and death over foreign aid. The attention devoted to foreign affairs in the Appropriations Committees was understandably somewhat desultory since only some $4 billion of the $80-billion budget was devoted to mutual security programs. Moreover, there was little carry-over from the hearings of the Committees on Foreign Relations or Foreign Affairs to the Appropriations Committees, since no congressmen held membership in both. The absence of overlapping memberships imposed further limitations on the effectiveness of the understaffed committees performing functions of congressional review.

Congress has tried to overcome its own staff limitations by using consultants for occasional reviews of mutual security. In 1957 a Senate Special Committee to Study the Foreign Aid Program contracted for eleven "studies" and ten regional "surveys,"[28]

[28] *Foreign Aid Program*, compilation of Studies and Surveys, prepared for the Senate Special Committee to Study the Foreign Aid Program, Doc. No. 52, 85th Cong., 1st sess. (Washington: GPO, 1957).

before issuing its own report calling for greater leadership (especially from the executive branch) in overcoming the weaknesses it found in the policies and administration of foreign aid.[29] Although the President declined the implied invitation to suggest corrective legislation, it is possible that the release of the studies and final report helped prevent a legislative catastrophe for foreign aid in 1958 and 1959.[30] Special reports commissioned by the Senate Foreign Relations Committee in 1959 included five foreign policy studies that favorably influenced public opinion on foreign aid, although leading to no major legislative changes. The call to leadership in the executive branch was also, in general, ignored.[31]

Congress has established two auditing agencies to supplement its own efforts to supervise executive performance. Both are useful means of disclosing malfeasance or inefficiency, but they have limited value for appraising program effectiveness, yielding new insights, or developing better policies. The first, the General Accounting Office (GAO), conducts spot audits and prepares financial reports for congressional use. The second, the Office of Inspector General and Comptroller of Mutual Security (IGC), was recently established in the State Department to perform inquiries of a broader character, principally in the field. Both have been placed under the direction of congressional auditors, although the IGC is staffed by foreign service officers as well. There are already indications that Congress may be denied access

[29] *Foreign Aid*, Report of the Senate Special Committee to Study the Foreign Aid Program, S. Report 300, 85th Cong., 1st sess. (Washington: GPO, 1957). For recommendations relating to executive leadership, see pp. 11, 16, 19, and 20.

[30] Only seven senators voted against the Marshall Plan in 1948, but by 1956 the votes against the mutual security appropriations had grown to thirty. Some observers ascribed the decline to twenty-five in 1959 to support generated by the publication of the special studies and surveys.

[31] *United States Foreign Policy*, compilation of studies, Doc. No. 24, 87th Cong., 1st sess. (Washington: GPO, 1961). The principal studies were: *Basic Aims of United States Foreign Policy* (Council on Foreign Relations); *The Operational Aspects of United States Foreign Policy* (Syracuse University); *Economic, Social and Political Change in the Underdeveloped Countries and Its Implications for United States Policy* (Massachusetts Institute of Technology); and *The Formulation and Administration of United States Foreign Policy* (Brookings Institution). Several of the regional studies also touched upon foreign aid requirements.

to some of the nonfinancial information developed by IGC on the grounds that it is confidential to the executive branch.[32]

The withholding of information from congressmen is a fine art and a dangerous one. Obviously the constitutional division of powers would be weakened if all information possessed by the executive branch were communicated immediately to Congress so that administrative decisions could be in effect shared; but in foreign aid operations the normal constitutional separation between establishing policy standards and executing them has dissolved in mutual distrust. The congressional appetite for information about foreign aid operations is insatiable; it is further stimulated by the executive's use of the "national interest" criterion to withhold certain privileged information, especially in cases of suspected wrongdoing. It has been impossible to avoid the suggestion of politics in the relationships engendered by the process of seeking and offering or denying information. This problem was aggravated by the fact that so often in recent years the congressional majority party has not been that of the president.

Congressional suspicions of evasion were not alleviated by the Eisenhower administration's avowed preference for "congressional" rather than "presidential" government. Even when the administration withheld information of an obviously confidential nature—such as personnel ratings, delicate matters under negotiation with foreign governments, and papers given a security classification by the United States or another government—the suspicion of "government by secrecy" remained. In these truly confidential matters, Congress may sometimes be satisfied with closed hearings and off-the-record meetings, disclosure of classified information to key congressional leaders, simplified declassification procedures, or even a few studied "leaks." But in some cases the executive branch has apparently yielded to the temptation to withhold testimony (and dam up "leakages") merely to avoid embarrass-

---

[32] Sec. 533A of the Mutual Security Act of 1954 as amended (in 1959) provides: "(d) . . . all documents, papers, communications, audits, reviews, findings, recommendations, reports, and other material which relate to the operation or activities of the Office of Inspector General and Comptroller shall be furnished to the General Accounting Office and to any committee of the Congress . . . upon request. . . ." This has been unofficially interpreted in the IGC as subject to the usual "executive privilege" of classifying and withholding from public inspection documents or information if such communication would be inconsistent with the national interest.

ment.[33] Evaluation reports dealing with the performance of over-seas missions have also been withheld, at least temporarily, in spite of their obvious usefulness to Congress.

Congress is capable of severe retaliation against executive secretiveness. In one extreme case, after repeated requests for an official evaluation of U.S. Operations Missions in Laos and Viet-Nam had been rejected, Congress voted to cut off funds from any foreign aid program on which such information was refused. This episode originated when Congressman Porter Hardy wrote to the Director of ICA on July 24, 1959, calling attention to a provision of the Mutual Security Act of 1959 which explicitly prohibited the withholding of any report.[34] The Director replied, on August 5, that this law did not "amend the Constitution of the United States," citing the President's statement on signing the Mutual Security Act of 1959 that that law "cannot alter the recognized constitutional duty and power of the Executive with respect to the disclosure of information. . . . Indeed, any other construction of these [provisions] . . . would raise grave constitutional questions under the historic Separation of Powers Doctrine." One month later Congress joined the issue directly by threatening to withhold funds unless the President personally forbade disclosure of the requested documents, and in December President Eisenhower capitulated by releasing a slightly edited version of the report. Seldom has Congress so openly, or so successfully, intervened between the President and his principal officers.

The nature and volume of congressional inquiries impose a heavy burden upon foreign aid administrators. It has been reliably estimated that one-third of the time of all ICA personnel, both in Washington and overseas, was spent preparing materials for

[33] Harold Stassen was accused of withholding information to avoid embarrassment when he laid down rules ordering Foreign Operations Administration employees not to submit to interviews by staff members of a Senate subcommittee except when he or his lawyers were present. The issue was raised by Senator Symington's inquiry as to why the highest bidder (from among five competitors) won an FOA contract to build three grain storage elevators in Pakistan. Russell Baker, in *The New York Times*, April 1, 1955.

[34] Sec. 533A (d) authorizes charging the costs of the IGC to mutual security programs, provided that all reports be made available to proper congressional agencies upon request. Sec. 534 (b) provides more directly that all communications relating to ICA shall be furnished to proper congressional agencies upon request.

presentation to Congress. One schedule of mutual security hearings called for thirty-two separate appearances by key officials between February 17 and March 25, 1960, and most of these involved several staff members and extensive preparation. Even in the field missions, substantial amounts of time have been given over to congressional and other official visits. When Representative Otto Passman visited Viet-Nam for two days in September 1958, the aid mission devoted 328 man-days to preparing staff papers and making other arrangements. During fiscal years 1958 and 1959, there were 1,123 official visits to Viet-Nam (mostly, however, by representatives of the executive branch, as shown in Table 3). Collecting and processing information is a relentless obligation of aid administrations, and one which may override other obligations directly connected with the implementation and success of American policy.

Table 3

Official Visits to Viet-Nam, 1958 and 1959

Visitors	Number	Number of Days
Congressmen	28	121
Congressmen's wives	6	28
Congressional Staff Aides	30	155
Executive Branch Visitors to Embassy	146	545
Executive Branch Visitors to USIS	62	156
Executive Branch Visitors to USOM	211	1,055
Executive Branch Visitors to MAAG	640	1,615
	1,123	3,675

Source: U.S. Operations Mission, Viet-Nam.

Initiating New Programs

Congress has on occasion been solely responsible for important changes in the scope and procedures of foreign aid. Through the legislative process Congress has directly participated in designing programs, determining country allocations, and administering projects. It was at the suggestion of the Senate that $100 million was added to the program in fiscal year 1952 for aid to Spain, and in both 1953 and 1954 Congress increased aid appropriations for Taiwan; at the other end of the political spectrum, an amendment in 1956 withheld all aid from Yugoslavia. Programs and administration have been repeatedly changed by congressional initiative; more than seventy of such changes occurred in the 1959 legislation alone. Congress originated the provision requiring the use of American vessels for one-half of all aid shipments; the Kem Amendment cut off aid to countries shipping materials of potential military value to the Communists; the Richards Amendment was designed to withhold aid from certain countries not participating in the European Defense Community; and the Kersten Amendment of 1951 provided $100 million for the benefit of escapees from iron-curtain countries.

The mutual security laws contain exhortations added by Congress favoring the promotion of free enterprise, nonrecognition of Red China, and the liberation of captive peoples. Congress once attempted to bring about the termination of "development assistance" by June 30, 1955; the Mansfield Amendment required the executive branch to report annually on its progress in phasing out aid in each country; and Congress initiated the requirement that all engineering and other planning be completed before any fund obligations or contracting could take place on any part of a major project.[35]

Congress has also introduced positive innovations in foreign aid practice. The use of agricultural surpluses as a means of augmenting aid was conceived jointly by Congress and the Department of Agriculture; congressional initiative lay behind the transition from

[35] This engineering requirement appeared in the Mutual Security Act of 1958 as a new Sec. 517, amending the basic Act of 1954. It provided that no project aid commitments in excess of $100,000 could be made until all important technical or financial planning had been completed, a "reasonably firm estimate of the cost" was available, and any necessary legislative action had been taken by the recipient country or might "reasonably be anticipated ... within one year." This provision was intended to reduce the lag between the appropriation of funds and their use, on the theory that ICA would not obligate funds until the projects were ready, a process which would keep aid appropriations closely adjusted to actual projects. No one claimed that Sec. 517 would save time or money. Local missions seemed to believe that its rigidity would at least afford them an excuse to delay dubious projects; but, they also pointed out that in practice major construction projects in unsurveyed territories could not be based on a "reasonably firm estimate of the cost" in advance of actual construction operations. (For an unexpected use of Sec. 517 to compel a government industry to change its rate structure, see pp. 120–121, above.)

a "balance-of-payments" to a "project" basis in the determination of aid levels; and finally, Congress provided the initial impetus for establishing the Development Loan Fund, the International Development Association of the World Bank, and the Office of the Inspector General and Comptroller of Mutual Security. These creative functions of Congress have been much less publicized than those of finding fault with a bureaucracy engaged in the somewhat suspect, if not downright unpopular, task of spending American tax money abroad.

Expediting Favored Projects

Congressmen have influenced foreign aid policies and administration in their individual as well as their collective capacities. Where constituents' interests are involved, congressmen are unexcelled as expediters. On one occasion ICA in Washington had repeatedly declined to approve the importing of surplus cheese and butter into Viet-Nam; finally, in response to a request for intercession from an American importer in Saigon, Senator Alexander Wiley of Wisconsin sprang into prompt and effective action. The call to arms to which he responded read in part: "You [would] . . . think that agriculture surplus is in short supply. Instead of using every opportunity to ship agricultural surplus to this country [Viet-Nam], [ICA] seems to think that [it] . . . is sitting not on the golden butter of Wisconsin, but on the gold of Fort Knox." In a matter of weeks American butter began to appear legally and in quantity in Viet-Nam.

Individual senators and congressmen sometimes become so closely involved with the fortunes of a particular country receiving aid that facetious references are made to "the Senator from Formosa" or "the Representative from Spain." By developing a special knowledge of Indo-China, for example, Senator Mansfield was able to influence American policy at decisive moments, and perhaps to change the course of Southeast Asian history. In 1953, after the fighting stopped in Korea, and the Chinese Communists had begun to increase the flow of military supplies to Ho Chi Minh, Mansfield strongly supported the policy of extending military aid to the French as a means of restraining "the Communist advance in Southeast Asia."[36] At the same time he urged the

[36] *Indochina*, Report by Senator Mike Mansfield for the Senate Committee on Foreign Relations, 83d Cong., 1st sess. (Washington: GPO, 1953), p. 6.

French (unsuccessfully) to make greater concessions to nationalist forces. After the fall of Dien Bien Phu and the partition of Viet-Nam at Geneva, Mansfield noted that U.S. foreign policy had "suffered a serious reversal," not because of inadequate arms support—quite the contrary—but because of the absence of "a sound political substructure," necessary for the effective employment of military aid already supplied.[37]

Viet-Nam's primary need was clearly a strong, unifying force which, in Mansfield's judgment, could most probably be supplied by Ngo Dinh Diem. But the Senator was forced to report that rival Vietnamese leaders south of the 17th Parallel were engaged in "quasi-suicidal political maneuvering and strife." While the United States was ready to offer Diem strong backing, the French were opposed to him, largely because of his intense, intractable nationalism. Fearful of the consequences of French efforts to weaken Vietnamese self-reliance, Mansfield warned: "In the event that the Diem government falls, . . . I believe that the United States should consider an immediate suspension of all aid to Vietnam and the French Union Forces there, except that of a humanitarian nature, preliminary to a complete reappraisal of our present policies in Free Vietnam."[38] This recommendation was communicated to the State Department officials who were then negotiating with a special French mission in Washington.

The French mission's opposition to the Diem regime collapsed in the face of State Department assurances that there would be no substantial aid for Viet-Nam unless Senator Mansfield gave wholehearted support. A few months later, however, French officials urged the American ambassador in Saigon to recommend abandoning Diem. Once more Mansfield firmly supported the State Department in its efforts to back the Vietnamese nationalists; and in the spring of 1955, when the French made their final effort to dismiss Diem, Mansfield spoke to the Senate in urgent tones, stating that our "national interests with respect to Vietnam can be furthered only if our policies serve to lead to a Vietnamese Government which is independent and which can put down solid roots in the Vietnamese populace." Even "France will not really

[37] *Report on Indochina,* by Senator Mike Mansfield for the Senate Committee on Foreign Relations, 83d Cong., 2d sess. (Washington: GPO, 1954), pp. 1, 6.
[38] Same, p. 14.

gain," he concluded, by destroying Diem and setting up a "coalition of the corrupt under a thin veneer of respectability."[39]

William Henderson later reported as one of Diem's achievements that he finally "got rid of the French," who had "continued to intrigue with the sects, to which they had given extensive economic and military support . . . ; and [whose] covert propaganda against Diem at times reached savage proportions. . . . At the height of the Binh Xuyen crisis in April 1955 Premier Faure openly tried to torpedo Diem. He gave up only when events in Saigon outran his policy and after the United States, overcoming grave apprehensions of its own, decided to continue its support of Diem."[40] When Senator Mansfield returned to Viet-Nam late in 1955, he observed that Diem had developed a satisfactory degree of political loyalty as well as institutions that could serve as "the nucleus of a government responsive to the people of Viet Nam."[41] In these achievements it is unquestionable that the Senator's intervention was an essential element.

Subsequent events illustrated the danger of permitting any lapse in relations between the executive branch and an influential legislator. Senator Mansfield, satisfied that the Diem government could survive, now began to turn his attention to the "long-range question of national development." He found that the existing aid program, dominated by military and emergency considerations, was not well adapted to this purpose: it was importing goods that "often fall in the luxury category and appear peculiarly out of place in a situation as serious as that which exists in Viet Nam," and its "crash basis . . . has undoubtedly resulted in a haphazard, wasteful, and ineffective" operation. What was needed, he concluded, was "a special group along the lines of the Bell Mission to the Philippines in 1950, to survey the present economic difficulties in Viet Nam and the functions of the aid program with respect thereto." Already concerned about the possibility of diminishing returns in foreign aid, even to the point of considering a terminal date for the whole program, he argued that the United States should begin devoting serious attention to reducing and eventually

[39] *Congressional Record*, v. 101, pt. 4, May 2, 1955, p. 5289.
[40] "South Viet Nam Finds Itself," *Foreign Affairs*, January 1957, p. 289.
[41] *Viet Nam, Cambodia, and Laos*, Report by Senator Mike Mansfield for the Senate Committee on Foreign Relations, 84th Cong., 1st sess. (Washington: GPO, 1955), p. 3.

terminating aid to Viet-Nam on the ground that a measure of stability had already been achieved.[42]

The executive branch took strong exception to this proposal. According to military and diplomatic observers wary of the maneuvers between Ho Chi Minh and Mao Tse-tung, the military threat to Viet-Nam's survival was by no means at an end, nor could internal stability be achieved without continued large-scale American assistance; moreover, if economic development planning was to be undertaken jointly with the sensitive, sovereignty-conscious Diem, they argued that the job could be done by the existing ICA staff with more effect and less friction than by a special temporary mission from the United States.

The administration never directly explained its point of view to Senator Mansfield, who, finding his recommendations unaccountably ignored once the emergency had subsided, became increasingly critical of the administration's performance in Viet-Nam and elsewhere. His doubts finally led him to recommend the virtual abandonment of ICA and Defense Department missions and the merger of their functions with those of the permanent diplomatic agencies.[43] He favored "recasting the foreign aid program in a fashion which will gain for it a greater measure of acceptance among the peoples of this nation and among recipient peoples abroad."[44] By the summer of 1959 when the Colegrove "exposé" of the Viet-Nam program suddenly burst upon Washington, the administration found that its erstwhile supporter in the Senate was no longer available as a shield against the enemies of foreign aid.

3. THE VIET-NAM "SCANDAL": A CASE STUDY IN CONGRESSIONAL RELATIONSHIPS

The 1959 hearings on aid to Viet-Nam offered the severest test to Vietnamese-American relations since the Geneva Conference in 1954. Arising out of a sensational journalistic attack and conducted in an atmosphere of cynicism and suspicion, the hearings left a trail of unresolved innuendoes, indecisive charges and countercharges, and administrative paralysis. Almost every congressional misgiving about foreign aid appeared to be confirmed; but, at least

[42] Same, pp. 10, 14.
[43] Letter to Secretary Dulles, cited in *The New York Times*, April 17, 1955.
[44] Rowland Evans, in the *New York Herald Tribune*, June 2, 1959.

the need for a new and stronger leadership in American aid diplomacy was irrefutably established.

The articles that occasioned the hearings appeared in eighteen newspapers of the Scripps-Howard syndicate, representing a total circulation of more than two and one-half million. Under the title "Our Hidden Scandal in Viet Nam," Albert M. Colegrove wrote six articles exploiting a public interest in American programs in Southeast Asia already stimulated by the publication of *The Ugly American*[45] and the beginning of the annual authorization hearings in both houses. The articles could hardly have been better timed. Scripps-Howard could be credited with a journalistic "scoop," although clearly no Pulitzer prize would be forthcoming for accurate reporting and public service.[46]

Colegrove charged waste, corruption, bad judgment, and incompetence on the part of both Americans and Vietnamese, and he flavored his articles with brief anecdotes that managed to convey the appearance of circumstantial evidence. Most of his evidence related to emergency projects conceived under the stress of the Indochinese war or to housing and other perquisites available to American personnel. The account made lurid reading. No public representative interested in upholding the American virtues of honesty, efficiency, and economy could fail to express horror at the conditions suggested by the "exposé."

The congressional reaction was all that a publisher could hope for. Subcommittees of both houses immediately started hearings: the House Subcommittee on the Far East and the Pacific began on July 27, and the Senate Subcommittee on State Department Organization and Public Affairs, on July 30. From Viet-Nam the American ambassador, the chief of the Military Assistance Advisory Group, and the director of the U.S. Operations Mission all flew to Washington to testify. The House subcommittee heard fifteen witnesses, the Senate seven. The issues were no longer the property of Scripps-Howard and its readers, but of the nation.

[45] William J. Lederer and Eugene Burdick's *The Ugly American* (New York: Norton, 1958) had by then sold 150,000 copies in book form, as well as being presented serially to the 5,700,000 readers of *The Saturday Evening Post*. For a thoroughgoing critique, see Joseph Buttinger, "Fact and Fiction on Foreign Aid," *Dissent*, Summer 1959.

[46] For an analysis of the factual basis and emotional tone of the six articles, see Appendix III.

The Hearings in Washington

The House subcommittee began its hearings with administration witnesses and ended with Mr. Colegrove. The results were indecisive; after the administration denied the charges point by point, Colegrove reaffirmed them, and the subcommittee members finally professed themselves unable to choose between the two incompatible versions. Representative Meyer suggested that "our committee actually should have its own independent staff . . . in the field" because "we rely too much entirely on the words and reports of the State Department and naturally, as Mr. Colegrove says in his report, they are going to paint it for us the way they want it painted,"[47] and Representative Judd agreed that official testimony would not convince critics of the program.[48] Indeed, six days of such official testimony failed to lay the suspicions of the House to rest.

Although duplicating most of the material presented in the House, the Senate subcommittee hearings were somewhat more compact and orderly; moreover, the inquiry was pressed to issues more basic than those raised by Colegrove. Senator Mansfield attempted to set the tone of the questioning by suggesting "five principal lines of exploration" relating to the program in Viet-Nam: the sense of purpose, the administrative integration and efficiency, the wisdom of project designs, the size and adequacy of the staff, and the mode of American life in Saigon;[49] but the hearings did not follow any such logical pattern. Mr. Colegrove reiterated his charges before the Senate group and added several new ones. He had avoided consulting the ambassador and the directors of the military and ICA missions during his nineteen-day, information-gathering stay in Saigon, he explained, because from them he "would get the official line" rather than the facts.[50] The administration witnesses then made categorical denials of the charges, their vehemence matching that of the original articles:

[47] *Current Situation in the Far East*, Hearings before a subcommittee of the House Committee on Foreign Affairs, 86th Cong., 1st sess., August 14, 1959 (Washington: GPO, 1959), p. 256.

[48] Same, p. 277.

[49] *Situation in Vietnam*, Hearings before a subcommittee of the Senate Committee on Foreign Relations, 86th Cong., 1st sess., July 30, 1959 (Washington: GPO, 1959), pt. 1, pp. 3–4.

[50] Same, pp. 77–78.

"no such scandals," "simply not true," "a most inaccurate statement," "incorrect," "reckless, sweeping charges," "in the range of fantasy." The director of the ICA mission and others expressed themselves on the validity of Colegrove's methods in similarly unequivocal language: "Had he taken the trouble to check these stories. . . ."; "Mr. Colegrove would have verified this fact by a direct inquiry. . . ."; ". . . had Mr. Colegrove desired to see these towers they would have been shown to him"; "Mr Colegrove, unfortunately, has not been thorough in his analysis of the phosphate fertilizer business. . . ."; and, almost summing up the criticism, "Mr. Colegrove should have done a more thorough job. . . ." The testimony of the ambassador and other high officials was peppered with specific denials of the Colegrove reports. That of the chief of the Military Assistance Advisory Group was above such denials, however; the military program had not been attacked in Colegrove's articles.[51]

The senators, like their colleagues in the House, showed a remarkable reluctance to accept the word of the ambassador and of ICA officials. As Senator Capehart expressed it: "I have no way of knowing . . . who is right and who is wrong"; his general distrust of public officials was revealed in his suggestion that if "private industry [had been] . . . given the contract to do the job over there" and more businesslike procedures had been followed, there would be less basis for criticism. Senator Lausche stated: "We ought . . . to send our representatives there and ascertain the truth," implying that the witnesses on both sides were suspect.

Most senators drew from the hearings only confirmation of previous beliefs, finding small basis for new conclusions. Senator Mansfield inquired into the exchange rate, the problem of delays caused by possibly excessive control from Washington, and the possible effects of the Colegrove articles on relations with the Vietnamese; but he agreed to the need for more facts on which to base a judgment, ignoring most of the new evidence made available in answer to Colegrove's allegations. Senator Morse addressed himself to the question of executive privilege, defined as an attempt "to invoke a government by secrecy upon a free people," although he was unable when challenged to mention an instance in which a congressional request for information had been denied,

[51] Same, pp. 4–6, 9, 10–21, 55.

except for the country evaluation reports.[52] Expressing himself as
dissatisfied with the results of the hearings ("just saying 'it ain't
so' doesn't prove it ain't so"), Morse defended Colegrove as one
"newspaperman against the crowd" and demanded an investigation
in Saigon exercising powers of subpoena.

Senator Mansfield resumed his questioning in a sharper vein,
revealing at several points that he still regretted the administration's rejection of his earlier proposal to send a special survey team
to Viet-Nam.[53] The subsequent discussion brought a revealing
insight into relations between the ambassador and the chief of the
Military Assistance Advisory Group, incidentally involving an
open disagreement in their testimony:[54]

> Senator MANSFIELD. Mr. Ambassador, Congress has stated in
> law, and the President, I believe, has stressed on occasion, the need
> for a single voice in speaking on foreign policy. Presumably that
> voice in Vietnam belongs to the Ambassador; is that correct?
> Mr. DURBROW. Correct
> Senator MANSFIELD. Have you, as Ambassador, ever directed
> the MAAG group to pursue or to refrain from pursuing a particular
> military aid project?
> Mr. DURBROW. Yes. We discussed various military aid proj-
> ects and made recommendations.
> Sometimes General Williams does not agree with them. We
> bring these back here and have them coordinated in Washington.
> Senator MANSFIELD. Could you give us one example or could
> you furnish one for the record?
> Mr. DURBROW. I would prefer to do it in executive session,
> if I may, sir.

[52] Although the evaluation reports as such were withheld, the actual raw
data that went into them were always available to the subcommittee. The
classified reports, prepared jointly by representatives of the State Department
and of ICA (usually a former mission director), were originally made available
only to some twenty-five interested members of the executive branch. Because
the reports were intended to set forth without any restraint "direct, candid
views," it is clear that they were strictly internal memoranda unsuitable for
publication in any form. Eventually the report on Viet-Nam, edited slightly,
was made available to members of the subcommittee.

[53] For all these statements, see *Situation in Vietnam*, Hearings, 1959, cited,
pp. 79, 92–95, 104, 111, 129, 136–137, 139, 152, 169–176.

[54] A minor difference occurring earlier had been passed over without comment when the ambassador described the suggestion that the army theater be
opened to Vietnamese nationals as "a very fine thing to do," and General
Williams opposed it entirely. Same, pp. 166, 167.

General WILLIAMS. Mr. Chairman, would you mind reading that question once more, please, sir?

Senator MANSFIELD. Have you, as Ambassador, ever directed the MAAG group to pursue or to refrain from pursuing a particular military aid project?

General WILLIAMS. The answer to that is "No."

Mr. DURBROW. I guess you are right on that.

Senator MANSFIELD. The answer is "No"?

Mr. DURBROW. What I meant to say was that in discussing various matters affecting MAAG, I have recommended things that I did not think were within policy guidance, and we have come back to Washington here to ask for coordination on that.

Senator MANSFIELD. Now, the answer to that question is "No."[55]

It was clear, as some had predicted from the outset, that congressional hearings in Saigon could scarcely be avoided.

The Saigon Hearings

In November and December, members of the House subcommittee and three senators representing the Senate Foreign Relations Committee held additional hearings in Viet-Nam which gave rise to incidents that bewildered and even distressed the Vietnamese. Representative Pilcher, reportedly offended at not having been met by either American or Vietnamese dignitaries at the airport (his plane having arrived slightly ahead of schedule), declined to attend any official functions, including a reception given by the President of Viet-Nam. Although the hearings were conducted in "executive session," Senator Gore apparently indulged in widely publicized "leaks" to a Scripps-Howard reporter which constituted an attack on the integrity of the USOM director. Since this official had been excused from the hearings, he was unaware of the charges made against him—which, incidentally, were false, as Senator Gore later conceded in an appendix to the report of the hearings.[56] The Scripps-Howard newspapers, three of which were in the Senator's home state of Tennessee, did not report Gore's retraction and apology.

The hearings in Saigon, which took place four months after those in Washington, were conducted by Senators Gore, McGee,

[55] Same, p. 183.
[56] *Situation in Vietnam*, Hearings, cited, pt. 2 (1960), pp. 366–367.

and Hickenlooper, and by Representatives Pilcher, McDowell, Fascell, Church, Curtis, and Judd. Limited to short question-and-answer sessions with American officials, the hearings held to no systematic agenda and yielded no consistent and coherent evidence. No final conclusions were drawn; indeed, it appears that the senators disagreed sharply over what the hearings had established.[57] While Senator Gore remained critical, Senator McGee later took pains to deny publicly newspaper stories that he had attacked the program on grounds of waste and inefficiency. "Quite the contrary," he wrote, "what I saw in Vietnam was the most exciting and imaginative of any program we examined around the world."[58]

The hearings devoted little time to the Colegrove charges, which had been generally discredited by the staff work preceding the arrival of the senators and representatives. The subject most discussed was supervision over construction (occupying thirty-nine pages in the transcript). The second most important issue, judging by its persistence through seventeen pages of the record, was the deep freezers and other furnishings in the USOM director's house, following by the use of vehicles in (and out of) the motor pool (fourteen pages); import taxes, coordination and control of the aid program, audit of counterpart funds and Vietnamese import taxes, and procurement procedures each occupied about the same portion of space (eleven pages); finally, bidding procedures and engineering fees (ten pages) and the exchange rate (seven pages) were also discussed. None of these subjects had played a significant role in either the Colegrove articles or the Washington hearings.

The general tone of the hearings was more querulous in Viet-Nam than in Washington. Senator Gore's investigation included strongly implied criticisms of seeming irregularities. The congressmen were generally impatient, and occasionally sarcastic, when witnesses attempted to give long and comprehensive answers, even when such answers were a response to unclear or irrelevant questions.[59] On occasion, off-the-cuff advice was given to the Viet-

[57] *The Christian Science Monitor*, December 18, 1959. Cf. *New York World-Telegram and Sun*, December 11, 1959.

[58] *The Reporter*, December 24, 1959, p. 6, and February 18, 1960, p. 11.

[59] *Situation in Vietnam*, Hearings, cited, pt. 2, pp. 247 and 248, 285–286, 334.

namese government as well as to American officials: "I hope that the Vietnamese Government will realize the gravity of [any] refusal of cooperation," said Senator Gore. "This is an action of mutuality. Obligations fall upon the part of both governments. I want to see our Government perform its obligation and responsibility and I would hope for reciprocal action on the part of the Vietnamese Government."[60]

The reports of both congressional missions cited numerous shortcomings; but also, perhaps surprisingly, they commended the Viet-Nam program in general. Three principal criticisms emerged from the hearings: procedures for bringing engineering and construction firms to Viet-Nam on contract were slow and costly, in part because of long-distance Washington controls; the government of Viet-Nam had refused to permit an audit of the indirect aid derived from import taxes levied on Commercial Import Program commodities; and finally, there was some looseness in the coordination of the country team and in administrative controls over the use of vehicles.[61]

Report of the Senate Subcommittee

When the final report of the Senate subcommittee appeared, a much higher level of criticism was evident; in fact, scant attention was paid to the many trivial matters discussed in the hearings. Senator Mansfield and his staff were the principal authors of the report, and they clearly had access to material hitherto unexploited, including a version of the original ICA evaluation report made available at the last moment. The subcommittee called its inquiry "a case study" of the type suggested in 1957 by a Special Committee to Study the Foreign Aid Program. It explained that while Viet-Nam had been chosen because of the Colegrove articles, such journalistic reports "do not generally lend themselves to proof or disproof by a legislative body."[62] In consequence, the

[60] Same, p. 257.

[61] Same, pp. 238ff, 285–305, 345–349; *Report of the Special Study Mission to Asia, Western Pacific, Middle East, Southern Europe and North Africa,* H. Report 1386, for the House Committee on Foreign Affairs, 86th Cong., 2d sess. (Washington: GPO, 1960).

[62] *United States Aid Program in Vietnam,* Report by a subcommittee of the Senate Committee on Foreign Relations, 86th Cong., 2d sess. (Washington: GPO, 1960), p. 5.

study was concerned with a "larger problem" than the issues presented in the newspaper "allegations."

The report dealt with many of the key issues of American aid: the respective usefulness of grants and loans; the problem of continuity of direction; the adequacy of the ambassador's authority; administrative simplification; the techniques of administering project and nonproject aid; "the American presence"; and the purposes and direction of the program. Senator Mansfield's views were conspicuous in the recommendations for more attention to the reduction and termination of grants and for strengthening the Secretary of State's role, and for stimulating at the same time greater initiative in the field at the expense of ICA in Washington. The executive branch was urged to revive the issue of the Vietnamese exchange rate and to consider a novel (if somewhat obscure) proposal to change "the present indirect system of financing Vietnamese imports by aid dollars, to one of supplying directly a substantial part of the requisite aid commodities in the fashion of Public Law 480." In effect, this proposal would have made the federal government a purchasing agent for all items supplied under U.S. aid to Viet-Nam, as it already was for surplus agricultural commodities. Some of the recommendations were merely hortatory: to make decisions and stick by them "despite criticism from one quarter or another"; to lighten the burdens of the "American presence" by improving "language and cultural training systems" and making efforts to scale down pay, allowances, and perquisites of overseas personnel; and even that "Congress . . . be prepared to forbear . . . occasional mistakes."[63] The report, though directed to the Senate Committee on Foreign Relations, also contained many injunctions to the executive branch.

There was no evidence that any senatorial opinions of the program had been significantly affected by the hearings in Washington or in Saigon. Those concerned with economic planning, program coordination, or eventual withdrawal all found vindication for their points of view; those who had found foreign aid incompatible with the free enterprise system continued to do so; those most interested in appealing to a mass audience found foreign aid as convenient a target as had Albert Colegrove. While the final report was constructive in outlook, it must be said that

[63] Same, pp. 3–5.

in this whole affair the processes of congressional hearings reinforced existing opinions and prejudices more than they contributed to enlightenment.

The Effects in Viet-Nam

In Saigon these events had the explosive effect of a series of Viet-Cong bombs. The publication of the first Colegrove article had occasioned great excitement in the American community; mimeographed transcripts and photo-offsets of the black headlines made their rounds of the city for many weeks. Top officials set aside other activities and hunted through the files for evidence relating to the charges; the ambassador and the chiefs of USOM and MAAG personally devoted three days to analyzing the charges and preparing replies; few important decisions could be made in Saigon during the three weeks that followed publication. A pile of cables several inches high was sent to Washington to brief ICA for the inevitable congressional inquiries. Even after the three key Americans had flown to Washington the excitement remained, and the mimeograph machines continued to turn out summaries of the hearings.

The Vietnamese government was distinctly offended by the articles. President Diem himself declined to comment directly on the inquiry, but he stated he "would fail in my responsibility as a human being towards our American friends who have been attacked wrongly for carelessness, if I did not say that, in my opinion, American aid has been extremely effective. Indeed, it is for that very reason that our common enemies—and they include others in addition to the Communists, of course—are concentrating their efforts on the aid question." He emphasized that while the U.S. government had the right to investigate the program, "my government, like that of the United States, is sovereign and does not permit any interference in our internal affairs."[64]

The press in Viet-Nam also resented Colegrove's attack. Even the English-language *Times of Viet Nam*, generally critical of American aid, objected to the tone and most of the allegations of the articles: on July 29, 1959, an editorial answered a few of the charges "which were the most insidious and/or patently false";

[64] Wesley R. Fishel, "Vietnam President Sees Laos as First Step in Red Campaign," *N.A.N.A. Special* (Saigon), August 31, 1959.

three days later, another editorial confessed itself "astounded by that man's ability to rake up mud in complete disregard for truthfulness and decency"; and a final editorial (entitled "Colegrove's Politico-Economic Weltanschauung") attacked the reporter's neo-colonial assumptions about American influence over Viet-Nam. Other opinion in Viet-Nam was equally vigorous. An article entitled "Une Tempête dans un Verre d'Eau," appearing in *Extrême Asie* on September 5, referred to the series as "Le plus beau cadeau que La Radio de Hå-Nôi ait reçu depuis longtemps," quoting a government official to that effect. In a piece called "Myopic Muck-raking Beclouds Aid Report," Fr. Raymond J. DeJaegher observed that "by wantonly perverting the authentic, Mr. Colegrove grossly insulted two groups: the Vietnamese, whose country he visited and disdained to look at, and his fellow countrymen. . . ."[65]

Repercussions in the United States and elsewhere convinced the Vietnamese that the Scripps-Howard publications carried weight. A department store in Cincinnati canceled orders resulting from a display of Vietnamese handicraft on the ground that there was a conflict between the American and Vietnamese governments. The American Friends of Vietnam, a private organization devoted to nothing more insidious than promoting a particular phase of international amity, reported that three members of its national committee resigned immediately after the Colegrove articles had appeared. Public contributions for a major conference it organized in October 1959, three months after the hearings, were only half those donated for a less important affair staged two months before Colegrove.

The Communist radio broadcasts took up the articles with understandable glee. On August 2, Radio Moscow broadcast in Vietnamese that the "scandal" had at last been "revealed" to the point where "the Senate Foreign Relations Committee has been obliged to open a special investigation." True, the broadcast continued, "the committee did not reach any decision. . . . They could not refuse to finance Ngo Dinh Diem because the United States needs South Vietnam as a military base. Hence their acquiescence in U.S. aid to a bunch of embezzling rowdies. . . . the United States is ready to support any rotten regime in order to

[65] *Free Front*, July 1959.

hold fast to dependent countries." A similar denunciation was issued by Peking's New China News Agency and from Hanoi, capital of Communist North Viet-Nam, came a steady stream of broadcasts citing the articles as proof of American imperialism and South Vietnamese knavery. The press of North Viet-Nam joined heartily in the exploitation of Colegrove's "exposé."[66]

Even in Burma, which seldom displayed public interest in news from Viet-Nam, a high official in the Ministry of Planning told the writer that, while willing to have American technicians invited to Burma, "we want decent chaps, not the kind they have in Viet-Nam. And if any American businessmen are brought here on ICA contracts, let them be firms with no Asian experience or familiarity with the techniques of palm-greasing."

The need for informing Congress about the central problems of development and execution of policy in Viet-Nam obviously was not satisfied by these hearings, partly because they placed the administration in a defensive position. While some of the administration's problems were of its own making—the lack of an aggressive leadership, the willful ignoring of legitimate congressional attitudes, a defensive and sometimes resentful posture before committees, and a scarcely concealed conviction of congressional ignorance—others had been thrust upon it by members of Congress and were subject to correction by more statesmanlike congressional action. But such action would not be forthcoming without the exercise of greater understanding and forbearance on both sides than had been evidenced in the immediate past.

4. The Case for Political Leadership

What continuity there is in American foreign aid programing has been more a function of bureaucratic perseverance than a result of deliberate policy. The absence of a political consensus has produced a vacillating and unpredictable program of operations, damaged the morale of foreign aid personnel, and encouraged widespread public acceptance of irrelevant or ill-founded views and judgments on foreign aid aired in the press and in the popular literature. The fact of administrative continuity has been

[66] Hanoi, radio broadcasts, July 23, August 1, August 14, November 6, 7, 10, 12, December 12, 1959. See also *Current Situation in the Far East,* Hearings, 1959, cited, pp. 337–338.

insufficient to arrest a deterioration in the effectiveness of the vast aid program to which the United States appears to be so reluctantly committed. The somewhat mechanical performance that has resulted has brought about a significant decline in international respect for America's role as a leading power and a questioning of the sincerity of the humanitarian gestures and political ideals which are a part of our approach to the world.

The remedy does not lie in the suppression of irresponsible criticism, even if this were possible in a democratic society. Mere criticism need not paralyze the functioning and threaten the very existence of a program of such importance. Nor is it inevitable that foreign aid must be, as President Eisenhower once described it, "the most misunderstood of any of the Federal Government's activities."[67] Clarification of national purposes as a prelude to the strengthening of the will to achieve them can provide a sufficient protection against these disabilities.

Political leadership must come from the President, the party chieftains, and Congress. The exercise of dramatic authority by the President cannot in itself resolve all of these problems, although it is clear that no national consensus is likely to develop without it. Both parties must restrain their appetites for spoils appointments, while the President must resolve to make exceptionally well-qualified appointments in foreign operations and afford them strong and continuing support. There are also important areas in which congressional performance can be improved, entirely apart from the exercise of presidential prerogatives.

Outstanding congressmen have, of course, been able to surmount the routines of their office and the difficulties of asserting congressional leadership in foreign aid, but the task has been immense and the rewards minor. The trivia that dominate public hearings, the preoccupation with sensations, the shortage of good staff, and imperfect liaison with the executive branch have prevented efficient legislative performance either in the passage of strong and timely laws or in the oversight of administrative operations. Major improvements in American aid diplomacy probably cannot take place without drastic revisions in congressional procedures, organization, and staffing.

[67] Quoted in Richard P. Stebbins, *The United States in World Affairs, 1957* (New York: Harper, 1958), p. 65.

The most important procedural change necessary for the development of a stable foreign aid policy relates to the authorization and appropriation of funds. The fourfold congressional obstacle course through which the agencies must pass each year not only occupies much more time than would be required for funding the program on a long-term basis, but also contributes to confusion when inconsistent views are developed in the various committees or at different times. Then authorization, even by an impressive majority, is not proof against substantial cuts at appropriation time; the Appropriations Committees, charged with different responsibilities and bringing to bear a new series of prejudices, can make deep cuts in the program before recommending it to Congress. On occasion these cuts are arbitrary responses to incidents of small relevance to program needs. In 1956, for example, some committee members were angered by the discovery that the Defense Department had obligated over $700 million for military aid on June 30, the last day of the fiscal year. Although this action was taken only to earmark the funds for approved projects, thus avoiding the laborious process of rescheduling the expenditures in the next fiscal year, exaggerated congressional reactions resulted in one of the most drastic program reductions in recent years.[68]

Theoretically the best solution would be for Congress to authorize foreign aid on a permanent or long-term basis, permitting the committees dealing with foreign affairs to concentrate on the general oversight of operations. Even if the Appropriations Committees declined to forgo the panoply of annual hearings, this proposal would eliminate the annual repetition of executive branch pleas for authorizing legislation and relieve the administration of a large part of its burden. The administration would be freed of the obligation to devise new justifications every year for the same operations, a course which is self-defeating and counterproductive. The enforced search for new ideas in the justification and rationale for foreign aid is fruitless: wise continuity is needed more than glittering novelty.

The hostility of the Appropriations Committees to foreign aid perhaps explains the reluctance of the executive branch to elimi-

[68] *The New York Times*, July 13 and 23, 1955, and the editorial, July 10, 1955.

nate the relatively friendly influence of the Foreign Relations and
Foreign Affairs Committees' annual hearings by seeking a permanent authorization for the 1961 Act for International Development. Political solutions to this problem are possible, however:
the defeat of the administration's Treasury financing approach in
1961, like those of the past, may have resulted from too direct an
assault on the appropriations process. Eliminating the annual
authorization hearings would still leave the present appropriations
cycle intact, with the possibility that joint subcommittee action
with the Foreign Affairs and Foreign Relations Committees could
be arranged. Even if this should fail, there is no reason to believe
that the change would make the Appropriations Committees
wholly irresponsible in spite of some well-founded fears in the
executive branch. Strengthening the information and influence of
Appropriations Committee members who are concerned with
foreign affairs could do as much to offset unfriendly committee
leadership as pitting it against the Foreign Relations and Foreign
Affairs Committees, as at present. Moreover, the continued responsibility of the latter over operations would encourage them to
play the same protective role when appropriations are voted as
they have in the past.

Congressional committees are properly jealous of their prerogatives. The committees concerned with foreign affairs may be
unwilling to leave their annual hearings on foreign aid operations
to the Appropriations Committees, even if the latter were to adopt
a position more favorable to the basic objectives of the program.
But no essential legislative responsibilities would be surrendered
if the number of hearings is reduced, either by creating special
joint committees, or by forgoing the luxury of trying to "second-
guess every administrative action" and instead concentrating upon
"broad questions of policy." These words are Senator Fulbright's,
who recently told the Senate:

> In my judgment, we have already gone so far that we allow our
> policy-making function to suffer and at the same time we seriously
> handicap the administrators of the program. . . . this program cannot
> survive many more annual authorizations. Every year there is a
> steady accretion of new restrictions. . . . The cumulative result of
> these provisions is to make the program so slow and cumbersome as
> to reduce its effectiveness very greatly. When, under these handi-

caps, the program fails to perform as it should, its opponents seize on this as an excuse to add more handicaps.[69]

The issue is not to prevent congressional surveillance but to improve it. Permanent agencies housed in the executive branch can provide detailed information to congressmen, but past experience suggests that the latter tend to rely upon financial audits to the neglect of operational problems and basic policy questions. Additional methods of acquainting congressmen with practical difficulties should be explored, including enlarging congressional staffs and employing more consultants, making greater use of Library of Congress studies, and appointing citizen or mixed citizen-congressional commissions to evaluate the impact of selected aid programs. Congressional responsibilities will also continue to require some personal inspection by members of Congress and their staffs, no matter how momentarily uncomfortable this may be for the agencies involved, for the host government, and for the travelers themselves. Field trips, if they are seriously meant and carefully planned, can be the most eloquent testimony to the importance and the need of foreign aid.

The constitutional separation of powers requires respect for the prerogatives of each branch, and the relationships between the legislative and executive personnel have been more strained over foreign aid policy and operations than good government can tolerate.[70] Congressional initiative and perseverance will be required to lower the barriers that impede ready communication between the two branches. Recently an effort was made to organize "consultative subcommittees" of the committees concerned with foreign affairs, along the functional lines of the State Department, to provide continuous access and consultation between Congress and staff members of the executive branch; but the press of other legislative duties and the absence of concrete questions on which

[69] Statement by Senator Fulbright on Conference Committee report, *Mutual Security Act of 1960*; reprinted in *Congressional Record*, v. 106, pt. 8, May 12, 1960, p. 10146.

[70] On the need for fundamental reconstitution of this relationship, see the writings of W. Y. Elliott, especially in *The Need for Constitutional Reform* (New York: Whittlesey House, 1935), pp. 182–184, 203; *United States Foreign Policy: Its Organization and Control* (New York: Columbia University Press, 1952), pp. 177–193, 257–260; and *The Political Economy of American Foreign Policy* (New York: Holt, 1955), pp. 365–381.

action would be taken discouraged regular meetings, and the institution withered on the vine. The executive has also made intermittent attempts to establish informal relationships, so far without notable success. Probably the initiative for closer co-operation on foreign aid must come from the Congress, since gestures by the executive branch are so easily misinterpreted: for example, the spontaneity of a recent cocktail party given by State Department officials for congressmen was marred by the suspicion —unfounded—that public funds were paying for it.

There are also opportunities at the working administrative levels to improve congressional understanding of foreign aid. The annual effort to justify the program has resulted in a frantic search for new ideas, and occasionally in overselling them. The 1960 presentation offered the new "islands of development" approach, under which U.S. economic aid would be concentrated on Taiwan and India as principal show places of development assistance. The idea was appealing in itself and as a rationale for the fiscal year ahead, but it may prove embarrassing if anticipated progress is not forthcoming. Not all economists would agree that these areas (with Pakistan added for reasons of international politics) are ready for "economic take-off" or that five years of massive aid will stabilize their economies at a high level of production. Another example of administrative "oversell" was a State Department memorandum for congressional use that spoke of Pakistan's "wholehearted and unequivocal support of SEATO and the Baghdad Pact," together with "enthusiastic support of SEATO" from Thailand. The same memorandum attributed "substantial armed forces" to Iran and a "small but reliable" army to Laos.[71] Actually, a plausible case can be made that at that time "Pakistan was a disgruntled ally and Thailand an opportunistic one; the Iranian army had to be supervised by the secret police to prevent it from following the example of the Iraqi army which, briefly before the coup, had been described by the State Department as one of the pillars of stability in Iraq; and the utility of the Lao army for effective combat or internal security functions was highly problematical."[72] Whether or not one accepts the full force of that critique of the State Department's estimate, the worst feature of the memorandum was that military considerations were assumed to be the basic criterion for political and economic support.

Confusion among political, military, and economic purposes remains a major weakness of U.S. foreign aid programs. Past disappointments and disillusionments have contributed to the defensive attitude of the executive branch, which has invited only further distrust and criticism. Economic failures of "defense support" and "special assistance" programs have been allowed to stand as a reproach against the International Cooperation Administration even though the political or military purposes may have been achieved while the economically feasible projects were left to the World Bank, the Export-Import Bank, or the Development Loan Fund: again, the reproach came largely because ICA felt it necessary to find spurious economic justifications for all its projects. The administration's defensive posture has led it to concentrate on justifying the minutiae of programing to the neglect of major policy issues in foreign aid operations. These are matters of national leadership, not merely of legislation or organization.

Domestic politics will continue to be heavily involved in the establishment of foreign aid policies and the administration of country programs, regardless of changes in laws or organization, of the exercise of strong executive, congressional, or administrative leadership, or even of the attainment of a high level of national consensus on foreign aid. The tensions imposed by constitutional checks and balances, the invitation to spoils appointments or patronage contracts, the absence of a geographical constituency and of politically effective interest groups, and the unstable nature of the operation itself will insure that. War and subversion will always require the use of temporary expedients that appear inconsistent with long-range national goals. But the terms in which Congress views and reviews the aid program should always be precise enough to focus clearly upon the divergent country programs, yet broad enough to encompass the full potentiality of the national effort.

In the past American aid has restored war-torn countries, strengthened the political and military defenses of free nations, and weakened the appeal of communism. Its present and future role is to stabilize and strengthen the underdeveloped countries, thus contributing to the peaceful world order envisaged as a basic aim of American foreign policy. The wise deployment of national resources available for these ends will require a resolution and a steadfastness of planning and purpose invoking the highest potentialities of political leadership.

In the final analysis, foreign aid can be no more effective than Congress and the nation will it to be.

VI THE PROMISE OF FOREIGN AID

AMERICA'S EMERGENCE to world leadership after the Second World War was a sudden change even for the fast pace of events in the twentieth century. Before the last overtones of isolation had died away, the United States had discovered that the demands of peace were to be as unremitting as those of war. And in the decade that followed, a substantial American involvement in the modernization of other nations was to be recognized as part of its commitment to world peace. Two great wars had shattered the possibility of returning to the old system, centered largely on the European powers, as a basis for relating the great and the small nations; and the United States had assumed its uncomfortable role as restorer of Europe, chief Western protagonist in the cold war, and protector of weak and inexperienced nations from involuntary subjection to communism.

Even now, after nearly two decades and $85 billion of foreign aid, the proposition that continued American involvement in the affairs of other nations might be necessary for the preservation of peace and the establishment of a decent world order is still unlikely to be found in the platform of either great national party. Virtually all leaders may accept the importance of other nations as a vital factor in American security; they may even agree that the threatened loss of any part of the non-Communist world is a potential threat to the United States. From a military point of view this agreement has led successively to the building of defensive alliances, a strategy of deterrence of aggression through the capacity to retaliate, and a series of preparations for limited war. But the advanced position of the United States has also required efforts to influence the domestic and foreign policies of many nations, great and small, allied, neutral, and unfriendly, in ways extending well beyond the defensive requirements of the cold war.

Those efforts have centered about programs of military, economic, and technical assistance. They have met with varying degrees of success, which, however, has never been great enough to permit either their discontinuance or a significant relaxation of other military and diplomatic efforts. For even after America's Western allies became able to participate as partners instead of as recipients in these programs, it was apparent that an end of American involvement was still neither desirable nor possible. The indications were to the contrary: greater demands and requests from the underdeveloped world; increases in the absolute size and complexity of aid programs, and in the number of sources of foreign aid; more multilateralism in offering and administering aid; greater integration of U.S. programs with the efforts of allied nations and with international agencies; a growth of neutralism in the underdeveloped countries resulting partly from the offers and aid programs of the Communist bloc; and acceptance by those countries of Communist aid as an economic factor capable of exploitation for their own benefit. The main question was not whether the United States was going to continue large-scale aid to underdeveloped countries, but how.

Recent developments pose a great new challenge to the concepts and management of American aid programs. The Kennedy administration, in response to this challenge of the 1960s, almost at once recognized the need for a greater sense of national political purpose and a clearer statement of the requirements for American involvement in the planning for economic and social development of other countries. The proposals for the new Act for International Development included unified administration and policy formulation, long-term planning and financing, and integrated country programing.[1] An attempted coup in Viet-Nam and a dramatic increase in civil disorder there soon forced the new administration to apply still more basic principles to one of the most troublesome

[1] President Kennedy's message to Congress on foreign aid, March 22, 1962; reprinted in *The Department of State Bulletin*, April 10, 1962, pp. 507–514.

problems in postwar diplomacy: to find economic and technical means of directly countering successful Communist subversion in a country whose government resisted repeated suggestions to introduce democratic reform. The findings of the Staley and Taylor missions to Viet-Nam in 1961 underlined the weakness of any external power's efforts to encourage another sovereign nation to sacrifice certain immediate advantages for its own survival. Past experiences in Viet-Nam suggest that a much stronger American position than ever adopted before may well be necessary if basic changes are to occur there before it is too late.

The American experiences in Southeast Asia recited in this volume suggest still further requirements for foreign aid operations in the next decade:

1) Greater delegation of responsibility for program design and flexibility in administration to American ambassadors, who, in turn, would be assisted by professional coordinators and planners of military, economic, and technical aid. The "country approach" remains essential.

2) Greater flexibility in the advance designing of special impact projects for use when speedy performance is necessary, especially in countries where U.S. aid is an innovation or a controversial issue.

3) Renewed emphasis on the possibility of introducing widespread consumer and public benefits as a legitimate end of foreign aid, recognizing the fact that the capacity to respond to mass needs and at the same time to dramatize the individual-oriented character of the American society is an important and thus far unique feature of U.S. bilateral aid programs.

4) Greater and better coordinated use of nongovernmental aid resources, emphasizing the unique and pluralistic nature of the American society, whose diverse resources are nevertheless capable of working toward common purposes.

5) Greater flexibility in using expert help not now generally available to U.S. aid operations, including short-term technicians, teachers, semiprofessional operating personnel, voluntary associations, and university research and consulting services.

6) Greater attention to the probable impact of U.S. aid upon political, social, and moral development of the receiving country, so that encouragement can be given to responsible democratic

tendencies within the traditional social framework of developing societies.

7) Acceptance of the implications of a continued Communist trade-and-aid offensive, and the development of criteria by which countries may be encouraged to receive aid from any source so long as it does not have injurious political or economic consequences.

Some of the changes that will be necessary to accommodate these requirements have already been suggested in this analysis of American experiences in Southeast Asia. Others touch the fundamentals of the American approach to foreign aid and the essence of relations among advanced and underdeveloped nations in the years ahead. Of these, none is more significant than the changing concepts of national sovereignty and of nonintervention in the affairs of other nations.

1. FOREIGN AID AND THE DOCTRINE OF NONINTERVENTION

The traditional doctrine of nonintervention is morally and politically unimpeachable. Like many principles of ethics and politics, however, it has never been and cannot be practiced as an absolute. Limitations on the doctrine on both sides may arise out of self-interest, or humanitarianism, or the very facts of international life in the modern world: security and survival, political morality, international justice, and national obligations have all been invoked as justification for various actions which might be called "intervention." When President Eisenhower called for the world to "refrain from intervening" in the new nations' internal affairs, he suggested at the same time that it was appropriate that the peoples of those nations "should be furnished with the mental tools to preserve and develop their freedom."[2] Similarly in the Act of Bogotá the inter-American community, whose basic treaties enshrine the doctrine of nonintervention, lists a variety of aid programs in which the United States would participate to speed social and economic progress in Latin America, to enable "the individual citizen of Latin America to live a better life and to

[2] Address before the 15th Session of UN General Assembly, September 22, 1960; reprinted in *The Department of State Bulletin*, October 10, 1960, pp. 551–557.

provide him the fullest opportunity to improve his status."[3] Intervention for the purpose of protecting the freedom and dignity of individual citizens or minority groups in other countries has often been sanctioned in international declarations and acts so long as the corrective action is nonmilitary in character. Whether there is a legal basis for it or not, the fact remains that economic relations between nations generally lead to a mutual involvement that subtly crosses national boundaries; and foreign aid is in many ways the most promising means of influence.

Circumstances in each country will determine the point at which "involvement" through foreign aid becomes "intervention." American insistence on using U.S. shipping, offering bids to small businessmen, or withholding aid from producers of certain agricultural commodities will be resented more in some countries than the suggestion that the host government take note of certain previously unrecognized needs among its own people, or that it diversify its crop production in order to minimize the effects of world price fluctuations. Most governments will object to an attempt to influence an election outcome, but will accept open efforts by Americans to persuade elected officials to take certain courses of action. And the requirement of measures designed to serve American administrative or political convenience, such as diplomatic immunities for aid technicians or widespread publicity for American aid efforts, may appear less legitimate than demands for engineering, planning, or adequate fiscal arrangements for a given project.

What is lacking, then, is not a redefined doctrine of nonintervention but a rationale for the legitimate and inevitable involvement that occurs in foreign aid relationships, and an understanding of both the opportunities and the limitations of such involvement. It is not enough to explain away interference in the domestic affairs of other nations on the ground that it is unintentional, for in international relations nothing is less impressive than mere intentions. Nor can such interference through the accidents of foreign aid be excused as the result of a nonrecurrent emergency such as the cold war. American aid is not regarded in most parts of the world as a temporary emergency operation. If noninterven-

---

[3] Act of Bogotá, Colombia, September 13, 1960; reprinted in *The Department of State Bulletin*, October 3, 1960, p. 537.

tion is to be a declared principle of foreign aid, then sustained involvement must be justified as a necessary consequence of acting on other equally legitimate principles. Both sides should be prepared to discuss and to reach understanding on its probable consequences as well as its original purpose.

No responsible American argues for interference for its own sake. On the contrary, it is important to preserve the principle of the independence of nations even though the international actions of the United States and other powerful states are increasingly influencing the domestic affairs of others. This problem cannot be resolved in terms of power calculations alone. The assumption of a leading or guiding role in the affairs of a weak country like Laos carries a responsibility for the eventual consequences even though no protest may be registered at the moment of crisis; while on the other hand a hesitance to play a role in domestic crises in Korea, Taiwan, or Viet-Nam might have mutually disastrous consequences even though occasioned by a concern for sovereign rights.

The most compelling rationale for America's involvements abroad has been that of national security or survival. In the cold war context, "intervention" through foreign aid is clearly relevant to a struggle which presumably is as mortal for the recipient as for the donor. But the cold war does not explain the content or operational patterns of foreign aid. Efforts to promote land reform, attempts to influence governmental organization, and concern over the status and accomplishments of public health and educational institutions are only vaguely associated with bipolar power politics. It is necessary to deal with the realities of involvement on other levels as well.

These realities spring from the community of purpose between U.S. foreign policy and the domestic aspirations of the underdeveloped world. The economic growth and political maturation of newly independent and other underprivileged nations are goals that clearly serve American interests. But certain consequences of these aspirations, and the detailed means for fulfilling them, are somewhat better understood in the developed than in the underdeveloped world. The certainty of social change implies that some losses will inevitably be sustained along with the gains; those who are responsible for the success of the new order may be among its first victims unless great foresight is exhibited. Because of long-standing and world-wide experience in foreign aid, America is gradually developing an understanding of these problems which can be communicated to the governments of the underdeveloped world. Efforts to minimize anticipated failures and undesirable consequences of change constitute a form of American interference that is almost inescapable.

Not all actions designed to benefit other nations, of course, represent purposes and techniques equally desired by the United States and the host government, as the experiences related in earlier chapters of this book indicate. Much of the activity of American aid is performed not for the benefit of the present host government, but for that of its successors. What may seem momentarily unimportant or unpalatable to the current regime may nevertheless have to remain high on the American list of priorities. Concern for the "next governments" represents an important element in American aid operations even though the aid programs as a whole tend to support existing regimes.[4] The case studies presented in this volume suggest a number of situations in which American policy tends to move in advance of the thinking of the host government and some in which its failure to do so has proved disastrous.

The vocabulary of foreign aid provides countless examples of the effort toward "political sterilization" to minimize the appearance of involvement. Many of these are tactics adopted in order to protect other governments against unfair charges of surrendering their sovereignty. The term "technical assistance" itself is intended to reassure, even though the programs involved include activities that may influence governmental organizations and attitudes, improve the economic status of a social class, or change social and economic beliefs. Efforts have been made to shift from the use of grants to "businesslike" and supposedly impersonal loans, which, being administered by a hard-headed bankers' operation, are thought to preserve the self-respect of the beneficiary— a sterilization device not entirely successful because in practice grants were often replaced by loans that were "soft" and therefore obviously politically motivated.

[4] See *The Operational Aspects of United States Foreign Policy*, a study prepared at the request of the Senate Committee on Foreign Relations by the Maxwell Graduate School of Citizenship and Public Affairs, Syracuse University, in *United States Foreign Policy*, Doc. No. 24, 87th Cong., 1st sess. (Washington: GPO, 1961), pp. 31–40.

Another effort to reduce the political charge of foreign aid has been the attempt to apply purely economic criteria in allocating funds. This is an important step away from the haphazardness of allocations based only on vague "political" standards, but it may still depend upon assumptions that are subject to political manipulation. The theory that some countries are ready for economic "take-off" involves judgments about political maturity and stability and the general climate of investment. At the first presentation of the "islands of development" proposals for massive aid, for example, it was clear that the selection of Taiwan, India, Pakistan, and Brazil for massive doses of dollar aid was based almost as much on political as on economic justifications. Economic need alone does not justify American aid. In fact, no adequate, objective rationale for the economic allocation of aid funds among competing nations has been discovered. President Kennedy stated that the nations "most willing and able to mobilize their own resources" should receive "special attention,"[5] but this use of aid as an inducement, in the style of federal-state "grants-in-aid," does not provide a measuring device of the "willingness" of other nations or of the amount of special attention needed. It also fails to allow for the fact that "special attention" may also be devoted to countries that are unwilling to undertake internal reforms. The economic vocabulary used in justifying foreign aid and in urging participation by other nations is appropriate to our concern for preserving sovereign prerogatives, but it does not, in the last analysis, relieve us or them of the responsibility for making political decisions.[6]

Perhaps the minimum policy requirement of the doctrine of nonintervention is that the United States should avoid interference that is needless or irrelevant to major foreign policy purposes. This principle is violated when the requirements of American merchant shipping, small business, and farmers' groups are served by imposing intolerable administrative and political burdens on foreign aid relationships. Indeed, through foreign aid, the Amer-

[5] Message to Congress on foreign aid, cited. The "efforts of resource mobilization" cited include land reform, tax reform, improved education, and social justice, which are political and social as much as economic.
[6] For a discussion of other efforts to develop standard, nonpolitical means of allocating foreign aid funds, see Charles Wolf, *Foreign Aid: Theory and Practice in Southern Asia* (Princeton: Princeton University Press, 1960).

ican politics of the 1950s touched virtually every country in the underdeveloped world. The working out of annual legislative programs presented an enlightening display of competing private interests, administrative rivalries, and partisan manipulations, all of which were closely followed overseas in anticipation of demands to come. Some political impact of external funds and advice is sustained wherever aid is offered, accepted, or even refused. Foreign aid provides ample evidence for the truism that international affairs are largely made up of the domestic affairs of other nations. Yet it is clearly our responsibility to minimize the influence of purely American politics abroad.

A further obligation imposed by respect for the sovereignty of other nations is to discover administrative means that will minimize the embarrassment surrounding the intrusion of foreign funds, personnel, and ideas. Already the foreign aid agencies have developed institutions that conform to special political circumstances. The Joint Commission on Rural Reconstruction in Taiwan, the substitution of a small staff of generalists for the usual aid mission in Burma, and the increasing use of contract agencies to render technical assistance in Thailand all represent responses to unusual political circumstances. It is likely that further concessions to the political requirements of other governments will be necessary, both in the negotiation of bilateral agreements and in the organizational formalities of aid diplomacy. The United States only deprives itself of needed flexibility by imposing rigid bureaucratic requirements across the board.

The interventionist tendencies of foreign aid are also minimized when several sources of funds and personnel become available. The possibility of choosing among aid agencies has at least reduced the sense of political involvement that might follow from substantial dependence on a single source. Private foundations have operated effectively in countries where official technical assistance was unwelcome. Special entrée is also available to the UN and other multilateral aid agencies, especially those in which the host government has a sense of full participating membership. The offering of unwelcome recommendations by such organizations sometimes takes place without giving offense and without appearing to endanger the independence or the neutral stance of the receiving government. Of course, there is no escaping the fact that insofar as foreign aid contributes to development and change it touches upon questions of sovereignty regardless of its source. But preserving the element of choice for the host government can convert "interference" into the more acceptable "involvement" from its point of view.

The doctrine of nonintervention, while obviously not eliminating American involvement in the affairs of other countries, has obscured the American vision of that involvement. Repeated assertions of the nonpolitical character of foreign aid have deceived Americans more than they have the leaders of the underdeveloped countries. As proof of American nonintervention, many examples can be cited of American helplessness in dealing with corruption or maladministration in governments accepting grants or loans. These examples only illustrate the fact that foreign aid has not fulfilled some political objectives of the United States; they ignore its other political consequences. Among these the most serious is that the noninterventionist dogma has been strictly followed to the point that the working out of the aid program has discouraged democratic forces in the host country and has restrained the expression of concern in cases where undemocratic forces have harvested the principal benefits of aid. Even in Korea, an American ambassador decisively supported democratic forces only after the Rhee dictatorship had shown signs of senility. Sensitivity on the subject of internal politics is a fact of which we have to take account, but it should set no rigid limits. There have been cases like Burma, where the presence of American aid was too vulnerable to afford the basis for offering any political advice at all; but also others like Taiwan in which American policy preferred the convenience of a friendly dictatorship to the exertion of helping to introduce democratic reforms; or like Viet-Nam in which political advice was offered so timidly that it could be safely ignored. The view that the American presence is divorced from the politics of a recipient nation and from the social progress of its people has contributed to the shallowness of much of the public and private debate over issues of foreign aid.

The most serious consequences of the doctrine of total nonintervention are the missed opportunities represented by the calls to action that have been denied or given the pocket veto of indecision. If the United States had decided a decade ago to accept the proposition that its aid should be offered in such a way as to strengthen the respect for individual rights to self-fulfillment, for example, the grim developments of Laos and now Viet-Nam might have taken significantly different form. There is much that could still be done in Taiwan and Viet-Nam to realize a more satisfactory political as well as economic and technical potential if such purposes became primary.

In some countries, to be sure, the intentional use of American resources to strengthen courts, legislatures, party organizations, the press, or other popular institutions would be outrageously inappropriate; but even this self-restraining judgment could best be made in a context of American policy concerned with political values subject to the political choice of the two governments. Political inertness is not required by the moral precepts of nonintervention. Missed opportunities, whether exploited by the Communist powers or not, represent a political liability rather than a neutral factor. The diplomacy of foreign aid should be evaluated by both its actual achievements and its failures, by its potentials as well as its history.

Legitimate involvement in the affairs of other nations is more than a matter of mutuality or even of consent. It may require an active role of studying, proposing, and innovating. The requirements for constructive involvement cannot now be stated abstractly or universally; the use of legislative and administrative rules is no substitute for informed local judgments. Ambassadors and their advisers can, however, be instructed to temper the traditional American concern for the sovereign rights of others by a consciousness of the necessary and appropriate role of involvement in the affairs of the developing nations whenever aid is offered and accepted. At the same time, the congressional and executive leadership should recognize the greater self-restraint called for by the fact that the domestic politics of American aid often become important issues overseas.

Nonintervention is still a useful concept in American diplomacy. It protects us against acting with the self-indulgent arrogance of a busybody and against excessive zeal in extending our own value systems. It calls attention to the fact that international relations in the free world must be based on mutual interest and consent, not on force. But ignoring the anticipated consequences of foreign aid destroys the basis for an adequate response to the problems of East and West and of North and South. Neither the Communists' invitations to revolution of their type nor the nationalist revolutions for a better life will permit the United States to ignore the desire for change. The end of the *status quo* in the underdeveloped world should bring with it a recognition of the inadequacy of the traditional view of nonintervention, just as it has marked the end of the colonial system. The problem is not how to keep from influencing the internal affairs of other nations, but how to do it legitimately and on a continuing basis.

2. The Need for Legitimizing Foreign Aid

Few predictions about the inherently unstable world order seem more probable than that foreign aid will continue in a variety of forms for a generation or longer. Efforts to ignore or deny the facts behind this probability have tended only to confirm it. Congressional reluctance to authorize the program on a continuing basis has only fixed another institution in its place: the annual authorization of the program and successive postponements of its termination date. The results have been exasperating both to congressmen and to the aid administrators who are forced to run an Alice-in-Wonderland treadmill of presentations and hearings in order to keep the program from disappearing. Repeated attacks on the program, including efforts to legislate it out of existence, have only forced it to take different forms.[7]

Most of the factors that have impelled the United States to offer foreign aid in the postwar years are still operative. Although the ruins of World War II have been rebuilt and European recovery has been achieved, the need for technical and economic assistance to underdeveloped countries is, if anything, even greater than it

[7] The Mutual Security Act of 1953, like its predecessors, put a time limit on the program, requiring the termination of economic assistance within two years, and of military aid within three years. S. Report 1799, 83d Cong., 2d sess. (Washington: GPO, 1954), p. 82, indicated that prolongation might be necessary, however, and the Mutual Security Act of 1954 reluctantly confirmed this decision, terminating FOA (Sec. 503) but authorizing the President to transfer its functions, powers, and personnel to other agencies (same, Sec. 525). It was this law that returned technical cooperation to the State Department (Sec. 521) and military aid to the Defense Department (Secs. 524 and 525, by implication). The Draper Committee report as summarized by the President's report to Congress (January 14, 1960, p. 7) argued that economic aid must continue almost indefinitely. A summary of these and other views on the prospects of foreign aid appears in Appendix II, "The Unsuccessful History of Economic Disengagement."

was ten years ago. A growing political consciousness has given expression to economic demands to which governments have become painfully attentive. Population increases are expected to occur with the greatest force in countries possessing backward technologies or inadequate resources; and the danger posed by Communist infiltration is all the greater because at the time when it is becoming apparent that requirements may exceed present Western capabilities, the Sino-Soviet bloc has demonstrated unexpected skill in rendering foreign aid for political purposes. The clumsy Soviet operations in Burma are by no means a typical phenomenon. Moreover, Communists are encouraging other governments to participate extensively in planning and designing projects to insure reasonably effective use, so that the lack of realism in the symbolic projects that characterized Soviet aid in the 1950s can be avoided in the future. In these respects the U.S.S.R. may be learning from its experiences and from those of the United States.

In addition to these essentially political factors supporting a continuation of aid, a more general historical influence may be at work. In the decades following the industrial revolution there has been an irreversible trend toward publicly supported welfare activities. Recognition by Western governments of responsibility for providing social services for their less fortunate citizens is a novelty of the nineteenth century, to which the twentieth has added the notion that nations have something resembling a humanitarian responsibility to noncitizens and even to people outside their borders.[8] Organized, systematic humanitarianism is a contagious and unfilterable virus of civilization. It not only encourages similar performance on the part of others; it also spreads to additional fields of activity in the same society. It cannot be readily dispensed with in the continuing presence of the needs that have stimulated it and of others that may become apparent later.

Practical considerations would probably require the United States to continue limited foreign aid operations for some decades even if Congress should decide to make no further financial commitments at all. U.S. aid is becoming increasingly self-perpetuating

---

[8] In a reversion to earlier attitudes, Elgin Groseclose, "Diplomacy or Altruism?" in James W. Wiggins and Helmut Schoeck, eds., *Foreign Aid Reexamined* (Washington: Public Affairs Press, 1958), argues that foreign aid is unconstitutional because of the use of tax revenues for purposes other than the general welfare of the American people.

as its "pipeline" of funds lengthens and as loans begin to be paid back into revolving funds. Loans extended to underdeveloped areas and repayable in local currency totaled nearly $1.8 billion in 1961. Excluding counterpart funds, the United States held an additional $1 billion of local currencies from which loans could be made.[9] The use of these funds for new loans, grants, or various forms of budget support will require careful, long-range planning on a country-by-country basis even if no further funds are forthcoming from fresh appropriations. It might be possible to turn the administration of them over to the United Nations or a regional consortium of interested nations; or, alternatively, the United States could extricate itself from this continuing responsibility by turning the principal and interest of these loans over to the national treasuries of the debtor countries. But the wisdom of relinquishing such a potentially useful instrument on a world-wide basis, to say nothing of the political consequences of canceling the loans, would surely be questioned seriously in and out of Congress. It seems probable, moreover, that the usefulness of this instrument will increase rather than the reverse as the United States gains experience in foreign aid projects financed out of local currency, especially if American aid is accepted at home and overseas as a continuing program rather than on the basis of a series of crisis-oriented projects.

The probable perseverance of an American foreign aid effort is also indicated by the extent and nature of parallel efforts throughout the world. Other nations and international organizations have made impressive beginnings in offering foreign aid to newly independent areas. This effort has sprung from a variety of motives, ranging from a desire to retain post-imperial spheres of influence to a slowly growing sense of the importance of foreign aid in forming world-community relationships transcending immediate economic or military gain. Economic and technical assistance has already begun to create new bonds of common interest among nations which otherwise have demonstrated little evidence of mutuality (between Israel and Burma, for example, and among Asian Colombo Plan nations). The nature and extent of these

[9] According to an informal but reliable estimate, the total of nearly $3 billion of local currencies might increase to $10 or $11 billion by 1964. (See Edward S. Mason, "Foreign Money We Can't Spend," *The Atlantic*, May 1960, pp. 79–86.) In India alone, U.S.-owned rupee deposits exceeded half a billion dollars in 1961.

tenuous but growing international ties are still largely unknown, but the fact that they exist at all will discourage any substantial American withdrawal from foreign aid.

Perhaps the most compelling argument in favor of a decisive recognition of foreign aid as a continuing and legitimate instrument of American policy is the consequence a vigorous reaffirmation could have. It was obvious beyond all doubt, as the 1950s drew to a close, that a congressional assurance of program continuity would lead to great improvements in American performance overseas. The myth that foreign aid is inherently temporary and must therefore be administered by *ad hoc* agencies and on the basis of expediency was being supplanted by a more substantial view of its organizational and administrative requirements. Plans were advanced for integrating foreign aid into other governmental operations serving the ends of American diplomacy, creating a focus of responsibility for all policies relating to military assistance, various forms of grant aid, loan operations, technical assistance, overseas assistance and information operations of individual government agencies, and certain aspects of foreign trade. Stronger and more coherent American positions were also being suggested on the aid functions of the UN and on other multilateral assistance policies. The exercise of vigorous leadership in a unified office for overseas operations, it was suggested, could achieve a collective impact from American efforts that even the best administration of the present array of independent agencies could not approach. At the field level the country team, under the ambassador, would find less fragmentation of direction from Washington, would have less to fear from appeals by the host government to Washington for reversals of its technical decisions, and could anticipate speedier answers to its requests for policy guidance because of better coordination among the agencies concerned. Independent staffs for program review of the operations of these agencies at the country level could provide Washington with more effective, policy-oriented oversight of field operations.

Other important administrative gains from such a step could be anticipated from the greater stability of staff and policy that would result. A genuine career service would be possible among a nucleus of the best qualified of the aid administrators and technicians, with a standing fully equal to that of the Foreign Service. Establishment of a career service would not only improve recruitment prospects but could also contribute to a better employment of skills already available. It would be possible to establish permanent training programs for the career development of officials which could eventually become a prerequisite for advancement to the highest administrative and technical positions, and at the same time serve as a focus of continuing research and evaluation of political, technical, and economic phases of foreign aid administration.

The largest single component of foreign aid—its military element—has been surrounded by a formidable *mystique* that has hitherto prevented adequate participation by professional outsiders. Assignment of career aid administrators to military service schools could develop a versatility on the civilian side that the military services already possess in reverse, and could even lead to a mixing of career personnel in the development and administration of defense support and military aid programs. In short, the developing professionalism of foreign aid could be recognized as such by systematic research and training programs designed to increase its capacity of service to the great national purposes abroad.

A decisive American recognition of the legitimacy of foreign aid as an integral and permanent part of foreign policy would also encourage other countries to join in multilateral arrangements including both donor and receiving governments. Some of these countries, under American leadership, have already established formal relationships among themselves with the view to creating a consortium of donors. But the apparently tentative nature of the American commitment has remained a bar to long-term arrangements. It has not only complicated efforts at increasing the financial participation by other countries but also reduced the effectiveness of the individual contributions of each. A working organization for planning purposes could develop a basis for specialization of function among the donors and reduce the friction and competition that have sometimes amounted to a form of gamesmanship among receiving countries.

The community of interest among underdeveloped countries receiving foreign aid could also be furthered by a more positive American commitment. The continuity implied by a recognition of the permanence of aid operations would help to break down two of the principal psychological barriers in present relationships: it would reduce the sense of dependence upon periodic acts of "charity" that is offensive to the pride of new nations, since the offering and receiving of foreign aid could become a normal pattern of relationship between the rich and the poor nations; and it would separate foreign aid for development from the predominantly military connotations of the mutual security concept of the 1950s. Foreign aid offered as a natural responsibility of the leading power of the Western world could be accepted out of a deeper sense of mutuality than that implied by emergency measures related to transient military considerations.

The probability of continued U.S. participation in bilateral aid operations does not rule out the need for planning systematically for the termination of programs that have fulfilled their objectives and withdrawal from those whose results are not serving American purposes. It is the U.S. commitment to foreign aid, rather than specific policies and programs, that should be permanent. Continuation of individual projects could be considered a voluntary action for both parties, once the principle of a continuing American participation in foreign aid is established. A change of government in the host country should be the occasion for a joint review of basic objectives rather than for its insistence on U.S. withdrawal from commitments no longer desired, especially if in the changed circumstances the prospects for the success of individual projects were significantly reduced. A continuing aid project would then constitute a freely undertaken obligation rather than a source of possible resentment against commitments of the past. At the same time, the U.S. commitment to unproductive aid activities should be subjected to much more critical review than is possible under the present uncertainties of American purpose and direction and the preoccupation with tactical considerations. No problem has been more difficult than that of bringing programs to an end at the right time and for the right reasons.

"Withdrawal" is considered here as a tactical maneuver, made for political reasons or as a result of unilateral dissatisfaction; while "termination" takes place when a program has fulfilled, or can no longer be expected to fulfill, its economic, technical, or political objectives. Withdrawal is usually a temporary, localized action. It may be undertaken at the initiative of either party. In Laos the United States used the threat of withdrawal in 1958 as an instrument to force the government to undertake fiscal reforms; in Burma it was the host government that asked the U.S. mission to withdraw in 1953 as a moral protest against apparent American sponsorship of Kuomintang activities within its borders. Total or partial withdrawal might theoretically take place at any time the cold war or other conditions altered sufficiently to permit it (although the United States has seldom actually indulged in a unilateral withdrawal). Future agreements on disarmament might permit major changes in certain types of aid, or shifts in international alignments or military strategy might bring about partial, local, or temporary withdrawals and changes of emphasis. But there should be a generally understood pattern within which such changes can take place without disaster to relations between the two nations.

Termination of aid implies a planned scaling-down as program objectives are achieved. Because of the difficulty of measuring economic recovery or development, a decision to terminate because of the achievement of such goals might be made politically rather than on purely technical grounds, but the rational and orderly manner of terminating a program could be distinguished readily from the politics of withdrawal. The Marshall Plan offers the most impressive example of termination, and the Mansfield Amendment to mutual security legislation offers a basis for applying scaled termination to programs in underdeveloped countries. In Greece, Japan, and Israel, an intended termination of aid was announced in 1960 without arousing resentment; indeed, Americans were surprised at the absence of disappointment. The host governments had seen the end before the United States had announced it.

It was not individual programs but the concept of foreign aid that had taken on the aspect of permanence by the end of the 1950s. What was still needed was full and formal recognition of that fact.

3. IDEOLOGICAL REQUIREMENTS

History will almost certainly include the relationships between the rich and the poor nations among the most crucial problems of the latter half of this century. The responses produced in the United States by these relationships were sporadic, temporizing, and improvisatory at first, inhibited by the unevenness of our own theoretical understanding of the requirements, by the doctrine of nonintervention, and by doubts about the economic advisability of such heavy commitments abroad. In spite of the erratic character of the programs that resulted, few can seriously question that the American responses have been creative and sometimes impressive. But enthusiasm for the cause of foreign aid and its specific achievements has still produced no national policy concept equal to its scope or its potential.

Although American contributions to the underdeveloped world have been generous, the uncertain sense of commitment and the manner of performance have detracted from their effectiveness. Even when the total amount of resources available in the 1950s was sufficient for mounting major developmental programs, conceptual limitations did not permit their optimum utilization. This was especially true in regard to political objectives, where there have been only loose connections between basic purposes and the actual programs. Because of a reluctance to regard foreign aid as a continuing function, economic objectives have also been formulated as piecemeal projects except where necessity forced some form of integration; and even technical objectives suffered from organizational and procedural handicaps because they were approached from professional or bureaucratic viewpoints not related to major purposes.

Among the political potentials of foreign aid is the promotion of stable institutions for the protection of individual rights, the principal limitations being those imposed by the sovereign relationships between governments giving and receiving aid. When foreign aid is considered from this standpoint and not merely from that of cold war strategy, the roles of local armies, internal police forces, and other public and private institutions receiving American aid can be identified as they contribute to the broad national purposes of the United States and of the host country. The nature, extent, and purposes of American concern over domestic affairs abroad would lose some of their mystery if placed in this perspective. Thus, while subject to constant review and negotiation, American support to undemocratic regimes like those in Taiwan or Viet-Nam, or in Pakistan or Spain, could yield more than anti-Communist strength, and eventually permit a more active role than the ambiguities of our previous, politically heedless support could tolerate. The general direction of American aid policy in countries of varying political complexions could be related to the basic diplomatic purposes of the United States.

One of the most perplexing political problems confronting American aid diplomacy has been the entry of the Communist bloc into direct competition for the ideological allegiance of the uncommitted world. The first automatic American response of rejecting the politics of neutralism failed to prevent the offer and acceptance of Soviet, Chinese, and East European aid in many Asian and African countries. Improvements in Communist skill, the vast need for development assistance, and various forms of American misjudgment or intransigence have combined to produce great increases in the volume of Communist-bloc aid in recent years. Regrets over this development are undoubtedly well founded, for there is no need to minimize the dangers of flirtation with communism. The successful entry of the Communist bloc into foreign aid is an accomplished fact, however, and American aid policies and operations must find means of blunting its political effects and, where possible, converting this additional aid resource into an asset.

To some extent this has already happened. Our own long-term objectives in the underdeveloped countries are served everywhere by the creation of economic and political conditions favorable to their independence and to the growth of individual and social freedom. Whatever activities contribute to that end can be accepted regardless of the source; whatever does not should be blocked or avoided if possible. Thus Soviet aid in general education is more dangerous to the potentials of freedom than gift hotels which are impressive and may even be necessary, and, but for the Soviet presence, would represent a legitimate claim on U.S. aid. Similarly, Soviet concrete-mixers to pave streets in Kabul or Rangoon are preferable to Communist-trained government officials. In situations where aid requirements are unlimited, the United States should try to concentrate its activities in areas that it considers politically productive, leaving to the Communists those that do not hold that promise.

We should also consider the economic potentials of foreign aid in broad terms of the requirements of the poor nations and the resources of the rich. It is imperative to see the Communist challenge over the next four decades as more than rivalry in military weapons systems and foreign aid operations: total systems are competing in the developing world south of the Tropic of Cancer. The forced capital reinvestment of the Communist system has made impressive statistical showings and developed an economic and military capability of intimidating proportions. American and Western efforts to counterbalance this showing could not equal in every underdeveloped country the resources available in the demonstration countries using Communist techniques. Such efforts should provide, however, external resources to augment maximum internal efforts to raise the necessary capital investments in the public sector, and also encourage the introduction of private capital even if it involves some internal displacement of economic power in the host country.

A different concentration or balance of aid efforts in each country and among sectors of its society is also essential.[10] In some circumstances the West must find means of supplying consumption commodities at costs that will free local capital for reinvestment without sacrificing (and, if possible, even improving) the popular standard of living. An Asian or African society that is visibly developing its capital potential, and at the same time enjoying a standard of living superior to that of the Communist models in Asia (or, perhaps, in Africa), can find means of refuting the appeal of Communist methods. Under such circumstances many forms of Communist aid could be absorbed and even welcomed, since they would not be accompanied by the sacrifices demanded in the Communist homelands. The Western world, in supplying consumer goods out of its own abundance, and in making substantial contributions to capital development as well, would be demonstrating important aspects of its superiority over the Communist economic model.

If these proposals suggest some aspects of the political and economic potential of foreign aid, they also imply the need for overcoming present inadequacies of resources, personnel, and knowledge. Although in a few countries financial aid has been poured in at (or above) the point of saturation, most of the underdeveloped world continues to be short of investment and operating capital and of adequate supplies of managerial and technical personnel. Even the development of proposals for loans

[10] A persuasive economic argument favors "imbalance" and concentration of funds to achieve maximum effect. This offers in many cases an alternative to the attempt to move forward simultaneously on all economic and technical fronts. See Albert O. Hirschman, *The Strategy of Economic Development* (New Haven: Yale University Press, 1958), pp. 50–75.

or grants on a project basis cannot occur quickly enough under the normal entrepreneurial processes to offset these shortages. Unfortunately, in spite of improvements in our theoretical understanding of economic growth, the practical arts of inducing and guiding it are still underdeveloped themselves.[11]

The ideological shortcomings in American foreign aid doctrines of the 1950s are readily apparent when results are compared with the potentials described above. The sterile preoccupation with nonintervention has often rendered the American presence a reflection of national incapacity. No effort was made to use U.S. aid to improve the performance and prestige of the Vietnamese National Assembly or the Legislative Yuan in Taiwan, although efforts in this direction need not have involved intolerable interference in internal politics, affected specific oversensitive public issues, or required any indication or approval or disapproval of members or candidates. There was no financial and technical aid to courts, bar associations, and civic and taxpayers' associations, although this could have been offered and administered through public channels without committing the United States to specific internal programs. No effort was made to encourage leading individuals and private organizations in Viet-Nam, Taiwan, and Thailand to consider systematically the major national purposes and problems of their own countries. There were no efforts to sponsor local centers of advanced study or publish serious studies of the institutions and political needs of new nations. Many of the institutional and ideological requirements of modern democratic statehood were ignored in the American effort to respect the whims as well as the sovereign sensibilities of other nations.[12]

Similar deficiencies in the conceptual basis of economic activity in American foreign aid are revealed in the detailed programs for Southeast Asia. Needless concern over "creeping socialism" has discouraged administrators from offering assistance to economic planning or even from projecting economic requirements as a basis for aid programs. Exaggerated noninterventionism has forced

[11] Some stimulating suggestions appear in Robert Theobald, *The Rich and the Poor: A Study of the Economics of Rising Expectations* (New York: Potter, 1960).

[12] See John D. Montgomery, "Public Interest in the Ideologies of National Development," in C. J. Friedrich, ed., *Public Interest*, Nomos, V (forthcoming).

aid missions to tolerate and even support unsound fiscal management of aid funds, inefficient and corrupt licensing schemes for dollar-backed commercial imports, and unwise economic policies for internal growth. Bureaucratic restrictions have been permitted to delay—and sometimes prevent—the importation of heavy capital equipment under the commercial import programs, although the introduction of large-scale capital equipment has been described as one of the economic objectives of foreign aid. Irrelevant requirements based on preferences for private capital have also slowed development assistance to existing or contemplated public enterprises in spite of the absence of alternative ownership; but at the same time aid missions were barred from offering technical assistance directly to private entrepreneurs.

Even the technical operations of foreign aid have hitherto been dominated by a limited, piecemeal approach for want of a full intellectual commitment to its possibilities. The institutional and technological implications of modernization, whether in agriculture, education, administration, industry, or engineering, have been considered separately, dealt with independently, and judged in accordance with American standards and procedures. Individual technicians, representing a distinct discipline and usually a distinct bureaucratic identity as well, have perceived the technical requirements of development only in their own specialized terms. This fragmented conception of the possibilities of technical assistance is perhaps more a matter of natural inclination and administrative convenience than of doctrine. Specialization must be respected if professional judgments are to achieve their maximum impact. The effort to prevent "laymen" from interfering with the professional activities of agricultural experts, public health officers, and engineers corresponds to the autonomy of departments in government or in a university. But interdisciplinary thinking about priorities and projects is unavoidable in working out adequate country programs and large-scale technical projects if they are to fulfill their promise.

Experience is improving American practice in developing this cooperation, at least in the larger, well-established missions in Southeast Asia. Unfortunately, however, little of it filtered back to technical services offices in Washington, and still less to universities and private contractors performing specialized and technical services with foreign aid funds. It is this lack of information rather than any doctrine that has prevented administrators and specialists from developing a fuller concept of the potentials of technical assistance. The ingredients of success in this field are not well known because our own experiences lie still unexamined. The example offered by military historians, recording decisions and events while the battle is still in process, and re-creating them for subsequent study and examination, might well be followed in foreign aid operations. If qualified historians and social scientists could periodically follow the campaigns against poverty, ignorance, and time itself, while they are taking place and from the vantage point of the regions in which they are being waged, successes and failures could be better weighed and converted into lessons for the future.[13]

The major potential of technical assistance is in the building of institutions capable of introducing and supporting the changes implied by modernization. Governmental and private organizations and associations, legal and administrative procedures and traditions, laws and attitudes toward property ownership and human rights are all subject to change through technical innovation. American aid has supplied technicians to advise in all these fields. Technical assistance has been offered in production, distribution, and finance, in labor relations and mass communications, in social welfare, legislative and constitutional law, and management. But these are not unrelated subjects. Technical assistance by its very nature is academically an interdisciplinary, and bureaucratically an interdepartmental, operation. It implies greater wisdom in the selection of goals than any fragmented technique can offer; it calls for the creation of models of development in each country which can be approached in well-conceived stages, an impossibility under earlier concepts of foreign aid; it demands, in short, an integrated country program of technical assistance for each situation.

The absence of an adequate conceptual basis for foreign aid has introduced vague dissatisfactions with performances which, viewed in purely administrative terms, have been predominantly successful and occasionally brilliant. The application of essentially irrelevant standards of efficiency, taken from either the bookkeeper's

[13] A further use of such studies is suggested in John D. Montgomery, "Crossing the Culture Bars: An Approach to the Training of American Technicians for Overseas Assignments," *World Politics*, July 1961, pp. 544–560.

or the engineer's approach, has augmented these dissatisfactions and undermined political support for foreign aid itself. These facts have doubtless underlain the almost frantic search for "new ideas," the "gimmicks" that would make foreign aid once more attractive. Expressions like "funds for growth" and "human resources development" have been used to replace "loans" and "technical assistance" with no enrichment of their content. Slogan terminology like "defense support" and "islands of development" has conveyed conceptual justifications for portions of the program, but they are no substitute for a general doctrine of foreign aid. Congressional disappointment over failures to disengage, as each crisis subsided in its turn only to be replaced by another, reflects the absence of an adequate understanding of what is required to fulfill the American hope for a stable and decent world order.

4. Practical Politics and Foreign Aid

Ideology, of course, is not enough. If foreign aid is to fulfill its promise as an instrument of American diplomacy in the years ahead, important political changes will be required. A national consensus must be built; congressional and party support must be adequate to withstand the threats of destruction to which the policies and program are periodically subjected; congressional participation in establishing and reviewing basic foreign aid policies must be broadened; and the administrative arrangements for foreign aid, both nationally and internationally, must be designed to achieve a maximum impact from the resources available. The form and texture of these requirements will depend upon many factors that lie outside the American experience in Southeast Asia. But their major dimensions can be perceived even from that limited context.

The desired national consensus will not emerge automatically, even if the recommended degree of congressional and party support were achieved along with an optimum organization of the foreign operations agencies of the government. The task is one of continuous public education about purposes, potentials, and programs, in which the President himself may have to participate constantly in support of executive agencies and friendly congressional leaders. Nor can the national leadership be satisfied with token approvals or annual authorization acts as a measure of congressional consensus. It is less the nominal support by congress-men that is at stake than their individual understanding of the nature, potential, and requirements of an integrated, well-managed aid program, and their willingness to transmit this understanding to their constituents. Few popular votes are gained or lost by a congressman's stand on foreign aid, but much is lost in American prestige and effectiveness when irrelevant and unworkable amendments are attached to aid bills or when an individual congressman insults foreign governments because of an animus against the aid program.

Congressional Problems

Political leadership and party discipline can avert the worst of these catastrophes, but the positive potential of Congress as a link to public opinion and a fruitful source of new ideas cannot be developed unless congressmen can better inform themselves about policy and managerial problems without participating in daily operations. The congressional view of government, taken collectively, is fundamentally broader than that of any single executive department, transcending lines of professional isolation and interests. But congressional information on foreign aid has not been substantially greater than that available to interested private citizens. Misleading newspaper reports have occasioned explosions among well-informed members just as they have in editorial columns, each compounding the injury done by the original accounts. A flood tide of leaks and complaints from disgruntled employees (of whom there has been an astonishing number in ICA, partly because of the frustrations inherent in foreign aid administration as it has been organized, and partly because of shortcomings in the personnel available on the present somewhat uncertain career basis) has provided another source for ill-informed public opinion.

Formal presentations by the administration have not always fulfilled the need for developing sympathetic participation by the legislative branch. The aid agencies have often given the appearance of being on the defensive before congressional committees, which is an invitation to further attack; at other times they have appeared to lack candor, taking refuge in the doctrine of executive privilege and thus giving it significance as an issue that invites controversy rather than cooperation. The executive branch has also tended to offer too much detail and not enough general, long-range policy guidance and analysis in its presentations. Both congressional committees and executive agencies were increasingly separating foreign aid from foreign policy during the 1950s, a practice which only reinforced the parochial outlook on foreign aid.

As a consequence of a general distrust of foreign aid, Congress has developed special sources of information on the program, most of which already have been described. Some have produced original insights and useful evaluations, but the total effect has been sometimes misleading.[14] It is true that the somewhat restricted view of the General Accounting Office has been supplemented by the work of universities and professional research organizations undertaken at congressional request. Their studies have been of real assistance to students of politics and economics and to congressmen and administrators, but they have been generally ignored in the legislation that followed in spite of the widespread publicity attending their first release. Some have strongly supported a long-range approach; some have criticized congressional preoccupation with details; while, on the other hand, some have produced results equally uncongenial to the administration. An individual senator's conclusion that foreign aid was often "utter waste" was supported by an impressive list of unsuccessful projects,[15] but although criticisms of the congressional role could be equally well supported, they have not found their way into print. Nor have the public responsibilities for failures been as evenly shared between the legislature and the administration as the facts warrant. Adequate congressional self-criticism is no more to be expected than executive apologies for inefficiency, but the potential for improvement in both branches is impressive.

Many congressional misconceptions of foreign aid arise out of the fragmented views developed among the dozen or more committees and subcommittees concerned with aspects of legislative inquiry or oversight that affect mutual security. In 1960 these in-

[14] See Hamilton Fish Armstrong, "Disturbing Portent for Africa," *The New York Times Magazine*, April 17, 1960, p. 76, for an observation of the effects of this distrust.

[15] *Report on Overseas Operations of the United States Government*, by Senator Allen J. Ellender, Senate Doc. No. 31, 85th Cong., 1st sess. (Washington: GPO, 1957), p. v. This report was marred, however, by a number of misconceptions about the purposes and potentialities of foreign aid; see pp. 290–291, 390, 428, 430, for examples.

cluded two subcommittees of the House Foreign Affairs Committee, as well as the committee as a whole; the Senate Foreign Relations Committee and subcommittees; the Government Operations Committees, Appropriations Committees, and Armed Services Committees of both houses, each with subcommittees; and the House Money and Banking and Senate Finance Committees. The unfortunate effects of this pluralism of responsibility and effort have already been described.[16] The development of party machinery for the study and review of foreign operations has helped dispel the appearance of party indifference to foreign aid,[17] but this has been insufficient to prevent the erosion of support from southern Democrats and midwestern Republicans, and the adventitious but continuing attacks from individual congressmen.

The total result is a legislative climate that is far from favorable in spite of annual affirmations of the principle of foreign aid. Radical improvement in American foreign aid operations cannot occur unless the Congress is prepared to devote responsible attention to its own role.

Executive and Administrative Problems

It is the responsibility of the executive branch to devise means of better informing the public and the congressional rank and file about the operating problems and requirements of foreign aid as well as to improve its own administrative arrangements. One de-

[16] See above, pp. 200–206, 237–238.

[17] See, for an important example, *National Security and Peace, A Task Force Report by the Republican Committee on Programs and Progress*, Republican National Committee (Washington, October 8, 1959). A later report from House Republicans, based on a series of 22 study papers dealing with cold war strategies, appeared on June 20, 1960, as "American Strategy and Strength," in *Congressional Record*, v. 106, pt. 10, pp. 13418–13502. The Senate's activities along these lines are discussed in Malcolm E. Jewell, "The Senate Republican Policy Committee and Foreign Policy," *Western Political Quarterly*, December 1959, p. 966. Among the Democrats, the reports of the Advisory Committee on Foreign Policy of the Advisory Council of the Democratic National Committee are notable. See Hugh A. Bone, *Party Committees and National Politics* (Seattle: University of Washington Press, 1958). The House Democrats sponsored James P. Warburg's "Re-examination of United States Foreign Policy," *Congressional Quarterly Weekly Report*, April 22, 1960, p. 684, and June 3, 1960, p. 966. Professor Holbert N. Carroll summarizes these developments and others in "Congressional Politics and Foreign Policy in the 1960's," paper delivered at 1960 meeting of the American Political Science Association, University of Pittsburgh, processed (September 1960).

vice would be more thoroughgoing reviews arranged by the executive with congressional support, as by special task forces to evaluate foreign aid programs in the light of major national policies and purposes. Such teams, consisting of executive and congressional appointees, could supplement the work of executive audits and well-staffed congressional investigations without undermining the independent position of the executive branch. Many of the administrative difficulties that have been amply documented by the Mansfield and other congressional reports and by ICA evaluations could be resolved without giving the appearance of an executive defeat under congressional attack. The Mansfield report rightly criticized the rigidities of aid administration from Washington and the resultant slowness and inflexibilities of operation at the country team level;[18] but the very fear of congressional criticism has contributed heavily to these bureaucratic, decision-suspending procedures. The Mansfield report also correctly noted that the aid program must run the gauntlet of ten separate clearances in Congress each year and that executive branch clearances are "hardly of less significance"; but sharing the responsibility for such procedural hazards made no contribution to the urgently needed remedy. A unification of aid operations capable of smoothing out this obstacle course would have to take place at a sufficiently high level of government to avoid interagency impasses. In short, even the best congressional thinking about foreign aid, represented by the Mansfield report in the Senate and the Richards report in the House,[19] has been unable to provide a substitute for concerted executive and congressional leadership in finding means of achieving maximum national effectiveness in foreign aid policies and programs.

Efforts in the executive branch to overcome these political disabilities have been handicapped by organizational diffusion of foreign aid policy. During the 1950s the State Department's relationship to ICA and its predecessors was anomalous, though legally

[18] *United States Aid Program in Vietnam,* Report by a subcommittee of the Senate Committee on Foreign Relations, 86th Cong., 2d sess. (Washington: GPO, 1960), pp. 12–15.

[19] *Report on Foreign Policy and Mutual Security,* H. Report 551, 85th Cong., 1st sess. (Washington: GPO, 1957). This perceptive report by the retiring chairman of the Foreign Affairs Committee was neither endorsed nor followed by the committee itself.

clear enough; its responsibility for dealing with congressional committees concerned with aid problems was divided with the aid agency, leaving the latter in an exposed and vulnerable position, especially when seeking budgetary support. The separation between traditional diplomacy and foreign aid also forced ICA to carry out public information roles it was ill-equipped to perform in the United States and policy roles it was unprepared to assume abroad. The new higher status given to the foreign aid agency in 1961, wisely maintaining the policy subordination to the State Department, offers a hope of achieving better integration between foreign policy and economic operations. But a more thorough integration of key career personnel among the policy and operating agencies would also be necessary for the sake of coordination in the field. Political and economic officers in the foreign service, as well as military attachés, could benefit from training in the theory and practice of foreign aid. An exchange of personnel and experience among economic, technical, and military aid staffs has never been attempted on a large-scale basis. The gap between diplomacy and foreign aid operations has remained formidable.

The basic administrative problem in foreign aid, like that of a military operation, is the marshalling and deployment of resources. Even after many reorganizations different agencies are offering various forms of technical, economic, and cultural assistance, making decisions and seeking funds independently. Present arrangements afford only rudimentary means for relating the American diplomatic and political effort to that of other nations operating similar or parallel programs, or for establishing effective working relationships with the planning apparatus of the receiving government. The scattered administrative mechanisms for these functions are loosely coordinated by the State Department; but such organizational "looseness" does not mean administrative flexibility. The tendency to rigidity is a normal phenomenon in large agencies exhorted to caution in the use of public funds, especially if their operations are widespread. But when operations are diffused among several large agencies, the rigidity may amount to calcification as each circumscribes its activities to avoid interagency competition.

Although it is clear that coordination among these agencies must take place at the national level, the country requirements described in earlier chapters also call for a high degree of administrative flexibility within the operating agencies as well. The use of short-term consultants and special contractors supporting a country team's permanent nucleus of planners and technicians often makes it possible to reduce the self-perpetuating tendencies of a standing administrative group; but this approach is not a substitute for long-term country planning. The use of contract personnel has not been skillful within many aid missions, in part because of problems posed in Washington. Some contract personnel have been denied logistical support in the field because of accidents of negotiation in the contractor's home office; nonprofit contracts have been subjected to the same refund provisions that were applied to private enterprise, so that university endowment resources or state taxpayers were liable for the reimbursement of expenses rejected by a government auditor; engineering and construction contract awards have been made on the basis of total cost estimates rather than competition over a firm fee with costs left subject to engineering requirements. In each case the denial of flexibility in the operations mission offered a rigid form of protection against corruption or malfeasance that could be better controlled by post-audit devices.

Operational flexibility would also make it possible for the United States to act more promptly on legitimate and urgent requests for aid. The long "wind-up" that has preceded the extension of American aid has involved requests, offers, negotiations, agreements, orders, announcements, bids, more negotiations, inspections, plans, further negotiations, and finally operations, accompanied, often enough, by announcements and speeches, and followed up by well-publicized investigations. The completed project is often an anticlimax. These procedures have been useful as a means of preventing waste or careless planning or as instructional devices for technicians in the host country. But there have been times when prompt performance was more important than preliminary publicity or incidental educational benefits. Some attention should be given to the appropriation of funds for projects to be administered under special or emergency provisions designed for speed and effectiveness; the Communists need have no inviolable monopoly on successful "impact" projects. Special task forces with procedures for entering quickly into contracts for services and supplies could match the best demonstrations offered by the Communists. Normal post-audit procedures could control misuse of funds, once the purposes had been clarified, the impact areas chosen, and the necessary agreements reached.

The requirements of administrative reform were eloquently summarized in the words of a successful and distinguished ICA mission director in an unpublished report submitted to Washington in 1960:

> The field missions ought to look upon Washington as a center of ideas and leadership; a promoter of forward motion; a defender of human errors committed in the field, a supplier of necessarily central judgments, and, on request, of very advanced technical information; a performer of central services such as training and recruiting; an articulate defender of the program; the keeper of the evidence of world-wide progress of the program and the place to go for help when the field gets into trouble.
>
> This is far from the picture which comes through to the field. Unhappily the recurrent and dominant picture is one of a great impersonal machine which examines minute details without any apparent pattern, which opposes decisions urged by the field until months elapse and opportunities erode, which is overworked and harried and hurried and arbitrary, and can only be moved to agree to actions which seem . . . obvious to those on the spot. . . . Certainly the overwhelming Washington influence seems to the field to be to oppose rather than to stimulate forward momentum. . . . It is because the overburdened Washington staff has been trying to make too many decisions for which it has inadequate time, local information, and technical manpower. It has attempted to perform a task which was doomed to failure no matter how high the competence or how deep the dedication to duty.

Multilateral and Bilateral Aid

The increasing internationalism of aid operations has been widely greeted as a means of avoiding the often irrelevant political restrictions placed on American funds by Congress, the increasing bureaucratic rigidities of U.S. aid administration, the aimless duplication of functions among agencies (especially as other donor nations undertake programs of their own), and the complications that arise from government-to-government relationships in giving and receiving funds and advice. The impressive successes of the World Bank and of some agencies of the United Nations in delicate negotiations have confirmed the usefulness of the multilateral approach, and American taxpayers can be grateful that the foreign aid burdens borne by the United States can be increasingly shared with such competent partners.

It is almost inconceivable, however, that multilateral approaches can wholly replace specifically American programs. The probability is that American involvement in some forms of bilateral aid will continue throughout the twentieth century. Certainly aid that is offered in connection with the use of military and naval bases and for maintaining agreed levels of military strength will continue so long as the need for cooperation in the military field exists. The large country programs recently classified under "defense support" appropriations will also have to continue so long as the cold war or other conditions force many of America's allies to maintain larger military forces than their internal economies would permit. It is possible that these costs may be increasingly shared with other allies, but however the requirements and the burden-sharing arrangements may be formulated, the United States will still be carrying a substantial operational burden.

A principal advantage of international agencies is their informal and uncomplicated use of individual technicians. At present the United Nations is not organized in such a way as to develop integrated country policies; its field apparatus is limited, and the procedures for augmenting existing staffs are slow and cumbersome. UN activities tend to leave the individual technicians to make their own recommendations to the government to which they are accredited, and the independent agencies involved in rendering technical assistance are seldom interested in developing interfunctional programs. Only under crisis conditions like those of the Congo in the fall of 1960 can country programs emerge from these international bodies, and even then a coherent policy cannot always be developed. Where UN activities succeed in transcending the limitations of the cold war, their financial and political base can still be undermined by the Soviet bloc at its own discretion. But entirely apart from the threat of Communist wrecking, international agencies are under no obligation to allocate aid under their theoretically neutral criteria in such a way as to serve the ends of American foreign policy. The absence of political coloration may be useful in many respects, but the cold war, after all, is not unrelated to foreign aid. UN programs cannot fill the need met by the military and political operations conducted under

American programs designated as "defense support" and "special assistance."

The amounts and types of aid required among the countries of the underdeveloped world will vary tremendously: they must meet the economic needs of the poorest and most primitive country of Africa and still serve relatively advanced India and the energetic but overburdened Republic of China on Taiwan. Leaving entirely to the United Nations or other international organizations the decision as to the amount and type of aid to be offered each country would surely not in itself satisfy American policy requirements. Even if objective means were available for determining aid needs, absorptive capacity, and prospects for maximum employment of aid resources, such standards would ignore other factors that will continue to compel the United States to offer aid on humanitarian or political grounds. Thus, while increased reliance on international agencies will be possible in the 1960s, especially for the coordination of bilateral programs, the use of aid to encourage the development of suitable and durable institutions in a stable political society, as for other purposes, will continue to be an important element in American development diplomacy.

5. Foreign Aid as an Instrument of Democracy

The cold war context does not embrace all political objectives served by foreign aid. In times of political uncertainty the exigencies of the cold war may require the use of aid funds as a contribution to governmental stability through support to whatever leaders may be found who possess enough organized strength to stave off collapse. But even in these circumstances American aid tends to strengthen other elements of stability within the society—the army, the bureaucracy, and the business, professional, or landowning community—and thus contributes to the development of alternative leadership. A political calculus of this sort is, to be sure, a dangerous procedure. The forces of presumed stability that emerge may not succeed in gaining the public confidence after all, or the leadership supported by aid funds may abuse its position at the expense of the public welfare, making the donors of aid its scapegoat.

In Viet-Nam it has been representatives of the rising middle class, a principal beneficiary of American operations, who have most freely criticized the U.S. aid program and expressed disappointment over the slow pace of reform. The existence of such criticism suggests the role many observers believe foreign aid should play in creating or supporting potential elements of purpose, strength, stability, and growth in developing countries. In spite of the support aid funds have given to existing leaders, in spite of signs of arbitrary rule and dictatorship to be seen in so many of the underdeveloped nations, probably the long-term tendency of American aid has been to contribute to trends toward a pluralistic society resembling that which in the Western world has afforded protection against government by and for the self-appointed few. The political implications of the pluralistic society encouraged by the processes of change suggest a significant role for future aid policy in pointing out desirable directions of political and social evolution in the underdeveloped world.

These are perhaps the most sensitive aspects of aid. They may arouse the greatest opposition from powerful and privileged groups in the receiving countries. Support to land reforms will enable peasants to share more abundantly in the fruits of their labor, but will offend landowners; the supplying of simple consumer goods in rural areas tends to run counter to the desire of city dwellers to concentrate on imported luxuries for themselves; the offering of loans to small business and industrial enterprise capable of a sizable collective contribution may make it necessary to curb the temptation to demand more impressive capital investments; the encouragement of a broad diffusion of stock ownership in industrial enterprises will give a broader base of interest in the economic development of the country, but may encounter resistance from privileged classes. Similarly, strong support to educational and health activities in rural areas runs counter to the desire for a concentration on impressive hospitals and universities in the cities; the offering of educational and travel opportunities to village leaders and private persons as well as to public officials may be objectionable to the regime in power; and activities in support of rural credit, farm cooperatives, youth programs, and public health needs may help develop resistance to domestic injustice or misrule, and may therefore have to be urged upon a suspicious or an indifferent government.

Projects in support of political or social reform are not always suited to immediate political objectives. The case studies from

Viet-Nam show how difficult they can be, and how damaging on occasion. Nor do they necessarily serve the long-term objectives of more broadly based and stable societies. No one should presume that foreign aid can produce or even sustain a particular form of government. But it can strongly support the elements capable of contributing to a better political and economic life if it is flexibly administered with such purposes in mind.

The "better life" in an immediate, consumer's sense is within the range of interests foreign aid can serve. It is not limited to capital development or long-term institution-building. One of the ironies of the past decade of Western policy has been the emphasis placed on military and capital goods as the only legitimate elements of foreign aid (apart from consumption commodities provided out of U.S. agricultural surpluses), when the most marked element of superiority of capitalist economics over the Communist system is the attention it can devote to satisfying consumer wants. The means for providing more people with the material good things of life are not far to seek in the affluent society of the West.

What about the "better life" in the matter of human rights and political institutions? Parliamentary democracy is neither the natural state of man nor the conscious desire of all nations. Its achievement in the West is the precarious result of centuries of experimentation and speculation. Its institutions, a product of history, convenience, and purpose, are not hardy enough to survive in all environments. And its ethic proscribes any effort at destroying legitimate individual or national aspirations of other peoples. For these reasons alone, apart from its own limited capabilities in that direction, American development diplomacy must refrain from attempting to enforce ready-made ideologies and unfamiliar institutions upon doubting or unprepared governments and peoples. The radical transplantation of Western institutions in the political hothouses of Asia and Africa has rarely proven either successful or desirable.

But foreign aid is not for that reason politically "neutral." Its effects are powerfully manifested in international relations and in the domestic politics of both the giver and the receiver. It represents a new international ethic, at least in that it compels nations to take a more sympathetic view of each other. Whether or not it is to become a normal relationship between the rich and the poor nations in the decades ahead will not depend upon

American decisions alone. What the American nation can decide, however, is the manner in which it presents the case for freedom by offering progress in order and decency. The kinds of freedom social and technological evolution has made possible in the West arise out of a respect for the moral aspirations of individual citizens. The devising of constitutions and institutions, legislation and organization, and systems of production and distribution can be left to themselves if the ethic is once accepted. The details alone have little intrinsic merit. Placing American policy on the side of these basic principles as long-term purposes of foreign aid is a political necessity because in the absence of such affirmation the impact of American operations may so easily strengthen exploiting and humanity-destroying forces.

Economic and technical advancement does not necessarily produce a stable and decent political order, and the agents contributing to such advancement must bear a responsibility for its political and social consequences. This obligation is not a franchise for the revolutionists, saboteurs, or subversives who accompany the Communist international operations; but it does justify a strong, conscious support of the forces for decency and orderly progress at work in any developing society. As a positive force engaged in building elements of democratic strength in an environment of change, foreign aid can help offset the destructive efforts of those who would submerge individual freedom in a sea of turbulent ideology and totalitarian institutions.

Appendix I-A

SUMMARIES OF U.S. AID TO BURMA, TAIWAN, THAILAND, AND VIET-NAM

Notes: Economic aid data are given as both obligations and expenditures, as indicated in each table; they include "defense support" funds. The term "obligations" is used to include loan approvals and authorizations. (For a breakdown of obligations, see Appendix I-B.) In the case of military aid the published figures are identical for obligations and expenditures. PL 480 data are Title I sales agreements, valued at market cost (including cost of ocean transportation), as provided for in the Agricultural Trade Development and Assistance Act of 1954.

Sources: Agency for International Development, Statistics and Reports Division, *U.S. Foreign Assistance and Assistance from International Organizations*, July 1, 1945–June 30, 1961 (Washington: Author, 1962); International Cooperation Administration, Office of Statistics and Reports, *Operations Report* (Washington: Author, annual issues).

TABLE 1

Summary of U.S. Aid to Burma

(in millions of dollars or dollar equivalents)

	1946-1954	1955	1956	1957	1958	1959	1960	1961
Fiscal year obligations								
Economic grant aid	21.2	0.1	0.3	0.4	11.6	1.2	1.2	0.6
Economic loans	5.0		17.3	0.8	32.7	7.3		
Total[a]	26.2	0.1	17.6	1.2	44.3	8.5	1.2	0.6
PL 480 sales agreements			21.7	1.0	18.0			
Fiscal year expenditures	18.4	1.0	0.2	0.1	0.3	6.3	3.9	1.9

(a) No military aid has gone to Burma.

281

TABLE 2

Summary of U.S. Aid to Nationalist China (Taiwan)

(in millions of dollars or dollar equivalents)

	1946-1954	1955	1956	1957	1958	1959	1960	1961
Fiscal year obligations								
Economic grant aid	1,092.5ᵃ	120.2	62.9	78.6	71.3	89.9	82.8	74.4
Economic loans	128.7ᵇ	20.0	20.0	20.0	30.9	11.1	40.2	44.6
Total, economic aid	1,221.2	140.2	82.9	98.6	102.2	101.0	123.0	119.0
Military grants	537.1ᶜ	308.4	351.2	171.6	162.1	239.5	139.9	91.0
Total	1,758.3	448.6	434.1	270.2	264.3	340.5	262.9	210.0
PL 480 sales agreements				9.3	12.1	13.4	6.0	21.4
Fiscal year expenditures								
Economic	570.4	105.8	96.5	96.3	68.2	68.1	74.2	102.1

(a) In the period, 1946-1954, three-fourths of the economic grant aid, chiefly for relief operations, went to the Nationalist Government when it was still on the mainland.

(b) Export-Import Bank loans and surplus property credits to the Nationalist Government on the mainland.

(c) Military grants of $141 million went to the Nationalist Government on the mainland. Most of the remainder was obligated to Taiwan in FY 1953 and 1954.

TABLE 3

Summary of U.S. Aid to Thailand

(in millions of dollars or dollar equivalents)

	1946-1954	1955	1956	1957	1958	1959	1960	1961
Fiscal year obligations								
Economic grant aid	31.4	46.5	24.5	24.6	24.2	24.2	23.5	25.4
Economic loans	7.2	1.9	10.0	11.0	1.8	34.8	2.1	
Total, economic aid	38.6	48.4	34.5	35.6	26.0	59.0	25.6	25.4
Military grants	111.2[a]	40.8	43.4	26.2	19.7	18.0	24.7	23.9
Total	149.8	89.2	77.9	61.8	45.7	77.0	50.3	49.3
PL 480 sales agreements		2.2		2.1				
Fiscal year expenditures								
Economic	17.8	6.9	24.8	42.5	26.5	39.5	34.3	29.3

(a) In the period, 1946-1954, 85 per cent of military aid was obligated in FY 1953 and 1954.

TABLE 4

Summary of U.S. Aid to Viet-Nam

(in millions of dollars or dollar equivalents)

	1946-1954a	1955	1956	1957	1958	1959	1960	1961
Fiscal year obligations								
Economic grant aid	825.6	322.4	185.0	257.2	187.6	187.9	170.6	137.3
Economic loans			25.0	25.0	1.5	19.5	11.4	13.2
Total, economic aid	825.6	322.4	210.0	282.2	189.1	207.4	182.0	150.5
Military grants	709.6		167.3	110.5	53.2	41.9	70.9	65.0
Total	1,535.2	322.4	377.3	392.7	242.3	249.3	252.9	215.5
PL 480 sales agreements					5.9		7.0	10.0
Fiscal year expenditures								
Economic	825.6	129.1	192.8	251.3	212.3	179.2	181.2	146.4

(a) Total aid program for the Associated States of Indo-China, including deobligations in the years since 1954.

Appendix I-B

U.S. ECONOMIC AID TO BURMA, TAIWAN, THAILAND, AND VIET-NAM

Notes: ICA project aid covers activities directed at specific undertakings; nonproject aid is designed to meet broad economic needs and includes emergency aid and assistance to refugees. Development Loan Fund figures are approvals and those for the Export-Import Bank are credits authorized. PL 480 figures are Title II grants authorized for emergency assistance and Title III donations for relief agencies (valued at CCC costs), provided for in the Agricultural Trade Development and Assistance Act of 1954. Local currency transactions are planned grants and loans of U.S.-owned foreign currencies acquired by sales of agricultural products under (a) Secs. 550 and 402 of the 1951 and 1954 Mutual Security Acts and (b) Title I of PL 480.

Sources: Agency for International Development, Statistics and Reports Division, *U.S. Foreign Assistance and Assistance from International Organizations,* July 1, 1945–June 30, 1961 (Washington: Author, 1962); International Cooperation Administration, Office of Statistics and Reports, *Operations Report* (Washington: Author, annual issues); U.S. President, *The 14th Semiannual Report on the Food-for-Peace Program Carried on under Public Law 480, 83d Congress, as Amended* (Washington: GPO, 1961), and earlier semiannual reports.

TABLE 1

U.S. Economic Aid to Burma, 1955-1961

(in thousands of dollars or dollar equivalents)

Fiscal year obligations	1955	1956	1957	1958	1959	1960	1961
Project aid							
Food and agriculture				7,790	2,500		
Industry and mining				1,863	600		
Transportation				6,949			223
Labor							
Health and sanitation				3,598			
Education						1,000	6
Public administration and safety				4,000	4,800		
Community development, social welfare, and housing							
Technical support						58	189
General and miscellaneous							
Total project aid				24,200	7,900	1,058	417
Nonproject aid							
Total ICA obligations				24,200	7,900	1,058	417
PL 480, Title III	91	302	356	551	554	74	240
Total dollar aid, economic	91	302	356	24,751	8,454	1,132	657
Local currency grants and loans		17,300	800	19,500			
Total economic aid	91	17,602	1,156	44,251	8,454	1,132	657

TABLE 2
U.S. Economic Aid to Nationalist China (Taiwan), 1955-1961
(in thousands of dollars or dollar equivalents)

Fiscal year obligations	1955	1956	1957	1958	1959	1960	1961
Project aid							
Food and agriculture	2,116	1,046	2,599	1,469	1,692	1,151	794
Industry and mining	29,347	17,017	30,609	21,014	17,771	2,829	4,628
Transportation	1,352	1,287	7,320	2,835	7,790	5,238	675
Labor	4	15					
Health and sanitation	1,005	3,177	1,560	751	399	667	531
Education	952	1,144	1,075	900	1,040	946	992
Public administration and safety	1,201	283	181	100	156	161	443
Community development, social welfare, and housing	16	438	44	18	14	28	412
Technical support			147	235	323	341	381
General and miscellaneous	6,154a	5,136	5,215	2,001	1,886	2,281	
Total project aid	42,148	29,544	48,748	29,322	31,070	13,640	8,857
Nonproject aid	75,441	23,748	15,000	30,700	41,975	56,800	43,248
Total ICA obligations	117,589	53,292	63,748	60,022	73,045	70,440	52,105
Development Loan Fund				27,886	7,100	40,250	38,900
PL 480, Titles II and III	2,603	9,612	10,529	5,330	9,911	7,251	10,850
Total dollar aid, economic	120,192	62,904	74,277	93,238	90,056	117,940	101,854
Local currency grants and loans	20,000	20,000	24,400	9,000	11,000	5,100	17,200
Total economic aid	140,192	82,904	98,677	102,238	101,056	123,040	119,054

(a) Includes $5,375,000 for "direct military support," i.e., civilian-type goods for the military forces.

TABLE 3

U.S. Economic Aid to Thailand, 1955-1961

(in thousands of dollars or dollar equivalents)

Fiscal year obligations	1955	1956	1957	1958	1959	1960	1961
Project aid							
Food and agriculture	1,008	1,785	1,126	541	525	592	1,168
Industry and mining	311	340	5,837	99	272	359	946
Transportation	9,683	8,537	19,134	3,386	3,700	2,633	757
Labor	32	38	49	3			
Health and sanitation	1,268	1,037	820	841	617	1,166	1,115
Education	1,213	1,802	1,186	1,038	811	956	676
Public administration and safety	632	363	339	1,420	1,349	888	822
Community development, social welfare, and housing		5	34	15	18	44	124
Technical support				450	489	658	780
General and miscellaneous	5,085a	239	975	634	729	671	472
Total project aid	19,231	14,146	29,500	8,427	8,510	7,962	6,860
Nonproject aid	27,304	20,310	5,000	15,720	15,600	15,229	18,400
Total ICA obligations	46,535	34,456	34,500	24,147	24,110	23,266	25,260
Development Loan Fund				1,750	20,750		
Export-Import Bank	1,200				14,000	240	
PL 480, Title III		37	67	105	60	66	62
Total dollar aid, economic	47,735	34,493	34,567	26,002	58,920	23,572	25,322
Local currency grants and loans	700		1,000			1,900	
Total economic aid	48,435	34,493	35,567	26,002	58,920	25,472	25,322

(a) Includes $4,933,000 for "direct military support," i.e., civilian-type goods for the military forces.

TABLE 4

U.S. Economic Aid to Viet-Nam, 1955-1961

(in thousands of dollars or dollar equivalents)

Fiscal year obligations	1955	1956	1957	1958	1959	1960	1961
Project aid							
Food and agriculture	1,168	1,964	4,814	2,204	2,498	2,276	1,698
Industry and mining	631	534	8,880	466	2,042	1,844	1,123
Transportation	1,896	6,083	18,804	16,029	21,335	11,034	740
Labor	5	58			7	1	5
Health and sanitation	927	1,138	4,469	1,795	1,936	2,640	3,181
Education	169	330	1,963	1,120	1,443	2,490	1,781
Public administration and safety	1,048	2,566	7,313	4,031	3,983	5,867	1,629
Community development, social welfare, and housing	166	8,468				7	
Technical support	1,191	1,580	1,430	3,143	2,704	2,417	2,566
General and miscellaneous			1,265	545	486	344	634
Total project aid	7,200	22,721	48,939	29,333	36,434	28,920	13,357
Nonproject aid	312,995	172,966	210,499	150,089	144,994	131,878	114,491
Total ICA obligations	320,195	195,687	259,438	179,422	181,428	160,798	127,848
Development Loan Fund					19,500	9,700	10,700
PL 480, Titles II and III	2,223	14,323	22,780	5,151	6,500	6,257	4,528
Total dollar aid, economic	322,418	210,010	282,218	184,573	207,428	176,755	143,076
Local currency grants and loans				4,500		5,200	7,500
Total economic aid	322,418	210,010	282,218	189,073	207,428	181,955	150,576

Appendix I-C

LOCAL CURRENCY PROGRAMS, 1955-1961

Notes: The United States has some degree of control over two kinds of local currency accounts: (1) Counterpart funds, which are generated by U.S. grants under the aid program. These funds are owned by the recipient country, which agrees that a small portion may be used to meet local U.S. expenses; the remainder is available for the recipient country's use, subject to U.S. approval. (2) U.S.-owned accounts. Local currencies are acquired by the United States from sales of surplus agricultural commodities under the Mutual Security Acts of 1951 (Sec. 550) and 1954 (Sec. 402) and under the Agricultural Trade Development and Assistance Act of 1954 (PL 480, Title I). The sales proceeds are available for U.S. foreign currency needs and for grants and loans to the purchasing country.

The data in the accompanying tables represent the amounts approved for country use (1955-1956) and the amounts withdrawn by the country after U.S. approval (1957-1961) under all local currency programs. The exchange rates used to arrive at dollar equivalents of local currencies are given in the country tables; for 1955-1959 they are the current deposit rates, for 1960 and 1961 the U.S. Treasury Department selling rates.

Local currency data should not be regarded as "additional" U.S. aid, since adding them to the totals in Appendixes I-A and I-B would involve substantial double counting.

Source: International Cooperation Administration, Office of Statistics and Reports, *Counterpart Funds and ICA Foreign Currency Accounts* (Washington: Author, annual issues).

TABLE 1

Burma: Local Currency Programs, 1955-1961

(approximate dollar equivalents, in thousands)

Fiscal year withdrawals	1955	1956	1957	1958	1959	1960	1961
Food and agriculture	195				1,505	a	
Industry and mining	60					160	117
Health and sanitation					221		
Education	544						
General and miscellaneous	30		4	−3	−33	−4	−5
Total, economic	829		4	−3	1,693	156	112

(a) Less than the equivalent of $500.

Exchange rates (number of kyats per U.S. dollar):

1955-1958	4.78
1959	4.76
1960-1961	4.74

TABLE Σ

Nationalist China (Taiwan): Local Currency Programs, 1955-1961

(approximate dollar equivalents, in thousands)

Fiscal year withdrawals	1955	1956	1957	1958	1959	1960	1961
Food and agriculture	9,309	11,509	10,012	8,576	5,404	12,524	9,537
Industry and mining	13,955	11,791	14,340	15,772	10,101	13,243	13,769
Transportation	2,884	4,838	5,574	9,595	1,976	5,863	2,475
Labor	28	6	–81	a			
Health and sanitation	1,078	8,991	7,215	3,120	1,565	2,196	1,758
Education	1,024	2,391	1,705	1,890	2,013	2,286	2,117
Public administration and safety	1,524	825	852	483	51	38	234
Community development, social welfare, and housing	1,874	4,605	2,946	1,045	384	2,208	311
General and miscellaneous	618	5,060	8,974	892	2,508	7,191	20,335
Total, economic	32,294	50,016	51,537	41,373	24,000	45,549	50,536
Direct military support	36,688	24,604	27,919	16,319	18,702	31,211	16,887
Total	68,982	74,620	79,456	57,692	42,702	76,760	67,423

(a) Less than the equivalent of $500.

Exchange rates (number of new Taiwan dollars per U.S. dollar):

1955	15.65
1956-1957	24.78
1958	36.38 (for counterpart accounts); 25.23 (for Sec. 402 sales); 24.78 (for PL 480, Title I sales). Of the total equivalent of $57.7 million, $26.6 million was counterpart, $30.8 million was Sec. 402.
1959	39.93
1960-1961	40.00

TABLE 3

Thailand: Local Currency Programs, 1955-1961

(approximate dollar equivalents, in thousands)

Fiscal year withdrawals	1955	1956	1957	1958	1959	1960	1961
Food and agriculture	1,374	1,157	1,658	1,330	1,041	1,048	402
Industry and mining	192	64	401	524	672	1,790	832
Transportation	189	3,341	7,833	9,979	5,731	7,202	6,330
Labor	73						
Health and sanitation	2,031	246	636	884	733	1,030	1,359
Education	868	342	461	530	592	676	624
Public administration and safety	−53	55	111	155	383	743	112
Community development, social welfare, and housing	408	130		−15			8
General and miscellaneous	427	2,548	2,263	2,822	1,919	4,041	3,455
Total, economic	5,509	7,883	13,363	16,210	11,071	16,538	13,122
Direct military support			2,501	4,950	8,239	4,783	1,452
Total	5,509	7,883	15,864	21,160	19,310	21,321	14,574

Exchange rates (number of bahts per U.S. dollar) :

1955	19.9
1956	20.43
1957-1958	20.78
1959	21.02
1960-1961	20.85

TABLE 4

Viet-Nam: Local Currency Programs, 1955-1961

(approximate dollar equivalents, in thousands)

Fiscal year withdrawals	January 1955 through June 1957	1958	1959	1960	1961
Food and agriculture	17,067	10,174	8,965	1,885	2,138
Industry and mining	345	830	1,388	697	438
Transportation	16,065	17,447	12,950	3,807	3,937
Labor	230	35	9	24	13
Health and sanitation	6,213	680	1,412	761	1,201
Education	6,020	1,389	2,277	683	1,706
Public administration and Safety	5,909	2,086	1,016	879	484
Community development, social welfare, and housing	29,106	2,822	594	127	367
General and miscellaneous	55,151	3,987	288	60	320
Total, economic	136,106	39,450	28,899	8,925	10,604
Direct military support	394,538	205,454	164,751	77,286	71,814
Total	530,644	244,904	193,650	86,211	82,418

Note: These figures do not include the equivalent (in French francs) of $164.5 million furnished to Viet-Nam under triangular trade arrangements; funds received by the United States from sales to France of surplus agricultural products were used by Viet-Nam for purchases in France.

Exchange rates (number of piasters per U.S. dollar):

1955-1959	35
1960-1961	72.77

Appendix II

THE UNSUCCESSFUL HISTORY OF "ECONOMIC DISENGAGEMENT"

The history of American foreign aid has revealed a continuously broadening scope of activities, beginning with well-defined tactical operations in Europe and extending to longer-range policies of a world-wide character. U.S. foreign aid is generally agreed to have started with lend-lease to the allies in World War II. It continued with funds for relief and rehabilitation in allied countries and for cautious reconstruction of wartime enemies under military occupations. In later years there came still more challenging problems that required the extension of foreign aid for the recovery and strengthening of Western Europe and of some Asian nations, and that transformed the military occupations into something resembling foreign aid operations. Each of these programs was defined in terms of somewhat limited goals capable of measurable fulfillment. The challenges of the cold war and the demands of the underdeveloped world later introduced the "open-end" programs of mutual security and technical and economic assistance that characterized the decade of the 1950s.

The transition from discrete, divisible programs to large-scale world strategy began to suggest basic differences between the well-defined, *ad hoc* efforts and those of a continuing and possibly expanding nature. American policy makers in the Congress and the executive branch of the government continued, however, to pace their thinking to a course whose end was in sight. The successive failures of efforts to bring about a disengagement from foreign aid activities in the 1950s reflect the fundamental character of the new problems posed to foreign aid rather than ineptness on the part of those who hoped and planned for imminent American withdrawal. As early as November 1950, the Gray report to the President noted that the original target date for the end of the European Recovery Program, June 1952, could not be met. Nonmilitary aid would have to be continued another three or four years (that is, through 1953 or 1954) to "enable Western European countries to remain effectively functioning partners while undertaking their full and necessary contribution in the joint effort to build adequate defenses for the free world."[1] It was hoped, however, that Japan might be self-supporting by fiscal 1952.

The House of Representatives in passing the Mutual Security Act of 1951 proposed that a date be legislatively designated for terminating the Mutual Security Program. The 1951 Act provided (Secs. 502[c] and 530) that ECA should end as of June 2, 1952, and that military and "limited economic assistance" programs under the Mutual Security Agency were to continue until June 30, 1954. The Mutual Defense Assistance Act of 1949, which covered military aid, "was never intended to be of indefinite duration." The addition of two years for Point Four was based on the assumption that "a fair appraisal of its accomplishments cannot be made for several years."[2]

The executive branch did not challenge the congressional fixing of target dates. Secretary of State Acheson in his testimony on this point stated: "If the termination date were put in, it would probably be desirable to pick out one which would permit the program which we have in mind to be carried out. . . . The important thing, I think, would be to say that here is a program which in so far as we see will last two or three years, and after that we do not know, but we will reconsider the whole matter at that time. . . . the administration of our country's economic help to military production will continue through 1954 anyway, and possibly longer."[3] The testimony of William C. Foster, ECA administrator, also seemed to concede the temporary political advantages of establishing an arbitrary cut-off date. Economic recovery could not be achieved to a sufficient degree in June 1952 to permit a cut-off, he admitted, citing Greece, Italy, Austria, and Iceland as examples. But he estimated that economic assistance under the mutual security program could be terminated in three to five years, when recipients had reached the point where they could maintain the equipment themselves.[4]

Point Four, however, was not in the same category. Later in the same testimony to Congress Mr. Foster presented the first long-range view of technical assistance to underdeveloped areas: "Certainly the concept of technical assistance to the underdeveloped areas is one that I did not intend to measure in terms of a 2-, or 3-, or 4-year program, because I think that may well continue for a long time." The Point

[1] Gordon Gray, *Report to the President on Foreign Economic Policies* (Washington: GPO, 1950), p. 38.

[2] *Mutual Security Act of 1951*, Report 872 of the House Committee on Foreign Affairs, 82d Cong., 1st sess. (Washington: GPO, 1951), p. 49.

[3] *Mutual Security Program*, Hearings before the House Committee on Foreign Affairs, 82d Cong., 1st sess. (Washington: GPO, 1951), pp. 65, 66, 70.

[4] Same, pp. 166, 199-200.

Four Program, he stated, "is considered to be a permanent and long-term and lasting activity, which I believe is a very useful thing for the United States to pursue."[5]

No significant discussion of termination occurred until the approach of some of the terminal dates that had been mentioned. Harold Stassen wrote in April 1954 that the international economic crisis had passed, and that foreign aid should be considered as a means of "building the economic and defense strength of the free nations, not on the basis of a certain year of maximum danger, but on the basis of continuing grave danger for many years." He agreed, however, that the free world must depend primarily on its own resources and efforts "and not on repeated extensions of grant aid from the United States."[6] General George C. Stewart, speaking for the Department of Defense, reported that although the United States had made the initial military contribution it had intended, the problem of the future still remained: "I don't know how many years you are going to have."[7]

At this stage the administration's recommendations for mutual security were ambivalent on the question of duration. It suggested that June 1958 would be a reasonable terminal date for the program, but conceded that: ". . . it is not possible to fix a precise terminal date in the future. In view of the current situation and the uncertainty of the future, the 4-year extension has been proposed as a reasonable estimate under the circumstances."[8]

The Senate Committee on Foreign Relations was unwilling to recommend the 4-year extension. It proposed a 12-month termination date for military and economic assistance authorizations, not because there would be no further need beyond June 1955, but because this would require the President to act "to establish that such programs are essential in the future" before further congressional commitment would be made. "The committee felt that if no termination date were included in the legislation, the tendency would persist to think of military and economic assistance programs of the type authorized in titles I and II of the bill as continuing indefinitely into the future." On the other hand, the committee decided not to suggest a termination date for technical assistance and Title IV programs (special fund, joint-control areas, refugees, children's fund, etc.) because "these pro-

[5] Same, pp. 179, 203.

[6] "The Case for Private Investment Abroad," *Foreign Affairs*, April 1954, pp. 405, 415.

[7] *Mutual Security Act of 1954*, Hearings before the House Committee on Foreign Affairs, 83d Cong., 2nd sess. (Washington: GPO, 1954), p. 104.

[8] *The Mutual Security Program for Fiscal Year 1954*, analysis prepared by the executive branch for use of the House Committee on Foreign Affairs, 83d Cong., 1st sess. (Washington: GPO, 1953), p. 6.

grams must be justified on a yearly basis."[9] The Act as subsequently adopted provided in Sec. 503 that the Foreign Operations Administration, which had authority for all activities except military aid, was to go out of existence in June 1955. Most of its functions were later taken over by ICA, which operated within the Department of State.

The strongest statement against indefinite continuation as a basis for aid was made by Secretary of State Dulles: "We do not believe that even the United States can prudently make vast economic grants a permanent part of its policies." The Secretary pointed out that the amounts requested for 1955 were "on a scale very much less than the preceding year, which is a healthy development." But his statement continued with an important proviso: ". . . as long as we operate on a mutual security basis, we will always have to put up money for that . . . [even though the burden was being increasingly shared by other countries] I think that this community effort, which I hope will continue indefinitely, will continually require some appropriation to support it." Thus the strongest single statement against the permanence of economic grants implied the necessity for continued aid in cooperation with other countries.[10] Mr. Stassen, aid administrator, returned to the optimistic vagueness that had characterized earlier testimony:

> While no one can foresee the unfolding of the world situation . . . . it is my current estimate that the developing world situation is so favorable in its economic aspects that we can contemplate a further sharp decline in the overall requirements in the future fiscal years beyond 1955, and that the trend line can properly now be anticipated to continue downward.[11]

Technical cooperation, he agreed, "should be a continuing, long-term program. . . . It is the kind of program that could continue as long as there are in the world large numbers of people who are suffering seriously from the lack of technical knowledge in the fundamental necessities of human life."[12]

A year later, Mr. Stassen reported that an outstanding achievement of the previous eighteen months

> . . . has been the growing, and by now general, recognition of the long-term nature of the problems which the Mutual Security

[9] *Mutual Security Act of 1954*, Report 1799 of the Senate Committee on Foreign Relations, 83d Cong., 2nd sess. (Washington: GPO, 1954), pp. 5, 83.

[10] *Mutual Security Act of 1954*, Hearings before House Committee on Foreign Affairs, cited, pp. 4, 21.

[11] Same, p. 33.

[12] Same, pp. 359, 365.

Program is helping to solve, and the realization that the Program has become in fact an integral part of our total foreign policy and national security system. This realization has led to the initiation of a more systematic and long-term approach to the solution of these problems. . . . the emergency atmosphere and short-run temporary approach for the total program have been abandoned.[13]

Events, as interpreted by the executive branch, did not appear to confirm the assumptions of the Stassen report, however. Secretary Dulles, in the Senate Hearings of 1956, stated:

It may be asked whether this mutual security program will have to go on forever. The answer, I think, is that that part of the program which contributes to the security of the United States will have to go on so long as our security is threatened.

I hope that that part of the task which relates to the development of the newly developing countries may, more and more, be taken over by private capital. But for that there must be a lessening of the political risks.[14]

In 1957 the President ventured to propose continuing authorization for military and defense support aid and "long-term development assistance" through the new Development Loan Fund.[15] The proposal to provide long-term financing for DLF through the Treasury's borrowing power was rejected by Congress by slow, tortuous degrees. The Senate Committee on Foreign Relations recommended as a compromise that DLF authorizations be funded for 1958 under regular appropriations procedures, with a 3-year planning basis.[16] Congress rejected even this, but agreed to a two-year authorization.[17] This

[13] Foreign Operations Administration, *Report to the President on the Foreign Operations Administration* (Washington: Author, 1955), p. 7.

[14] *Mutual Security Act of 1956*, Hearings before the Senate Committee on Foreign Relations, 84th Cong., 2nd sess. (Washington: GPO, 1956), p. 26.

[15] Message from the President, *Mutual Security Programs*, House Doc. 182, 85th Cong., 1st sess. (Washington: GPO, 1957), pp. 5-6.

[16] The proposal was for a $500-million authorization for FY 1958 and two annual capitalizations of $750 million each in 1959 and 1960 as a "public debt transaction" under the Treasury's borrowing power, "unless disapproved in the act of appropriating these funds." *The Mutual Security Act of 1957*, Report of Senate Committee on Foreign Relations, Senate Report 417, 85th Cong., 1st sess. (Washington: GPO, 1957), p. 11.

[17] The House Committe on Foreign Affairs proposed an annual authorization of $500 million and two annual Treasury advances of $500 million each. *Mutual Security Act of 1957*, Report of Committee on Foreign Affairs, House Report No. 776, 85th Cong., 1st sess. (Washington: GPO, 1957), p. 22. The Conference Committee's report, however, authorized $500 million for

decision doubled the previous time scale for planning, but still did not constitute long-term financing.

In 1958 the President, apparently yielding to advice from the Treasury Department,[18] asked for an ordinary appropriation for the DLF. No mention was made of long-term financing again until 1959, when Senator Fulbright reopened the proposal that the Treasury's borrowing power be made available to the DLF on a long-term basis. His proposal, coupled with the trend from "grants" to "loans," now won approval in the Committee (even Senator Capehart supported the proposal); but the administration was no longer willing to endorse this approach. Mr. Dillon tried to justify the change of policy as follows:

In the first place, we have now only about one year of full-scale operations of the Fund behind us. The additional experience that will come with another year's operation will be invaluable in judging the size and form which longer term capitalization of the Fund should take. You will recall that when the President originally proposed the establishment of the Development Loan Fund 2 years ago he asked for a 3-year capitalization, and, as he stated in his recent message to the Congress, it was his intention, based on observation of its progress within that period, to ask for longer term capitalization commencing in fiscal year 1961. The request for fiscal year 1960 will complete this original 3-year trial period.

Another reason for postponing the decision on long-term capitalization until next year flowed from our desire to insure that the Development Loan Fund fits carefully into the pattern

---

FY 1958 and $625 for FY 1959 as regular appropriations, in view of "the strong sentiment in the House against any appropriations in the form of authorization of borrowing from the United States Treasury in future years." Mutual Security Act of 1957, Conference Report, 85th Cong., 1st sess. (Washington: GPO, 1957), p. 4.

[18] On May 25, 1959, Mr. Dillon, speaking for the State Department, explained: "while it is true that two years ago we [the executive branch] recommended borrowing authority such as you now propose, and that Congress refused such authority, the *fiscal agencies* of the executive branch have since generally gone on record in favor of financing operations such as this through the appropriations process." Mutual Security Act of 1959, Hearings before the Senate Committee on Foreign Relations, 86th Cong., 1st sess. (Washington: GPO, 1959), p. 1238. (Emphasis added.) On p. 1245 he specifically mentioned the Bureau of the Budget and the Treasury Department as recommending the regular governmental financial procedures as a basis for funding DLF operations.

of other development institutions [i.e., the Inter-American Bank and the multilateral International Development Association].[19]

Senator Fulbright continued to defend the adoption of the long-term Treasury-financed approach immediately rather than after another year: "Then you run into an election year. I don't see why you want to delay it. You have had experience; I am willing, so far as I am concerned, to do everything I can this year to help you, and I think you have to face this matter."[20] "I just don't think you can get continuity any other way," he added. Senator Capehart agreed: "You cannot operate a business on that basis [i.e., on year-by-year appropriations]. You have got to operate a business on a long-term basis."[21] Dillon's response indicated the quandary in which he felt himself:

> I am not the fiscal agencies of the U.S. Government. . . . That is my problem. . . . The fiscal agencies of the Government have developed a theory that they would like to put all possible financing through the appropriations process, and I think if we were starting the Export-Import Bank now they would try to get that money appropriated.[22]

In the last analysis Mr. Dillon accepted Senator Capehart's assertion that lending money on a one-year basis invites inefficiency because everyone is in a hurry to get in under the deadline. The administration's position was a retreat, he implied, "because there is a difference of view as far as the fiscal agencies of the Government are concerned."[23]

The final outcome was a committee recommendation greater than the administration's request: instead of the $700-million appropriation for fiscal year 1960 proposed, the committee recommended approval of a $1 billion-a-year borrowing power for 5 years. In the Conference Committee the two houses scaled down this proposal and authorized $1.8 billion, of which $700 million could be advanced in FY 1960 and the remaining $1.1 billion in FY 1961.[24] In 1960 the administration asked for the appropriation of $1.1 billion for FY 1961

[19] *Mutual Security Act of 1959*, Hearings before the Senate Committee on Foreign Relations, cited, p. 26.

[20] Same, p. 1246.

[21] Same, p. 1247.

[22] Same.

[23] Same, p. 1248.

[24] *Mutual Security Act of 1959*, Report of the Senate Foreign Relations Committee, Senate Report 412, 86th Cong., 1st sess. (Washington: GPO, 1959), p. 15.

that had already been authorized. The House Government Operations Committee reported unfavorably on the unbusinesslike practices of the DLF,[25] but there was no evidence that the Congress or the administration was planning to remedy this situation by extending its financial basis.

During the hearings of 1959 the administration seemed to abandon its hopes for longer-term grant aid and to seek ways of using the Development Loan Fund as a vehicle for large-scale programs even though no long-range financing was contemplated. However, Leonard Saccio, speaking for ICA, pointed out that more problems would be created than solved by proposals for terminating defense support and special assistance and providing compensatory increases in amounts available to banking agencies like the DLF. The functions of these two categories of aid, he said, were "crucial" because they permitted the United States to furnish aid "speedily, and on a flexible basis, as needed to meet requirements determined to be important to the U.S. foreign policy objectives." This might be done through the banking approach, but he believed that a revamping of their operations would be required.[26]

Later in 1959 the testimony by Mr. Dillon stated:

It is difficult to foresee how many years ahead this [the mutual security program] will continue. Certainly, the activities of the Development Loan Fund and the activities of our technical assistance program will continue, we think, for quite a few years until such time as these underdeveloped countries can gradually begin to take care of themselves.

The military part of the program, also, is frankly dependent on our relations with the Soviet Union and the Communist bloc. As long as they keep up military pressure and maintain a threatening attitude that will have to continue, presumably, in roughly the same amounts as it has been in the past few years. . . .

We would hope that items for defense support and special assistance would gradually be able to be reduced and absorbed in the funds that are available for loans for Development Loan Fund type of cooperation.[27]

[25] *Operations of the Development Loan Fund*, 14th Report of the House Committee on Government Operations, House Report 1526, 86th Cong., 2nd sess. (Washington: GPO, 1960).

[26] *Mutual Security Act of 1959*, Hearings before the Senate Committee on Foreign Relations, cited, pp. 800-801.

[27] *Mutual Security Appropriations for 1960*, Hearings before the Senate Committee on Appropriations, 86th Cong., 1st sess. (Washington: GPO, 1959), p. 113.

He predicted that development loans would have to continue "until these different countries can begin to carry their own weight." Mr. Dillon expected the loan program to continue for ten years at least: "I think it would go more toward twenty," he added.[28]

The President's 1960 report to Congress referred to the Draper Committee's conclusion that many forms of U.S. economic aid "must continue for as long as the Communist threat exists, and certainly until greater economic progress has been made in underdeveloped nations."[29] This statement suggests that the progress may be made before the Communist threat has subsided, and that it will be the latter that provides the motivation for continued aid. If the contrary view be assumed, suggesting that the threat of communism may recede before an adequate level of economic progress has been achieved, then the Draper report would still imply the necessity for continuation of American aid. It has not appeared politically prudent to stress this probability, however, and in spite of unsuccessful previous flirtations with economic disengagement, it is still considered good congressional manners to anticipate the termination of large-scale grants for foreign aid in a few years.

[28] Same, pp. 119-120.

[29] *Report to Congress on the Mutual Security Program for the Second Half of Fiscal Year 1959*, Department of State Publication 6926 (Washington: Author, 1960), p. 7.

Appendix III

THE SCRIPPS-HOWARD ARTICLES ON
THE VIET-NAM PROGRAM

The Colegrove articles of July 1959 criticizing the American aid program in Viet-Nam may not have been of great importance in the long perspective of foreign aid as an aspect of U.S. foreign policy. Because the affair proved so disruptive, however, and because it illustrated so well the vulnerability of the program in its relations with the Congress and with the press, it was discussed at some length in Chapter V. Additional details, with particular reference to the specific charges made, are given below, in order to show the sharp differences, on questions of fact, between Mr. Colegrove's version and that given by U.S. officials. There follow comments on the differences in interpretation and on the context in which the affair took place.

General Tone of the Articles

Albert M. Colegrove's six articles, "Our Hidden Scandal in Viet Nam," appeared in the following Scripps-Howard newspapers:

Newspaper	Circulation
Albuquerque Tribune	28,536
Cincinnati Post and Times-Star Covington (Ky.) Post and Times-Star }	265,831
Cleveland Press	314,053
Columbus Citizen	88,384
Denver Rocky Mountain News	160,155
El Paso Herald Post	42,933
Evansville Press	46,720
Fort Worth Press	57,861
Houston Press	106,259
Indianapolis Times	92,756

Newspaper	Circulation
Knoxville News-Sentinel	97,018
Memphis Commercial-Appeal	205,710
Memphis Press-Scimitar	147,519
New York World-Telegram and Sun	454,224
Pittsburgh Press	301,730
San Francisco News	101,786
Washington Daily News	174,626
	2,686,101

The articles concentrated on cases of profligacy with American funds, poor judgment and indifference, and high living on the part of American officials, and incompetency or venality on the part of the Vietnamese government. The vivacious, anecdotal style of the reporting conveyed the impression that much more "dirt" had to be withheld because of government secrecy involving "phony" grounds of security (July 22). Loyal and honest officials were described as silenced by a fear of reprisals against anyone who "rocked the boat" by exposing the "whole fantastic story" (July 20 and 22). The articles contrasted the few Americans who worked in the rural areas—"a sweat-soaked handful of dysentery-ridden unfortunates[1] assigned to duties in the provinces, where they train troops, spray village huts to fight malaria, show American movies to wide-eyed peasants, help engineer roads and dredge canals, and do similar tasks" (July 20)—with the many who lived "high on the hog" in Saigon. " 'But really,' I was assured by a $1,160-a-month-plus-free-rent public relations specialist paid to toot the horn for our economic aid program, 'you can get the whole picture in Saigon. No sense tramping around out there in the boondocks. Terribly hot and dirty, you know, and you can't get much from the peasants except disease. All the key people are here.' " (July 20).

The tone and emotional content of the articles, drawing heavily on the lexicon of affective writing, were calculated to appeal to many reader appetites: American idealism betrayed, the scandals uncovered, the petty foibles of the bureaucrats—all at the expense of the taxpayer. "America is spending more than $1 million a day to keep this country alive and on our side—but the well paid U.S. bureaucrats who supervise the program are not preventing serious waste. . . . Dollars vanish by the millions with little or no explanation offered" (July 21).

[1] Like Father Finian in *The Ugly American*, most Americans in Viet-Nam suffered dysentery, but few found in it the satisfaction of heroism that Messrs. Lederer and Burdick did; and its usefulness as a leveler of men was no contribution to Vietnamese-American solidarity.

Questions of Fact

Many of the facts as reported in the Colegrove articles were directly contradicted by official reports. The differences can best be compared in the parallel columns below.

Facts (Colegrove Version)

(a) "Only in Korea have we spent more" than in Viet-Nam (July 20).

(b) Total aid to Viet Nam was $2 billion (July 24).

(c) There were "only 300 trained technicians and engineers by [Vietnamese] government count" (July 21).

Facts (Official Sources)

(a) More military assistance alone had also been given to France, Taiwan, Italy, Greece, Turkey, Pakistan, India, Belgium, Britain, the Netherlands, and other countries. In economic and military categories combined, other countries would also have to be added.

(b) The "grand total" was reported to the Senate as $1.15 billion.[2]

(c) A tabulation of technicians in Viet-Nam should have included the following trained by USOM: over 2,700 engineers and technicians in transportation, communications, and power; over 3,400 agricultural technicians; almost 300 graduates of the National Institute of Administration; and over 33,-000 technicians and engineers trained in the Military Assistance Advisory Group.[3]

[2] *Situation in Vietnam*, Hearings before the Subcommittee on State Department Organization and Public Affairs, Senate Committee on Foreign Relations, 86th Cong., 1st sess. (Washington: GPO, 1959), p. 197. The USOM director suggested that Colegrove's error might have come about from adding "defense support aid" to "military aid" although "they were the same funds."

[3] Same, p. 10. Colegrove's statement might have referred to the total membership of a society of engineers. Obviously the term "technicians" was loosely defined on both sides.

Facts (Colegrove Version)

(d) 14 radio towers costing $28,-500 had been paid for three years earlier, but "no one has yet laid eyes on those towers. . . . When [an American technician] persisted in making inquiries . . . he was called on the carpet and royally bawled out for stirring up trouble" (July 21).

(e) Of the $71 million given to the Vietnamese government to provide for refugees, only $34 million had been immediately accounted for, and $22 million was still "missing" (July 21).

(f) $8 million of the funds given for transporting refugees had been "burned in a 1955 fire" (July 21).

(g) 2,700 vehicles had been "given to one branch of the Viet Nam government," which made no accounting for them and wound up,

Facts (Official Sources)

(d) Only 10 towers had been purchased in 1956. They had been bought with piasters rather than dollars, at a cost equivalent to $11,305.38. One was in use and the others were erected or awaiting erection.[4]

(e) Audit reports were completed in 1958, and were available for public inspection. Accounts were complete for sums greater than the total U.S. contribution.[5]

(f) The fire destroyed documentation but no funds. The funds themselves were from Vietnamese sources, since the U.S. contribution had been accounted for.[6]

(g) USOM gave 1,730 vehicles to various agencies of the government, the largest number given to any single agency being 690 distributed for

[4] Same, pp. 11, 55; *Current Situation in the Far East*, Hearings before the Subcommittee on the Far East and the Pacific, House Committee on Foreign Affairs, 86th Cong., 1st sess. (Washington: GPO, 1959), pp. 40, 122.

[5] *Situation in Vietnam*, Hearings, cited, p. 11. According to the Final Audit Report, "Expenditures totaling VN $1,430,889,967 have been fully documented by various ministries and agencies of the G[overnment of] V[iet] N[am]. This is VN $20,444,967 in excess of the ICA-financed contribution of VN $1,410,445,000." The ICA contribution was equivalent to $40,298,428 U.S., to which some $15.8 million was added for "U.S. Navy costs and some off-shore procurement." Same, pp. 42, 45.

[6] Same, pp. 158-159.

Facts (Colegrove Version)	Facts (Official Sources)

after much delay, with "a few dozen still missing" (July 21).

public administration and police purposes.[7]

(h) The Deputy Director of the Voice of America had promised to give Radio Vietnam a 50,000-watt transmitter, found he had violated the law by so doing, and withdrew the promise. Subsequently, to save "face," the equipment was "quietly sandwiched into the USOM budget for Viet Nam" (July 22).

(h) The Deputy Director had made no commitment. In any case, he would have been authorized by law to do so if the equipment were available. The USOM decision to supply the equipment arose out of "discussion following the reorganization of Radio Vietnam."[8]

(i) "Many American Government families here enjoy homes and villas that cost U.S. taxpayers upward of $600 a month (July 23).

(i) Of 269 leases held in 1959, only one cost more than $600 per month, and only three others exceeded $500 per month.[9]

(j) "To compensate for a nonexistent high cost of living, an unmarried civilian receives $400 extra a year, while the family man draws $800 extra" (July 23).

(j) There were no cost-of-living allowances for civilians in Saigon after September 1957.[10]

(k) "At least 90 per cent of the Americans never leave Saigon overnight" (July 23).

(k) "Roughly 17 per cent of the Americans in Vietnam are [i.e., live] outside of the Saigon-Cholon area."[11] Moreover, "American personnel visited every accessible region

[7] Military vehicles of all kinds were lost during the Indochinese War between 1945-54, but no accounting was required of them. Approximately 10,000 vehicles were given by MAAG but none were unaccounted for. Same, pp. 152-158.

[8] Same, p. 147.

[9] Current Situation in the Far East, Hearings, cited, p. 22. The confusion might have been caused by the use of different conversion rates.

[10] Same.

[11] Situation in Vietnam, Hearings, cited, p. 188.

Facts (Colegrove Version)　　　　*Facts (Official Sources)*

in Vietnam . . . ICA personnel perform an average of 90 official trips outside of Saigon each month [i.e., overnight on travel orders]. During 1959 fiscal year, USIS officers made 35 trips out of Saigon for a total of 170 days. . . . Military personnel averaged more than 450 trips to the field each month."[12] Such trips occurred despite the fact that on frequent occasions, for security reasons, travel on the highways outside Saigon was prohibited at night.[13]

(1) "We are also giving, outright, millions in cold U.S. cash to a country that has a desperate scarcity of skilled accountants. . . . Nonetheless once we arrange to deliver a batch of money . . . American officials wash their hands of further responsibility" (July 21).

(1) No cash has been given to Viet Nam since the emergency period ending in 1956. All assistance of other types was subject to audits and end-use checks, and the Vietnamese government was asked to make refunds in cases of improper use, although this procedure had little practical significance in a country whose public economy was 75 per cent dependent upon various forms of U.S. aid and related revenues. The scarcity of skilled accountants was minimized by the effective use of IBM equipment in the National Budget and Accounting Office.[14]

[12] *Current Situation in the Far East,* Hearings, cited, p. 121.
[13] Same, p. 23.
[14] Same, pp. 302-303.

Facts (Colegrove Version)	Facts (Official Sources)
(m) "Some U.S. 'jamming' equipment is on the way [to prevent reception of broadcasts from the Communist north]" (July 22).	(m) No jamming equipment was supplied by the United States, or was under consideration.[15]
(n) After a $25,000 building had been constructed for Radio Saigon, it was discovered that no tower over 90 feet in height could be built near the airport (July 22).	(n) The restrictions would permit a 273.9-foot tower.[16]
(o) "In addition to all the standard government benefits there are 20 official no-work holidays annually—including a 3-day lay-off for the Vietnamese New Year and a day's rest on the anniversary of Confucius" (July 23).	(o) There were eight U.S. holidays and seven and one-half days off for the major national Vietnamese observances.[17]
(p) "The typical civilian employee . . . receives . . . [a total income of] $12,200 a year . . ." (July 23).	(p) The actual average total, with allowances, was $10,142.40.[18]
(q) An American company bid on 2,000 metric tons of phosphate fertilizer but lost to a foreign bidder charging $30,000 more, on the trumped-up excuse that the fertilizer was required to be 10 per cent soluble in citric acid, although no such fertilizer existed (July 24).	(q) The fertilizer actually supplied was 12.27 per cent soluble by the Wagner standard method. It was "the type of phosphate fertilizer to which the farmers of Vietnam are accustomed and which they will pay for." This fertilizer "takes effect quicker than the less readily soluble kind."[19]

[15] Same, p. 312.
[16] Same, p. 311.
[17] Same, p. 318.
[18] Same.
[19] Same, pp. 118, 321. Not all authorities agreed on the relative merits of the types of fertilizers used in Viet Nam.

Questions of Interpretation

The Colegrove series also contained criticism based on undisputed facts, although these were not always presented in a context regarded as fair by the ICA. The "byword" to "keep your mouth shut, smile and don't rock the boat" (July 20 and 21), irritating and frustrating as it was to technicians who saw their Vietnamese counterparts performing inadequately, describes a form of self-restraint generally considered essential to success in technical assistance or almost any other form of diplomacy. Reticence or hesitation to criticize one's superiors to a newspaperman (July 20) was surely not a unique condition in a large bureaucracy.

The "hardship" allowances and PX privileges enjoyed by technicians in Saigon (July 23) might have seemed unnecessary to a journalist or a passing visitor, but they represented standard compensation established by law for work overseas in conditions hazardous to health and life and in the face of shortages of items Americans deem essential. It was also true that most technicians remained in Saigon most of the time: they were rendering advice to government officials working in Saigon. Again, it was true that "after almost five years of American aid, the Saigon water system remains so inadequate that the poorer people line up for blocks . . . to fill their buckets with water . . ." (July 21); but the water supply in Saigon had not been given a top priority in the early war-dominated days by the Vietnamese government itself, and no request for such aid had been forthcoming. Moreover, there were technical problems not yet resolved by engineers, although by 1959 "negotiations were well advanced to obtain financing . . . from the Development Loan Fund."[20]

It was also true that "we've done little to guide Vietnam toward the day when she can support herself," since the American effort had been toward survival, but to add that "our solution" had been to put her on the dole . . . [and that] "she may be there 10 years, 25 years, or forever" (July 20) did not recognize the economic progress that had been made or the trends already in evidence.

Major Cuu, Director of Radio Vietnam in 1956, had in fact been charged by the Vietnamese government with financial irregularities, but no U.S. funds were involved (July 22); a Vietnamese contractor had failed to perform satisfactorily in installing air-conditioning equipment in Radio Vietnam (July 22), although U.S. funds were not lost

[20] *Current Situation in the Far East*, Hearings, cited, p. 310. An agreement involving a $9 million loan had actually been signed in the spring of 1959, but the funds had not yet come forth because DLF wanted the services of a third engineering survey to evaluate two conflicting proposals.

thereby, and the faults were later corrected; and the Vietnamese government had indeed "rejected most of [an American technician's] designs for radio equipment" (July 22), at least at first, although this was clearly within its prerogatives and in most cases the "rejection" was only temporary. It was true that the "American movie house" was closed to Vietnamese; as a military facility it was closed to them by regulation (par. 17g of AR 28-62/AFR34-32), and the commercial motion picture producers in Saigon were especially anxious that the regulation be strictly enforced.[21] To take another example, describing the commissary as a "fantastic horn of plenty" (July 23) offered no explanation of the fact that 75 per cent of all meats, 83 per cent of the fruits, and 70 per cent of all vegetables purchased by American housewives in Saigon were bought directly in the local market.

The articles contained a generous amount of free-swinging criticism of the Vietnamese government as undemocratic, oppressive, and corrupt, with colorful and derogatory references to individual officials. The Scripps-Howard newspapers accompanied the series with editorials and other articles (such as "The Mess in Vietnam," July 20). The effect on Congress of the alleged exposure of "scandal" was immediate, leading to calls for investigations both in the Senate and in the House.

The Journalistic Context

Albert Colegrove testified that he had not been dispatched to Viet-Nam to do a "hatchet job,"[22] but had been assigned to report on aid in the Far East and decided, on arriving in Saigon, to concentrate on the Viet-Nam program. According to USOM officials, he spent 19 days there, with only a perfunctory call on the Ambassador and no contact at all with the director or division chiefs of the aid program. He spoke no Vietnamese or French. Much of his source material was derived from interviews with an American businessman who had lost several bids, as he believed, because of discrimination. He also drew material for his stories on Radio Vietnam from an ICA employee who was being returned to the United States and separated from ICA employment. Of course, it is normal journalistic practice to use sources likely to be free of official restraints, and even to seek out informants who hold grievances; the administration's complaint that these reports were not thereafter verified or placed in perspective by recourse to official sources seems justified, however.

Other negative reports on the Viet-Nam program had appeared in the American press (and more were to follow) but so had a far more

[21] *Current Situation in the Far East*, Hearings, cited, p. 319.
[22] Same, p. 206.

numerous and more substantial series of reports favorable to the program.[23]

When the congressional hearings were continued in Saigon, the Vietnamese government declined to admit Mr. Colegrove to the country to continue his reports. Another Scripps-Howard reporter was accredited to cover the proceedings. His reports were somewhat more friendly to the program than the Colegrove series but, as he pointed out to several American officials, he was compelled by the force of circumstances to attempt to corroborate his Scripps-Howard colleague. There was no change in the editorial attitude of the Scripps-Howard press.

The Colegrove reports and the Scripps-Howard campaign were by no means an isolated example of newspaper criticism of specific aid programs, but they represent a unique combination of a journalistic venture, in the best "scoop" tradition, evoking a political response and extended congressional hearings with inevitable damage to the effectiveness of the program and to U.S.-Vietnamese relations.

[23] See *Current Situation in the Far East*, Hearings, cited, pp. 47-76, including John T. Dorsey, "South Vietnam in perspective," *Far Eastern Survey* (December 1958); Ralph Lee Smith, "South Vietnam: A Success Story," *Foreign Policy Bulletin* (July 1, 1959); Ernest K. Lindley, "An Ally Worth Having," *Newsweek* (June 25, 1959); Vermont Royster, "Up from Chaos," *Wall Street Journal* (April 2, 1959); a series of articles by Tillman Durdin in *The New York Times* (April 2, 5, 6, 11, 12 and 13, 1959), and other articles (April 6, May 19, and July 7, 1959); Takashi Oka in *The Christian Science Monitor* (July 7, 1959); Igor Oganesoff in *Wall Street Journal* (June 16, 1959); *Business Week* (July 18, 1959).

SOURCE NOTES AND FURTHER READINGS

Apart from current project reports and official documents, most of the material presented in this book was derived from 300-odd interviews conducted with technical assistants and diplomatic personnel in Viet-Nam, Taiwan, Thailand, and Burma. In most cases the interview notes were reviewed and verified by the respondents or their supervisors. Many of the project reports consulted have not been published, but are available in mission files and in the technical offices of the present Agency for International Development. Annual reports by the various overseas missions are usually available for limited public distribution.

Among the congressional hearings, special studies, and administrative reports cited in the footnotes or the text, the following are of most general interest:

Mutual Security Program, Hearings before the House Committee on Foreign Affairs, 82d Cong., 1st sess. (Washington: GPO, 1951).

Mutual Security Program for Fiscal Year 1954, analysis prepared by the executive branch for use of the House Committee on Foreign Affairs, 83d Cong., 1st sess. (Washington: GPO, 1953).

Mutual Security Act of 1954, Hearings before the House Committee on Foreign Affairs, 83d Cong., 2d sess. (Washington: GPO, 1954).

Mutual Security Act of 1954, Report 1799 of the Senate Committee on Foreign Relations, 83d Cong., 2d sess. (Washington: GPO, 1954).

Mutual Security Act of 1957, Report 417 of the Senate Committee on Foreign Relations, 85th Cong., 1st sess. (Washington: GPO, 1957).

Report on Overseas Operations of the United States Government, by Senator Allen J. Ellender, Senate Doc. No. 31, 85th Cong., 1st sess. (Washington: GPO, 1957).

Mutual Security Act of 1958, Hearings before the Senate Committee on Foreign Relations, 85th Cong., 2d sess. (Washington: GPO, 1958).

Mutual Security Appropriations for 1960, Hearings before the Senate Committee on Appropriations, 86th Cong., 1st sess. (Washington: GPO, 1959).

The Mutual Security Program, Fiscal Year 1960, a summary presentation by the Department of State, Department of Defense, and ICA (Washington: GPO, 1959).

Mutual Security Act of 1959, Hearings before the Senate Committee on Foreign Relations, 86th Cong., 1st sess. (Washington: GPO, 1959).

Operations of the Development Loan Fund, 14th Report by the House Committee on Government Operations, H. Report 1526, 86th Cong., 2d sess. (Washington: GPO, 1960).

International Cooperation Administration, *U. S. Foreign Assistance and Assistance from International Organizations,* Obligations and Commitments, July 1, 1945 through June 30, 1960 (Washington: GPO, 1961).

Other annual hearings on the Mutual Security Act are also useful historical documents. Each year there has been a summary presentation of the Mutual Security Program and the Act for International Development prepared by the Department of State, the Department of Defense, the International Cooperation Administration, the Development Loan Fund, and the Agency for International Development. *Operations Reports* are also available for each fiscal year, presenting valuable cumulative information of a statistical character.

Congressional reports and general studies of foreign aid are also a useful source of information. Among these, the following are particularly valuable:

Foreign Aid, Report of the Senate Special Committee to Study the Foreign Aid Program, S. Report 300, 85th Cong., 1st sess. (Washington: GPO, 1957).

Foreign Aid Program, Compilation of Studies and Surveys, prepared for the Senate Special Committee to Study the Foreign Aid Program, Doc. No. 52, 85th Cong., 1st sess. (Washington: GPO, 1957).

Report on Foreign Policy and Mutual Security, H. Report 551, 85th Cong., 1st sess. (Washington: GPO, 1957).

Criticisms of the Foreign Aid Program and Comments Supplied by the Department of State, the International Cooperation Administration, and the Department of Defense, for the House Foreign Affairs Committee, 86th Cong., 1st sess. (Washington: GPO, 1959).

The President's Committee to Study the United States Military Assistance Program, *Composite Report* (Washington: GPO, 1959).

The Operational Aspects of United States Foreign Policy, a study prepared at the request of the Senate Committee on Foreign Relations by the Maxwell Graduate School of Citizenship and Public Affairs, Syracuse University, in *United States Foreign Policy,* Doc. No. 24, 87th Cong., 1st sess. (Washington: GPO, 1961).

United States Foreign Policy, Compilation of Studies for the Senate Committee on Foreign Relations, Doc. No. 24, 87th Cong., 1st sess. (Washington: GPO, 1961).

The President has convened several committees for the purpose of studying foreign aid problems, among which are the Randall Commission (Commission on Foreign Economic Policy, which reported in January, 1954), the Eric Johnston Board (International Development Advisory Board, January 1957); the Fairless Committee (Committee of President's Citizen Advisers on the Mutual Security Program, March 1957); and the Draper Committee (President's Committee to Study the United States Military Assistance Program, August 1959).

There are many general studies of foreign aid and the problems of the developing world. Among the most important of these are the following:

Walter Adams and John Garraty, *Is the World Our Campus?* (East Lansing: Michigan State University Press, 1960).

Brookings Institution, *Development of the Emerging Countries: An Agenda for Research,* by Robert E. Asher and others (Washington: Author, 1962).

William Adams Brown and Redvers Opie, *American Foreign Assistance* (Washington: Brookings, 1953).

Harlan Cleveland, Gerard J. Mangone, and John Clarke Adams, *The Overseas Americans* (New York: McGraw Hill, 1960).

Leonard W. Doob, *Becoming More Civilized: A Psychological Exploration* (New Haven: Yale University Press, 1960).

Leonard W. Doob, *Communication in Africa: A Search for Boundaries* (New Haven: Yale University Press, 1961).

Everett E. Hagen, *On the Theory of Social Change: How Economic Growth Begins* (Homewood, Ill.: Dorsey Press, 1962).

Albert O. Hirschman, *The Strategy of Economic Development* (New Haven: Yale University Press, 1958).

Institute of Research on Overseas Programs, Michigan State University, *The International Programs of American Universities* (East Lansing: Author, 1958).

John H. Kautsky, ed., *Political Change in Underdeveloped Countries: Nationalism and Communism* (New York: Wiley, 1962).

William J. Lederer and Eugene Burdick, *The Ugly American* (New York: Norton, 1958).

Daniel Lerner, with Lucille W. Pevsner, *The Passing of Traditional Society: Modernizing the Middle East* (Glencoe, Ill.: Free Press, 1958).

George Liska, *The New Statecraft* (Chicago: University of Chicago Press, 1960).

David Clarence McClelland, *The Achieving Society* (Princeton: Van Nostrand, 1961).

Max F. Millikan and Donald L. M. Blackmer (eds.), *The Emerging Nations: Their Growth and United States Policy* (Boston: Little, Brown, 1961).

Max F. Millikan and W. W. Rostow, *A Proposal: Key to an Effective Foreign Policy* (New York: Harper, 1957).

Fred W. Riggs, *The Ecology of Public Administration* (New York: Asia Publishing House, 1961).

W. W. Rostow, *The Stages of Economic Growth: A Non-Communist Manifesto* (Cambridge: Cambridge University Press, 1960).

Robert Theobald, *The Rich and the Poor: A Study of the Economics of Rising Expectations* (New York: Potter, 1960).

Barbara Ward, *The Rich Nations and the Poor Nations* (New York: Norton, 1962).

James W. Wiggins and Helmut Schoeck (eds.), *Foreign Aid Re-examined* (Washington: Public Affairs Press, 1958).

Charles Wolf, *Foreign Aid: Theory and Practice in Southern Asia* (Princeton: Princeton University Press, 1960).

Maurice Zinkin, *Development for Free Asia* (Fair Lawn, N.J.: Essential Books, 1956).

Among the many articles describing foreign aid problems and operations, the following may be especially useful:

Joseph Buttinger, "Fact and Fiction on Foreign Aid," *Dissent*, Summer 1959.

Harlan Cleveland, "Fits and Starts of Foreign Aid," *The Reporter*, April 16, 1959.

Huntington Gilchrist, "Technical Assistance from the United Nations —As Seen in Pakistan," *International Organization*, Autumn 1959.

Paul G. Hoffman, *One Hundred Countries, One and One-Quarter Billion People* (Washington: Albert D. and Mary Lasker Foundation, 1960).

Edward S. Mason, "Foreign Money We Can't Spend," *The Atlantic,* May 1960.

John D. Montgomery, "Crossing the Culture Bars," *World Politics,* July 1961.

John D. Montgomery, "Public Interest in the Ideologies of National Development," in C. J. Friedrich (ed.), *Public Interest,* Nomos, V (forthcoming).

Hans J. Morgenthau, "Preface to a Political Theory of Foreign Aid," *Congressional Record,* March 13, 1962, pp. A1886-A1890.

Henry Reining, Jr., "The Government Contract as an Administrative Device," *The Annals of the American Academy of Political and Social Science,* May 1959.

Harry L. Spence, Jr., "A Resident Representative's View of Technical Cooperation," *The Annals of the American Academy of Political and Social Science,* May 1959.

Discussion of American domestic politics and the foreign policy process, particularly as they relate to aid operations, appears in the following books and articles:

Hugh A. Bone, *Party Committees and National Politics* (Seattle: University of Washington Press, 1958).

Holbert N. Carroll, "Congressional Politics and Foreign Policy in the 1960's," paper delivered at 1960 meeting of the American Political Science Association, University of Pittsburgh, processed (September 1960).

W. Y. Elliott, *The Need for Constitutional Reform* (New York: Whittlesey House, 1953).

W. Y. Elliott, *The Political Economy of American Foreign Policy* (New York: Holt, 1955).

W. Y. Elliott, *United States Foreign Policy: Its Organization and Control* (New York: Columbia University Press, 1952).

Richard F. Fenno, Jr., "The House Appropriations Committee as a Political System," paper delivered at the 1961 meeting of the American Political Science Association (Rochester: University of Rochester, processed).

H. Field Haviland, Jr., "Foreign Aid and the Policy Process: 1957," *The American Political Science Review,* September 1958.

Roger Hilsman, "Congressional-Executive Relations and the Foreign Policy Consensus," *The American Political Science Review,* September 1958.

Roger Hilsman, "The Foreign-Policy Consensus: An Interim Research Report," *The Journal of Conflict Resolution*, December 1959.

Malcolm E. Jewell, "The Senate Republican Policy Committee and Foreign Policy," *Western Political Quarterly*, December 1959.

James N. Rosenau, *National Leadership and Foreign Policy: A Case Study in the Mobilization of Public Support* (Princeton: Princeton University Press, forthcoming).

In supplying information about the countries discussed here, the following official reports have been helpful to the author:

Indochina, Report by Senator Mike Mansfield for the Senate Committee on Foreign Relations, 83d Cong., 1st sess. (Washington: GPO, 1953).

Report on Indochina, by Senator Mike Mansfield for the Senate Committee on Foreign Relations, 83d Cong., 2d sess. (Washington: GPO, 1954).

Viet-Nam, Cambodia, and Laos, Report by Senator Mike Mansfield for the Senate Committee on Foreign Relations, 84th Cong., 1st sess. (Washington: GPO, 1955).

Technical Assistance in the Far East, South Asia, and Middle East, Report by Senator Theodore F. Green for the Senate Committee on Foreign Relations, 84th Cong., 2d sess. (Washington: GPO, 1956).

Current Situation in the Far East, Hearings before a subcommittee of the House Committee on Foreign Affairs, 86th Cong., 1st sess. (Washington: GPO, 1959).

Situation in Vietnam, Hearings before a subcommittee of the Senate Committee on Foreign Relations, 86th Cong., 1st sess. (Washington: GPO, 1959).

U.S. Operations Mission, Division of Agriculture and Natural Resources, *Land Development* (Saigon: 1959).

Report of the Special Study Mission to Asia, Western Pacific, Middle East, Southern Europe and North Africa, H. Report 1386, for the House Committee on Foreign Affairs, 86th Cong., 2d sess. (Washington: GPO, 1960).

United States Aid Program in Vietnam, Report by a subcommittee of the Senate Committee on Foreign Relations, 86th Cong., 2d sess. (Washington: GPO, 1960).

Additional books and articles about the four countries, many of which have been referred to in the text, include the following:

American Friends of Vietnam, *Aid to Vietnam—An American Success Story* (New York: Author, 1959).

Burma, Ministry of Finance and Revenue, *Economic Survey of Burma, 1956* (Rangoon: Director of Information, 1956).

Wesley R. Fishel, ed., *Problems of Freedom: South Vietnam Since Independence* (New York: Free Press, 1961).

J. Price Gittinger, "Progress in South Vietnam's Agrarian Reform, I and II," *Far Eastern Survey*, January and February 1960.

International Bank for Reconstruction and Development, *A Public Development Program for Thailand* (Baltimore: Johns Hopkins Press, 1959).

Adrian Jaffe and Milton C. Taylor, "A Crumbling Bastion: Flattery and Lies Won't Save Vietnam," *The New Republic*, June 19, 1961.

Knappen-Tippetts-Abbett-McCarthy, Pierce Management Inc., and Robert R. Nathan Associates Inc., *Comprehensive Report, Economic and Engineering, Development of Burma, Prepared for the Government of the Union of Burma*, Vols. I and II (Rangoon: 1953).

Richard W. Lindholm, ed., *Viet-Nam, the First Five Years* (East Lansing: Michigan State University Press, 1959).

John D. Montgomery and the NIA Case Development Seminar, *Cases in Vietnamese Administration* (Saigon: National Institute of Administration, 1959).

Lucian W. Pye, *Politics, Personality, and Nation Building: Burma's Search for Identity* (New Haven: Yale University Press, 1962).

Lucian W. Pye, *The Spirit of Burmese Politics* (Cambridge: Massachusetts Institute of Technology, Center for International Studies, 1959, processed).

Arthur F. Raper, *Rural Taiwan: Problem and Promise* (Taipei: 1953).

Robert Scigliano, "They Work for Americans: A Study of the National Staff of an American Overseas Agency," *American Sociological Review*, October 1960.

Milton C. Taylor, *The Taxation of Real Property in Viet-Nam* (Saigon: Michigan State University, Viet-Nam Advisory Group, 1959).

Vu Van Thai, "Our Concept of Development," *Vital Speeches of the Day*, December 1, 1959.

John Seabury Thomson, "Burmese Neutralism," *Political Science Quarterly*, June 1957.

Frank N. Trager, *Building a Welfare State in Burma, 1948–1956* (New York: Institute of Pacific Relations, 1958).

M. N. Trued, "South Viet-Nam's Industrial Development Center," *Pacific Affairs*, September 1960.

INDEX

Accounting requirements, 105, 106–9, 113, 158; *see also* Auditing; Post-audit procedures

Acheson, Dean, *quoted*, 296

Act for International Development (1961), 238, 244

Administration of aid programs, 102, 105–9, 134, 159–61, 257–58

and ambassadors, 245

American "presence," 172–78

coordination of, 152–59, 192–94

counterpart relationships, 162–65

decentralization, 178–82

and efficiency, 100, 151–52

friction in, 107

joint relationships, 161–62

and leadership, 215–16, 235–36

liaison relationships, 165

multilateral, 182–92

and nonintervention, 251

"master pattern" of ICA, 165–72

problems of, 270–74

reforms in, 109–13, 118–21

Africa, 7, 188, 195, 202–3, 276

Agencies in foreign aid, governmental, 152–56, 213 n.

international economic, 182–85

Agency for International Development, 34–35, 213

Agrarian Ministry (Viet-Nam), 164

Agrarian reform in Viet-Nam, 121–28

Agricultural and Rural Development Corporation, 53

Agricultural Surplus Disposal, Staff Committee on, 156

Agricultural Trade Development and Assistance Act of 1954 (PL 480), 155–56

Agriculture, 130–33, 154, 191, 205, 211–12

aid to, *see specific countries*

Agriculture, U.S. Department of, 153

and surplus commodities, 131–33, 155, 156, 210–12, 220–21

Aid, bilateral programs, 104–50, 185–86, 191, 259, 274–76

Communist, 40–43, 158, 255

continuation of, 254–60

and forms and procedures, 156–59

multilateral, 182–86, 251, 257, 274–76

reform as a condition of, 109–28

resources, nongovernmental, 245

see also Economic aid; Foreign aid; Military aid; Technical assistance; *specific countries*

Akyab Harbor, 144, 145

Ambassadors, role of, 245, 253, 257

American Friends of Vietnam, 234

Amoy dialect, 26 n.

Appropriations, amendments to bills, 202–6

and foreign aid policy, 237–39, 250

mutual security, 1948–60 (table), 211

committees, 214, 215, 270

Armed Services Committees, 215, 270

Army Corps of Engineers, 35

Asia, *see* Colombo Plan; Southeast Asia Treaty Organization; *specific countries*

Assassinations in Viet-Nam, 21, 64, 82

Aswan Dam, 135

Attitudes, unilateral, in host country, 134–48

Auditing, 163, 216, 231; *see also* Accounting requirements; Post-audit procedures

Australia, 31, 47, 189

Austria, 296

Ba Gyn, U, 141

Baghdad Pact, 240

"Balance-of-payments" basis, 221

Banana weevil pestilence, 170

Bangkok, 8, 110, 171

Banking operations, and multilateral aid, 182–85

Banmethuot, 78

Bao Dai, 123

Bell Mission, to Philippines, 223

Bilateral aid programs, 185–86, 191, 259, 274–76

  unilateral policies in, 104–50

Binh Xuyen, 64, 223

Bogotá, Act of, 246–47

Brazil, 250

Brookings Institution, 115

Buddhism, 55, 146

Budget, U.S. Bureau of the, 155–56, 210

Bulganin, Nikolai A., 41

Bulgaria, 40

Bureaucracy and Civic Action, in Viet-Nam, 70–71

Burma, 6–7, 173, 188, 235, 259

  agriculture, aid to, 31, 53

  and capitalism, 101–2

  and Colombo Plan, 189

  competition in extending aid, 40–43

  cotton to, 34, 42, 53, 143

  and grants, policy of, 137–38

  and Israel, 256

  liaison approach in, 161, 165

  malaria control in, 54

  Ne Win government, 35, 52, 112 n., 137–38, 146, 188

  neutralism, 32–35, 40–43, 52–53, 137–38, 165

  objectives of aid program in, 19–20, 31–35, 37

  planning in, 111–12

  and politics, 140–46, 251, 252

  press in, 140–46

  results of aid program in, 52–53, 157

  and Thailand, 55–56

  U.S. aid to, tabular summaries of, 281, 286, 291

Burmese Journalists' Association, 141–42

Butter, 221

Buu Loc, 123

Cadillacs, in Saigon, 86 n.

Cai San reclamation project, 47, 127

Cambodia, 16, 54, 55, 147, 189

  and Thailand, 28, 56

  and Viet-Nam, 15, 21, 78

Canada, 31, 55, 189

Capehart, Homer E., 227, 300–301

Capital, aid, 190

  goods, 40–41, 87, 88, 90, 92

  and industrialization, 37, 93–96, 97–99

Capitalism, Vietnamese attitude toward, 100–101; *see also* Free market; Free enterprise

Capitol Engineering Company, 147

CARE, 47

Career service, 257–58, 272

Cartels, Vietnamese, 129–30

Census-taking, 110

Centralization, organizational, **and** ICA, 166–67

Ceylon, 189